MURDER MOST FOUL

MURDER
MOST
FOUL

HAMLET THROUGH THE AGES

David Bevington

OXFORD
UNIVERSITY PRESS

OXFORD
UNIVERSITY PRESS

Great Clarendon Street, Oxford OX2 6DP

Oxford University Press is a department of the University of Oxford.
It furthers the University's objective of excellence in research, scholarship,
and education by publishing worldwide in

Oxford New York

Auckland Cape Town Dar es Salaam Hong Kong Karachi
Kuala Lumpur Madrid Melbourne Mexico City Nairobi
New Delhi Shanghai Taipei Toronto

With offices in

Argentina Austria Brazil Chile Czech Republic France Greece
Guatemala Hungary Italy Japan Poland Portugal Singapore
South Korea Switzerland Thailand Turkey Ukraine Vietnam

Oxford is a registered trade mark of Oxford University Press
in the UK and in certain other countries

Published in the United States
by Oxford University Press Inc., New York

© David Bevington 2011

The moral rights of the author have been asserted
Database right Oxford University Press (maker)

First published 2011

British Library Cataloguing in Publication Data

Data available

Library of Congress Cataloging in Publication Data

Data available

Typeset by SPI Publisher Services, Pondicherry, India
Printed in Great Britain
on acid-free paper by
MPG Books Group, Bodmin and King's Lynn

ISBN 978-0-19-959910-3

1 3 5 7 9 10 8 6 4 2

For Stephen Greenblatt and Ramie Targoff

Preface

What a piece of work is a man! How noble in reason, how infinite in faculties, in form and moving how express and admirable, in action how like an angel, in apprehension how like a god! The beauty of the world, the paragon of animals! And yet, to me, what is this quintessence of dust? (*Hamlet*, 2.2.304–10)

The central argument of this book is that the staging, criticism, and editing of *Hamlet* go hand in hand over the centuries, from 1599–1600 to the present day, to such a remarkable extent that the history of *Hamlet* can be seen as a kind of paradigm for the cultural history of the English-speaking world. Indeed, the play is able to speak to persons and societies of all nations and all ages who have turned to it for a better understanding of themselves. The very nature of the *Hamlet* story shifts and develops in cultural meaning from its earliest days as a Scandinavian heroic saga to Shakespeare's bold dramatization in the late sixteenth century, and thence to a vehicle for exploring cultural values in late seventeenth-century Restoration England and then in the eighteenth and nineteenth and twentieth centuries, until it has now evolved into a cultural expression of what we as a society have become today. As the process has unfolded, *Hamlet* has taken on ever-expanding complexities of meaning, with the result that the play is more controversial and multidimensional than ever before. The multiple pasts of *Hamlet* have been cumulatively folded into what the play can signify to us today.

The critical method of this claim is not in itself new. Gary Taylor's *Reinventing Shakespeare: A Cultural History, From the Restoration to the Present* (1989), to cite one important instance, looks at the Shakespeare canon as a whole in similar terms. Still, Hamlet and the play named for him have a special hold on our imagination, and have done so since Shakespeare first brought Hamlet to life. Hamlet has become a cultural hero for us, all the more so because he is such a troubled and problematic character. He asks questions of profound importance that need to be re-evaluated with each new generation of readers and viewers because he probes with such extraordinary insight into the angst of the human condition. In one sense he transcends historical change, and yet he seems to address the existential dilemmas of each new generation with particular and timely relevance. *Hamlet* has thus provided, over the centuries, a kind of mirror, a touchstone, a key to understanding the collective and individual self. The notable prominence of this play among Shakespeare's works, and indeed among literary creations of all places and all times, invites us to explore the reasons for its astonishing and continued success. I hope that a book devoted entirely to the cultural history of *Hamlet* can provide new insight and perspective on the play. It attempts to cover the entire history of *Hamlet*, including the prehistory of the *Hamlet* saga and the state of the play in 1599–1601, rather than (as in Taylor's *Reinventing Shakespeare*) focusing on the play's long afterlife. Much attention is paid in this present book to performance history as a product of, and contributor to, cultural change.

This book is addressed to general readers and theatre enthusiasts and anyone fascinated by *Hamlet*—as who among us is not? Among recent books which I would like to emulate for their success in addressing general readers and students of Shakespeare alike, let me mention especially Jonathan Bate's *The Genius of Shakespeare* (1997) and *Soul of the Age: A Biography of the Mind of William Shakespeare* (2009), Katherine Duncan-Jones's *Ungentle Shakespeare: Scenes from His Life* (2001), Stephen Greenblatt's *Hamlet in Purgatory* (2001) and *Will in the World: How Shakespeare Became Shakespeare* (2004), James Shapiro's *A Year in the Life of William Shakespeare: 1599* (2005), and Stanley Wells's *Shakespeare For All Time* (2003).

My indebtednesses are many, and are (partially) listed in "Further Reading" at the end of this book. Shakespeare is so extraordinarily thoughtful as a writer that he has inspired many who have written about him to say wonderful things about the ideas and the dramaturgy in *Hamlet*. I am particularly grateful to the scholars and critics named above (Bate, Duncan-Jones, Greenblatt, Shapiro, Taylor, Wells) and to Janet Adelman, Fredson Bowers, John Brewer, Anthony Dawson, Andrew Gurr, Francis Fergusson, and Maynard Mack. This list could easily be expanded. Richard Strier has graciously given me notes that have substantially improved the accuracy of what I was trying to say. Collegiality is at the heart of scholarship, in my view, and this book attempts to be collegial in that best sense of building upon and synthesizing what my *confrères* and predecessors have done so well.

Contents

List of Illustrations

Introduction

As its subtitle, "*Hamlet* Through the Ages," is meant to suggest, this book embraces a rich and complex story of one of the great literary creations of Western Civilization. The story begins with an account of Shakespeare's sources in ancient Scandinavian legend, in classical tragedy, and in the London theatre of Shakespeare's youth. From such beginnings the play evolved as a script that took various forms. It was written perhaps in more than one draft, transcribed, marked up for performance under diverse circumstances, shortened for acting on one or more occasions, modified presumably in rehearsal, and possibly changed in some of its wordings as the play ran in production. When the play reached the hands of publishers, it was set into print a number of times, with results that varied substantially from one text to the next. These differences among the early printed versions point to changing circumstances as the play evolved. What we call *Hamlet*, then, will hardly stay still even as a text.

From its inception as a play, the text of *Hamlet* interacted with a host of other shaping influences. The physical characteristics of Shakespeare's theatre helped determine what staging arrangements were possible in order to present soldiers on watch, ghostly appearances, courtiers in attendance on royalty, private conversations, overhearings, the staging of a play for an onstage audience, marching armies, a graveyard, a scene of dueling, and much more. The socially diverse nature of Shakespeare's first audience for *Hamlet* was bound to be reflected in what he wrote for his viewers. Styles of acting, the organization of Shakespeare's troupe, and competition among London's acting companies were part of the story in 1599–1601. Ideas about religion and the supernatural, family relationships, re-marriage after widowhood, romantic infatuation, friendship, political ambition, and class difference were all certain to bear down upon *Hamlet* in its original contemporary setting and then, in later centuries, in the new social environments of those who would watch or read the play.

As will be argued in chapter 2, *Hamlet* on stage in 1599–1601 was probably viewed as an action drama in the popular genre of the revenge play. The chances are that Elizabethan viewers took seriously, at least for theatrical purposes, the "reality" of ghosts. No evidence suggests that they puzzled over Hamlet's delay; not until much later would readers start wondering if the delay was psychological. Audiences may have been willing to take Hamlet at his word when he explains his mad behavior as an act calculated to confuse his adversary, Claudius. Stage madness was for those audiences a theatrical convention graphically illustrated by Ophelia's inability to know to whom she is speaking or where she is. Many spectators would have understood why the ghost of Hamlet's father has come from Purgatory and how Purgatory differs crucially from hell, though others, especially those of a militantly Protestant persuasion, might have suspected that any ghost purporting to come from Purgatory must be lying. The spectators would have been familiar with Hamlet's paradoxical view of humankind as both "the beauty of the world" and an innately depraved "quintessence of dust." They would have understood how Hamlet and his father's ghost could use the words "incest" and "incestuous" to describe the marriage of Hamlet's widowed mother to her dead husband's brother. In these and many other ways, Elizabethan audiences would have been able to interpret the play in contemporary terms that future generations of critics would see in very different lights.

The Restoration of the Stuart monarchy to the English throne in 1660 fostered a strikingly new theatrical world. How would Shakespeare's plays fare in this new cultural environment? Two theatres were licensed to put on plays in London after an enforced eighteen-year hiatus during the Civil War. Conditions of performance were greatly changed from those of Shakespeare's day. *Hamlet* seems to have been the first Shakespearean play to use perspective scenery, with movable painted flats to represent the various scenes. Indoor performance limited audiences to the well-to-do, many of them socially and politically connected at court. Artificial lighting and evening performances enhanced an aura of courtly entertainment. New comedies, by Wycherley, Congreve, Farquhar, and others were often rakish.

Actresses assumed the female roles previously taken by boy actors, and sometimes acquired notoriety as mistresses of royalty or other aristocrats. Shakespeare revivals were refashioned to please Restoration tastes in elegance and refinement. Actor-managers like Thomas Betterton demanded scripts that enhanced their roles on stage. *Hamlet* accordingly was shortened for performance and simplified in its scenic arrangement. Acting focused on the leading player, center stage, histrionically exploring the vast range of Hamlet's moods from despondency to satirical scorn to fury and finally to resignation, while the other actors did their best to stay out of the actor-manager's way.

In this new cultural environment, critical appraisals of *Hamlet* demanded elegance and correctness. They faulted Shakespeare for his lack of neoclassical sophistication and his failure to meet the demands of poetic justice that evil characters be punished and that the virtuous be rewarded. Critics uniformly wished that Shakespeare had been born into a more refined age. Some early editors of Shakespeare, notably Alexander Pope, regularized many features of Shakespeare's texts to conform with Enlightenment and neoclassical concepts of metrical regularity and decorum. Stage adaptations of Shakespeare's plays often imposed on his texts the neoclassically prescribed regularities of time, place, and action: that is to say, limiting the fictional time of the play to one day or at most two, locating the action in one city at least or preferably in one specific locale, and avoiding the "irregularity" of multiple plots that typically mixed comic with tragic or potentially tragic action. Performance texts adopted many such features in their acting scripts. Late eighteenth-century actors and critics, notably David Garrick and Samuel Johnson, continued and amplified the neoclassical reinterpretation of *Hamlet*, though in Johnson and some later eighteenth-century critics and editors we can also perceive a willingness to interpret the neoclassical "rules" of time, place, and action in a flexible way that allowed for Shakespeare's native genius. More or less simultaneously, performance and criticism alike developed a fascination with Shakespeare's characters, asking what they would be like if we could meet them as real people.

The late eighteenth and early nineteenth centuries recast Hamlet in the role of a melancholy and introspective Romantic hero, too noble for this world and hence ill-equipped to avenge the murder of his father. For the first time in the history of *Hamlet*, the major critical problem became that of explaining Hamlet's apparent reluctance to

avenge the murder of his father. The answer was found in his suppo-
sedly vacillating, brooding, and procrastinating temperament. His
abusive treatment of Ophelia became a major subject of concern
for readers who could not bear that such a beautiful and innocent
young woman should suffer so. Simultaneously, the play of *Hamlet*
came to be regarded by William Hazlitt and some others (as we shall
see in chapter 5) as singularly unsuited for theatrical performance: it
was perceived instead as a philosophical poem attuned to Romantic
ideals of the sublime. Despite this uneasiness about staging the play,
theatre managers built larger and larger theatres to attract audiences of
increased size, even if not to the satisfaction of some literary critics.

As the nineteenth century moved on into the Victorian era
(1837–1901), stage productions became more and more costly and
elaborate. Critical interpreters, meantime, attempted with increasing
urgency to understand Shakespeare's moral values and his presentation
of characters from whom readers could gain valuable ethical insights.
Horatio was seen as a model of virtuous friendship, Ophelia as tragic
victim, Hamlet himself as a thoughtful providential reader of history.
Representations of favorite scenes from *Hamlet* flourished in the visual
arts. Editing and scholarly work on the play moved towards becoming a
Shakespearean industry. Learned societies flourished. To an ever-expanding degree, even more so than in the eighteenth century, Shakespeare
became the national poet and symbol of what made England great.

As stated briefly in the preface, the central argument of this book is
that over the centuries, criticism, staging, and editing of *Hamlet* have
gone hand in hand, in such a way that the history of *Hamlet* can be seen
paradigmatically as a history of cultural change. The Restoration age
refashioned *Hamlet* within the bounds of neoclassical regularity. The
Ages of Reason and Enlightenment found in *Hamlet* a text for the
moral appreciation of character. The Romantic and Victorian eras re-
imagined the play, on stage and in the study, as a philosophical work
devoted to the ruminations of a delicate and poetic sensibility. These
cultural movements all happened, and continue to happen, with
striking synchronism: shifts in philosophical outlook have inspired
corresponding changes in theatrical productions of *Hamlet* and other
plays, while those shifts in theatrical styles have helped in turn to shape
changes in philosophical outlook. *Hamlet* has thus become a micro-
cosm, a little world, containing within itself the elements that go to

make up cultural history. And nowhere is this more true than in the twentieth and twenty-first centuries.

The modern era has proved to be one of continual and often revolutionary change, as signaled in the late nineteenth and early twentieth century by the writings of Charles Darwin, Sigmund Freud, Karl Marx, George Bernard Shaw, T. S. Eliot, and many others, and by the momentous events of World War I and the Russian Revolution of 1917. More or less concurrently, a revolution in the staging of *Hamlet* and other Shakespearean plays turned away from opulent verisimilar realism to experimental presentational methods on bare platforms and in modern dress. Productions on the Continent, in Prague, Berlin, or Moscow, were apt to be particularly daring. The mood of interpretation veered sharply in new directions, responding to widespread disillusionment following World War I. The era between the two great world wars saw productions that made use of *Hamlet* to ponder the uncertainties and anxieties of a world in economic and political stalemate. Post-World War II *Hamlets* often interpreted the play as an attack on political tyranny and the curtailment of individual freedom, whether in Russia or Germany or indeed just about any country.

A deepening sense of apathy, of impasse, and of utter helplessness lent itself to stagings and critical readings of *Hamlet* that were deliberately bleak and disorienting. Actors in the role of Hamlet learned to be gruff, sardonic, snarling, studiously informal in dress, more working-class than aristocratic, more virile and rough-edged than poetically sensitive. Hamlet turned out to be a lot like the Angry Young Men of John Osborne's generation (*Look Back in Anger*, 1958), educated beyond their ability to find suitable employment and longing for massive changes in the entire social structure. Critical movements like the New Historicism and Cultural Materialism of the late twentieth and early twenty-first centuries rebelled against traditional humanist teachings of politics, preferring to see all political activity as a power struggle. Feminism and gender studies promoted the thesis that gender is largely a matter of social construction. Texts were increasingly interpreted as open to multiple meanings. The idea of artistic genius as innate was strenuously contested in favor of seeing great art as socially constructed. All of these exciting and unsettling movements found their way into modern productions of, and critical writings about, *Hamlet*.

As a result, *Hamlet* is a more controversial play today than ever before. The relationship and reliability of its early texts are heatedly debated by textual scholars, with no consensus in sight. Critical writings and stage productions run the gamut from a preference for traditional costuming and interpretation to updated resettings of every imaginable sort. Audiences reflect their widely varying cultural standards by the ways in which they deplore or applaud what they see. Some revisionary productions and interpretations are admittedly, even designedly, over the top, as if intended to trumpet the ingenuity of the director's concept; but overall (in my view at least) the process has been liberating and healthy. It has opened new vistas, asked new questions, and challenged audiences to rethink their preconceived ideas in ways that are invaluable and that literature, especially drama, can best set in motion.

No doubt this a major reason why Shakespeare, in a modern world that often mistrusts and dethrones the traditional icons of literary history, has not only survived but has risen to ever-increasing prominence. He may be a Dead White European Male, but his relevance today, and in *Hamlet* especially, is both astonishing and all the more admirable because it is not simply the result of his being a Required Author.

The ever-expanding horizons of *Hamlet* today can be sampled in many ways: by the role of the play in shaping cultural experience, by its success on film and in television and in Shakespeare festivals worldwide, by the proliferation of spin-offs, parodies, and multitudinous borrowings, by literary quotations, and by the impact *Hamlet* has had on the very language that we speak. Debates about method acting versus more traditional styles, ethnic and multi-racial casting, and the use of controversial settings that interpret the play in terms of drug dealing and military conflict, all vividly indicate the extent to which *Hamlet* provides never-ending insight into contemporary culture, as it has done for readers and spectators over the centuries. As we continue to reinvent *Hamlet*, the play enters ever more remarkably into the way we see ourselves.

I

Prologue to Some Great Amiss: The Prehistory of *Hamlet*

The legend of Hamlet comes down to us from prehistoric Denmark. Like most such legends, its own early history is obscured in the mists of time. The oral versions of the story that must have circulated are lost to us. Not until a Dane called Saxo Grammaticus wrote in Latin his *Gesta Danorum*, or *History of the Danes*, some time around 1200, does the story of Hamlet loom into view. There it occupies the conclusion of book 3 and into book 4 of Saxo's *History*. We know nothing of Saxo's sources, but the story itself is by this time fully developed.[1]

In order to make clear what use Shakespeare has made of Saxo's *History* and of other probable sources, let me first offer a brief summary of Shakespeare's play. (Skip this paragraph, if you know the story.) Prince Hamlet, recently returned to Denmark from his studies in Wittenberg to mourn the sudden death of his royal father (also named Hamlet), is deeply distressed by his widowed mother's over-hasty marriage to Hamlet's uncle, Claudius. When Hamlet learns from the ghost of his dead father that Claudius has secretly murdered his older brother in order to steal the crown of Denmark and the Queen (Gertrude), Hamlet determines to revenge the murder, but is then held back by uncertainties as to the identity of the ghost: might it be a malign spirit tempting him to evil? He adopts a stance of madness to throw Claudius off the scent, managing in the process to fool the aged counselor, Polonius, into thinking that Hamlet is truly mad as the result of having been rejected as a suitor by Polonius's daughter, Ophelia. Aided by visiting players, Hamlet stages at court an enactment of a murder resembling that of King Hamlet, and determines from Claudius's abrupt response to the play-within-the-play that Claudius is in fact guilty. Proceeding to his mother's chambers, Hamlet arraigns her of moral weakness. When Polonius, having hidden behind a curtain to overhear this interview of mother and son, cries out in concern for Gertrude's safety, Hamlet stabs the old man, thinking him to be Claudius. This homicide leads to Hamlet's being banished to England under the escort of his one-time boyhood friends Rosencrantz and Guildenstern, with a secret request from Claudius to the King of England that Hamlet be executed, but Hamlet manages to evade this sentence by cannily substituting the names of Rosencrantz and Guildenstern for his in the order of execution. Returning to Denmark, he encounters Laertes at the grave of Laertes's sister Ophelia, who has drowned, seemingly having lost her sanity over her father's death and Hamlet's rejection of her. Laertes demands satisfaction from Hamlet for the deaths of Polonius and Ophelia in a gentlemanly duel, in preparation for which event, however, Laertes, in secret conspiracy with Claudius, procures a rapier with poisoned tip. A cup of poisoned wine is at hand as a backup stratagem. A foppish courtier named Osric acts as referee of the fencing match. Queen Gertrude, by now penitently reconciled with her son, drinks the wine as a toast to him and dies. Hamlet, learning from Laertes of Claudius's complicity in the poisoning of the rapier and cup, kills the King and then dies in the arms of his dear friend, Horatio. Fortinbras, nephew of the King of Norway, who has earlier attempted an invasion of Denmark but has been prevented from doing so by the diplomatic sagacity of Claudius, now arrives in time to mourn the death of Hamlet and to claim Denmark as his own.

In Saxo's account, Amlethus or Amleth (Hamlet) is the son of Ørvendil or Horwendil, brother of King Rørik of Denmark, and Guruth or Gurutha, the King's daughter, whom Horwendil has bravely won as his bride by killing King Koller of Norway in single combat. King Rørik has entrusted the governance of Jutland, in central Denmark, to Horwendil and to a second brother, Fengi or Feng, after the death of their father, Gervendil, the Jarl or Earl of the Jutes. The envious Feng, corresponding in Shakespeare's play to Claudius, murders his brother Horwendil, takes the widowed Gurutha (compare Shakespeare's Gertrude) as his wife, and rules Jutland alone, having deprived his brother, as Shakespeare puts it, "Of life, of crown, of queen" (1.5.76).

Amleth, plausibly fearful that Feng wants him dead, adopts the guise of a fool or madman to confuse his enemy. Feng, too canny to be taken in entirely by such a ruse, tests Amleth's supposed madness by arranging for him to encounter an attractive young woman (compare Ophelia) in the woods. Feng's notion is that Amleth, if sane, will succumb to erotic temptation and have sex with the woman. Amleth, having been secretly warned of Feng's malice by a kindly foster brother, manages to avoid this trap by spiriting the woman off to a hideaway where they can make love unobserved by Feng's agents. Because she and Amleth have had the same foster parents in infancy and are thus tied in strong bonds of friendship, the woman reveals Feng's plot to Amleth and assures him that she will keep silence on his behalf.

Feng's next move is to arrange for a counselor "who had more confidence than he had judgment" (compare Polonius) to conceal himself under some straw in a dark corner of Gurutha's chambers in order to overhear her conversation with her son, but again to no avail. Amleth, suspecting a trap, adopts his mad disguise and prances up and down on the straw, beating his arms and crowing like a rooster. He finds the courtier in the straw, hauls him forth, stabs him to death, hacks the body into bits, boils the morsels, and tosses them through the mouth of an open sewer or outhouse for the swine to eat. Amleth turns next to his mother, arraigning her of harlotry, and winning her to repentance and to a promise not to reveal his secrets to Feng. When Feng, having returned from a journey, asks about the spying counselor, Amleth grimly jests that the man fell into an outhouse and was devoured by swine. Amleth is, of course, mostly telling the truth in this, but the story seems so bizarre that it is attributed to Amleth's craziness.

Feng now determines to do away with Amleth, but dares not do so openly in Denmark for fear of angering his wife Gerutha and her father. Feng therefore determines to send Amleth to England with two escorts (compare Rosencrantz and Guildenstern) with a request to the King of England that Amleth be executed. Amleth manages to rewrite the letter of request so that it asks for the execution of the two escorts instead, and stipulating also that the English King's daughter be given to Amleth in marriage. A year later, Amleth returns to Denmark just in time to take part as cup-bearer in a festive celebration of his own supposed funeral. By secret prearrangement, his mother has decked the hall with woven tapestries for this event. Having encouraged Feng and his followers to drink themselves into an alcoholic stupor, Amleth flings over them the tapestries knitted for him by his mother, secures the weavings tightly, and sets fire to the palace. Feng escapes this holocaust, but is cut down by Amleth with Feng's sword (Amleth's own weapon having been secured fast into its scabbard by Feng's henchmen). Saxo does not tell what happens to Amleth's mother.

In a continuation not included by Shakespeare, Amleth goes back to England and claims his bride there, but soon finds himself plotted against by his new father-in-law, who feels himself obliged by oath to avenge the death of Feng. This English King cunningly arranges for Amleth to negotiate on the English King's behalf for the hand in marriage of Queen Herminthrud of Scotland, knowing that it is her grim practice to put to death any and all suitors. Amleth manages to win her for his own second and bigamous wife with her own cunning connivance: preferring the prospect of marriage with the young Amleth to a union with the older King of England, Herminthrud alters the English letter of petition to read that she is to marry the bearer. Amleth thereupon vanquishes the King of England in battle by the ruse of propping up the dead bodies of his slain soldiers as if they were part of a huge army. Returning to Denmark with two wives, Amleth eventually falls in battle against Viglek, the successor to King Rørik (and thus a distant analogue to Shakespeare's Fortinbras). Herminthrud, despite her vows of eternal loyalty to Amleth even in death, yields herself to Viglek as the victor's spoils, thus confirming the narrator's unshakable conviction that "all vows of women become void with changes in fortune, are dissolved by the shifting of time, and disappear with the play of fate, for their faith stands on slippery feet." Perhaps Shakespeare had this misogynistic observation in mind when he dramatized the story of Gertrude and the Player Queen in *Hamlet*, even though the rest of Saxo's continuation was to be omitted from the play.

Saxo's account thus provides for us the prototypes of Hamlet, Hamlet's father, Claudius, Gertrude, Polonius, Ophelia, Rosencrantz, and Guildenstern. The narrative outline of the story is strikingly similar in many particulars: the bravery of the hero's now-dead father, the murder of that chivalric ruler by his own brother, the incestuous marriage of the villainous brother to his own sister-in-law (as Saxo puts it, the villainous uncle "added incest to fratricide by taking the wife of the brother he had butchered"), the hero's feigning madness to confuse his enemy, the use of a woman as a decoy, the eavesdropping by a counselor who is thereupon killed by the hero, the hero's confronting of his mother with the sinfulness of her new marriage, the trip to England with the substitution of the letter intended to bring about the hero's execution, the execution instead of the two escorts, the hero's return to Denmark and reconciliation with his mother, and a final scene in which the hero avenges the murder of his father by killing the uncle.

Of course much is changed, most notably the hero's relationship to the ethic of revenge. Saxo's story of Amleth in *History of the Danes* is unapologetically a tale of revenge, derived from ancient Norse legends. Amleth must bide his time and feign madness because he is coping with a canny enemy, but the young man has no scruples about killing Feng in cold blood. He plots his course of vengeance and then, assisted by his mother, carries it out with sudden violence. Saxo as narrator applauds the intrepidity of a hero who "not only saved his own life but also managed to avenge his father. Because of his skillful defense of himself and his vigorous vengeance of his father, it is hard to say which was the greater, his courage or his cleverness." Throughout, Amleth is seen as admirably cunning. Saxo's account savors the wit of Amleth's deceptions and half-truths; we take ironic pleasure in knowing the full purport of what the hero is misleadingly saying to his enemies. We are invited to nod approvingly as he takes his sexual pleasure with a young woman employed as a decoy against him. We hear no authorial disapproval of his deliberately stabbing to death the nosey counselor he finds in his mother's chambers; Saxo offers no counterpart to Hamlet's quick regret at his having mistakenly killed the unseen man whom Hamlet plausibly assumed to be his uncle. Hamlet disposes of Polonius's dead body with ironic and matter-of-fact coolness, but with far less grisly effect than in Amleth's disposing of the counselor's dismembered body into a privy frequented by swine.

Amleth never encounters his father's ghost, and has no need to ascertain whether Feng is guilty of murdering his brother; indeed, Feng makes no secret of what he has done. The young woman in Saxo's story is not the old counselor's daughter. She does not go mad and then drown herself, as does Ophelia. She has no brother to seek vengeance for her death. Amleth has no dear friend like Horatio in whom he can confide. The counterparts to Rosencrantz

and Guildenstern in Saxo are only unnamed escorts who convey
Amleth to England and are killed in his stead, not his boyhood
friends. The whole story of Fortinbras has only a distant connection
to the saga as told by Saxo.

These observations of difference are not meant to imply that
Shakespeare went directly to Saxo as his source. Other versions had
intervened between 1200 and 1599–1601 when *Hamlet* was probably
written. Saxo's work itself was first printed (in Latin) in Paris in 1514,
to be followed by two more editions in the sixteenth century. François
de Belleforest translated parts of Saxo into French in his *Histoires
Tragiques* (1570), adding some significant details. The murdered
Horvendil's ghost or shade (*les ombres de Horvendile*) now appears to
his son. Hamlet (his name now spelled thus) adopts a disguise of
madness for reasons of personal safety; that detail is in Saxo, but
Belleforest's Hamlet also suffers from the genuine melancholy that
we find in Shakespeare's play. Belleforest portrays Hamlet's mother
Geruth as having entered into an adulterous relationship with Fengon
before the murder of Hamlet's father. The translator dwells on the
excessive drinking of the Danes and other northern peoples. His
setting is, anachronistically, more a court of Renaissance Europe,
replete with palace, courtiers, and pages, than the abode of an ancient
Scandinavian chieftain. By translating the Latin *stramentum*, straw, as
the French equivalent of "quilt," he provides an elegant flooring in the
Queen's chambers more suited to the French sixteenth century than to
the Danish twelfth or thirteenth centuries. Belleforest provides a
Christian justification for Hamlet's killing of his uncle, in that Fengon
is guilty of an "abominable guilt and twofold impiety," his "incestuous
adultery and parricide murder."

Belleforest's version is longer than that of Saxo, enabling the translator and redactor to enlarge upon psychological insights and moralizations. More dialogue is provided, especially in Hamlet's prolonged
interview with his mother in her chambers on the subject of her sinful
transformation from loyal spouse of Horvendil to the brutishly fleshly
bedpartner of Fengon. From the very beginning of his account,
Belleforest lays stress on the barbarous cruelty and faithlessness of an
ancient Danish kingdom not yet having received the gospel of Jesus
Christ. He inveighs against wicked and bold women who cast off the
bonds of honor and chastity. He represents Hamlet and the unnamed
decoy lady as genuinely attracted to each other and desirous of sex, yet

virtuously inclined to resist the blandishments of those wicked courtiers who have brought them together to endanger Hamlet's physical
body and soul.

Shakespeare could certainly afford, in his play, to eschew the heavy
moralizations of Belleforest, but he may well have read with interest
the account of Hamlet's begging forgiveness of his mother for his bold
lecturing to her, his insistence that the advice is offered for her own
good, and her contrite begging for her son's understanding for her
having entered into a second wedding under duress. Belleforest's
Queen is a mother who, despite her lamentable lapse into adultery,
does fondly hope to see her son restored to his rights as heir and
monarch of Denmark, and does undertake to distance herself from
her new husband out of loyalty to her son and his cause of rightful
revenge. None of this is in Saxo.

Most of Belleforest's account is retained in an English version, *The
History of Hamlet*, 1608, an unacknowledged translation of Belleforest.
Shakespeare cannot have known this version when he wrote *Hamlet*
some nine years earlier. One or two changes may show instead that the
English translator was influenced by Shakespeare's play, as when
Hamlet detects the counselor hidden behind the arras or hangings in
the mother's bedchamber by beating with his arms against those
hangings and then thrusting his sword into the arras, crying "A rat, a
rat!" Even so, the 1608 text does provide us with an English translation
of Belleforest, a work that Shakespeare does appear to have known.
(His French was evidently adequate enough for him to have read
Belleforest in that language.)

The changes in Shakespeare's version, assuming that he knew
Belleforest, are of course stupendous. The characters are much more
fully developed. A whole new family unit emerges: Ophelia, provided
by Shakespeare with her name, is now the daughter of the previously
unnamed counselor, who has become Polonius, and Ophelia now
has a brother, Laertes. The two escorts are now Rosencrantz and
Guildenstern, with a detailed history of their earlier friendship with
Hamlet and their attachment as ambitious young men to the service of
the new king. (This king, named Fengon in Belleforest, is called
Claudius in the stage direction of his first entry in the 1604 quarto
and 1623 folio texts of Shakespeare's play, and in 1604's first speech
prefix; he is never named in the dialogue.) Horatio, perhaps hinted at
in the gentleman in Saxo and Belleforest who befriends Hamlet by

warning him of a plot against him, is importantly enlarged into an intellectual and moral companion with whom the Prince can share secrets and discuss philosophy.

The plot is changed as well. Shakespeare transforms Saxo's Viglek into young Fortinbras of Norway, ready to invade Denmark and then willing to bide his time until at last he is seemingly named by Hamlet as the next ruler of Denmark. Claudius, in Shakespeare's play, murders his brother in secret. He learns that Hamlet has killed Polonius, whereas in the earlier accounts Hamlet's mad disguise has misled his enemies into a misapprehension. Without a Laertes to return from Paris so intent on avenging his father's death that he conspires with Claudius to poison Hamlet by means of a poisoned sword or cup, as told in Shakespeare's account, the denouement in both Saxo and Belleforest focuses instead on Hamlet's cleverness in outwitting his opponent. Nothing corresponds in the sources to the way in which Shakespeare's Hamlet passively attunes himself to the unknowable intent of Providence. Belleforest's Hamlet is "subtle," like Saxo's. Aided indeed by the devilish powers of magic he has acquired in his father's day, Belleforest's Hamlet proceeds to amaze the King of England by revealing that he, the King, is in fact the illegitimate son of a slave and that his Queen is of no less base parentage.

On Hamlet's return to England, the overthrow in Belleforest of Fengon and his followers is fully as bloody and savage as in Saxo, even if in the French version the holocaust is morally sanctioned by the flagrant debauchery of those who perish in the flames. To Fengon, as he lies fallen with his head cut clean from his shoulders, Hamlet declares (quoting from the 1608 English translation of Belleforest), "This just and violent death is a just reward for such as thou art. Now go thy ways, and when thou comest in hell, see thou forget not to tell thy brother whom thou traitorously slewest that it was his son sent thee thither with the message, to the end that, being comforted thereby, his soul may rest among the blessed spirits and quit me of the obligation that bound me to pursue his vengeance upon mine own blood." Belleforest's attempt here to reconcile the pagan ethic of revenge with Christian idealism of salvation and damnation is confused and contradictory to the point of seeming to say that Hamlet's father's ghost, now in hell, will be transported into heavenly rest once the revenge has been accomplished. Shakespeare's Hamlet will choose a very different path, that of resigning himself to the will of heaven in the hope and expectation that heaven will indeed fashion a resolution far more perfect than Hamlet could devise for himself. We will return to this crucial matter in chapter 3.

Stylistically, Shakespeare's *Hamlet* is strikingly different from the accounts of Saxo or Belleforest. As a drama, the play has no omniscient narrator. We witness the story from conflicting points of view, and must sort out as best we can its profound ambiguities as we attempt to discern the truth, much as Hamlet himself struggles to know what he must do. The handling of time is recast for dramatic presentation: instead of pursuing a continuous linear narrative, the play's account begins in the middle of things, after the death of the old King Hamlet. Only later do we learn of the murder, just as Hamlet himself must attempt to reconstruct the past. The secrecy of the murder necessitates on Hamlet's part a quest for certainty that is not imposed upon the protagonist in Saxo or Belleforest, since Feng makes no attempt to conceal the fact of his having assassinated his brother. Time in Shakespeare is foreshortened by compression, especially in the account of Hamlet's journey to England; drama shows us the episodes of this voyage as an onrush of events and by reporting of offstage action, as when Hamlet relates to Horatio, by letter and then in person, his discovering in the packets of Rosencrantz and Guildenstern the royal commission ordering his death, and his boarding a pirate ship during a sea-fight (4.6, 5.2).

Structural design becomes a marked feature of Shakespeare's treatment of the story: by adding Laertes and enhancing the saga of Fortinbras, Shakespeare provides his play with three sons who are called upon to avenge the deaths of their fathers. As a result, the play features more parallels and interactions of related plot lines than in Shakespeare's sources. Shakespeare is more interested in providing a plausible sixteenth-century Danish setting than are Saxo and Belleforest; Saxo's Denmark is of course that of an earlier era. The names of Rosencrantz and Guildenstern, not in Shakespeare's sources, are those of aristocratic sixteenth-century Denmark.

Meantime, a more imponderable element enters into the history of Shakespeare's sources. An old play of *Hamlet* appears to have been in existence on the London stage in the late 1580s and early 1590s. The theatre owner and manager Philip Henslowe entered in his diary for 11 June 1594 a record of performance of a *Hamlet* at Newington Butts by "my Lord Admiral's Men" or "my Lord Chamberlain's Men," probably the latter, though Henslowe does not specify. The item is not marked as "new," as was Henslowe's custom for a new play. Thomas Lodge, in his *Wit's Misery and the World's Madness* (1596), refers to "the vizard of the ghost which cried so miserably in the theatre, like an oyster wife, 'Hamlet, revenge!'" Most significantly, perhaps, Thomas Nashe wrote a prefatory Epistle to Robert Greene's *Menaphon* in 1589 with the following observation:

It is a common practice nowadays amongst a sort of shifting companions, that run through every art and thrive by none, to leave the trade of noverint [i.e., copier of writs], whereto they were born, and busy themselves with the endeavors of art, that could scarcely Latinize their neck verse [i.e., a Latin scriptural verse, usually the fifty-first psalm, the reading of which could enable an accused person to claim benefit of clergy and thereby save himself from hanging] if they should have need; yet English Seneca read by candlelight yields many good sentences, as "Blood is a beggar" and so forth; and if you entreat him fair in a frosty morning, he will afford you whole *Hamlet*s, I should say handfuls, of tragical speeches. But O grief! *Tempus edax rerum* [Time is the devourer of all things], what's that will last always? The sea exhaled by drops will in continuance be dry, and Seneca, let blood line by line and page by page, at length must need die to our stage; which makes his famished followers to imitate the Kid in Aesop, who, enamored with the Fox's newfangels, forsook all hopes of life to leap into a new occupation; and these men, renouncing all possibilities of credit or estimation, to intermeddle with Italian translations ...

Nashe's testimonial confirms the evidence of a *Hamlet* on the Elizabethan stage by 1589 and adds several fascinating details. The play was evidently the work of someone whom Nashe denounces as an opportunistic scribbler, deficient in Latin and yet turning to the ancient Roman dramatist Seneca for inspiration. This authorial portrait is generic in its satire; a number of men such as Robert Greene, Christopher Marlowe, and Thomas Lodge, searching for gainful employment but not socially qualified for positions at court, were now offering their talents to the adult acting companies in London. Some of these writers were so-called University Wits, educated at Oxford or Cambridge beyond their means of finding a position unless they were willing to become ministers of the Anglican Church; others, like Shakespeare and Thomas Kyd, were not university educated but flocked also to London, attracted by the same siren call of writing for the acting companies. The companies themselves gravitated to

London, where a rapid growth in population and improved education helped to foster an appetite for live drama.

The economic advantage of touring, as practiced successfully by the Queen's Men in the 1570s and 1580s, was quickly losing ground to the appeal of addressing much larger theatre audiences in the London area in large, new, purpose-built playhouses, of which the Theatre, erected in Moorfields, just to the north of London's city walls, by James Burbage in 1576, was evidently the first (though acting had taken place earlier in more improvised locations). Once the acting companies discovered the advantages of staying put in the city and its environs, they needed lots of new plays, exponentially more than they had required on tour. The young writers quickly set to work. In Nashe's mordant view, they did so in good part by pillaging the classical tradition of Seneca and Italian neoclassical writers (such as Ariosto). Nashe is dismayed by the hyperbole that has resulted from such imitative borrowing. The idea of classical or neoclassical sources points in quite a different direction from that offered by Saxo Grammaticus and the Scandinavian north.

The likeliest candidate for authorship of a lost *Hamlet* play in the years around 1589 would appear to be Thomas Kyd. His profile fits Nashe's satirical description of one who has left the trade of "noverint" or copier of writs to become a hack writer turning out whole *Hamlet*s, that is to say, handfuls, of overwrought tragical speeches. Nashe could be punning with Kyd's name when he refers to "the Kid in Aesop." If so, Kyd is being likened to the gullible young lamb in the Aesopian fable who incautiously jumps at the Fox's disingenuous offer of something new, to the kid's infinite cost.

The identification is not certain, but the idea does invite us to think about Kyd's enormously popular and long-lived *The Spanish Tragedy* (*c.* 1587) and its many affinities to Shakespeare's *Hamlet* (see Illustration 1). The ghost of a murdered man (Don Andrea) is on stage in Kyd's play throughout as a chorus figure, aided and abetted in his desire for vengeance by a personified representation of Revenge. Kyd could have found a similar device, for example, in Seneca's *Agamemnon*, in which the ghost of Thyestes urges his son Aegisthus to avenge the crime of Thyestes's old brother, Atreus, in having set before Thyestes a dish containing the flesh of Thyestes's own children. (Seneca's plays were translated early in the English Renaissance and were thus available to playwrights like Kyd.) *The Spanish Tragedy*'s chief character, Don

The Spanish Tragedie:
OR,
Hieronimo is mad againe.

Containing the lamentable end of *Don Horatio*, and
Belimperia ; with the pittifull death of *Hieronimo*.

Newly corrected, amended, and enlarged with new
Additions of the *Painters* part, and others, as
it hath of late been diuers times acted.

LONDON,
Printed by W. White, for I. White and T. Langley,
and are to be fold at their Shop ouer againft the
Sarazens head without New-gate. 1615.

Illustration 1. The 1615 title page of Thomas Kyd's *The Spanish Tragedy, c.*
1587. Don Horatio, hanged in an arbor, is discovered by his father, Don
Hieronimo. Belimpera cries for help as she is seized by her villainous brother,
Don Lorenzo.

Hieronimo, burdened with the solemn responsibility of revenging the murder of his son, Don Horatio, has difficulties (like Hamlet's) in ascertaining who committed the crime and whether the Ghost's words are believable—another Senecan trait. The motif of madness, derived in good part from Saxo and Belleforest, is a feature also of Seneca's *Hercules Furens* or *The Madness of Heracles*, dramatized earlier by Euripides, relating the hero's slaughter of his wife and children; and of Sophocles's *Ajax*, in which the protagonist slowly recovers from having madly slain a flock of sheep, taking them for his enemies. The device of the play-within-the-play, found in Kyd and in Shakespeare, is derived from classical tradition, not Saxo or Belleforest. Hieronimo's eloquent soliloquies, agonizing over his inability to find justice in this world despite his being the minister of justice for the Spanish state, are Senecan in tone and rhetoric.

Thomas Kyd, writing his *The Spanish Tragedy* in about 1587, is thus exploiting a tradition of Senecan revenge that had gained currency in English drama of the late sixteenth century in such plays as *Gorboduc* (1562), *Jocasta* (1566), *Gismond of Salerne* (1566–8), and *The Misfortunes of Arthur* (1588). Kyd's huge success with his play propelled the genre forward into something like the status of a fad. If he also wrote the lost *Hamlet*, he is even more worthy of being hailed as the great progenitor of Elizabethan revenge tragedy.

We, of course, cannot know exactly how much Shakespeare took from the lost *Hamlet*, but its very existence raises the possibility, and perhaps even the likelihood, that a number of details found in his *Hamlet* and not in Saxo or Belleforest were available to him in the lost play. These might include a name for Ophelia and an expanded role for her as the once-beloved of Hamlet and the daughter of Polonius; a greater role for that counselor; a brother for Ophelia, furiously intent on avenging his murdered father; a friend for Hamlet in the role of Horatio; a son and heir of the King of Norway, armed for an invasion of Denmark; and still more. Even so, how much would the lost *Hamlet* and Shakespeare's play have resembled each other?

The other instances we have of Shakespeare's recasting of older plays suggest two contrary responses to that question: plot and character roles may have been extensively though by no means entirely similar, while on the other hand the Shakespearean play is sure to be incomparably greater in idea, in language, and in dramatic force. Shakespeare's *King John* (*c.* 1594–6) is a reworking of an anonymous two-part play called *The Troublesome Reign of King John*, published in 1591; at least that is the consensus view of most scholars, though the matter of which came first, and who wrote what, is still disputed. In *Henry IV, Parts I* and *II*, and *Henry V* (1596–9), Shakespeare fashioned three superb English history plays out of the chronicles and also out of the plot materials he found in the anonymous *The Famous Victories of Henry the Fifth* (*c.* 1588), relating the story of Prince Henry all the way from his robbing escapades with a fat Falstaff-like roguish knight named Sir John Oldcastle down through King Henry V's triumph at the battle of Agincourt in 1415. Shakespeare's immediate source for his *King Lear* was an old play called *The Chronicle History of King Leir*, first published in 1605 but acted probably by the Queen's Men as early as 1586–8 and still occasionally seen on stage in 1594, when Philip Henslowe recorded in his diary the performance of a "King Leare" at the Rose Theatre on April 6 and 8. George Peele, Robert Greene, Thomas Lodge, and Thomas Kyd have all been suggested as possible authors.

Shakespeare was thus not averse to reworking old plays, just as he also adopted plots and characters in his other plays from chronicle sources, short stories, long narrative poems, and the like. Two of his very greatest tragedies, *Hamlet* and *King Lear*, were based to a significant extent on earlier plays. A recent production of the old *King Leir* in Toronto, in 2006, demonstrated that the play can be rollicking good fun and at times quite moving, even though it pales by comparison with Shakespeare's great achievement. So too with *The Troublesome Reign of King John*. Might not the same be true of the lost *Hamlet*? Shakespeare knew a good story when he saw it.

The lost anonymous *Hamlet* appears to have been popular enough in its day that it may have been acted by English actors travelling in Germany in 1586. (A later touring production of the play in Germany, in 1626, could obviously have been influenced by Shakespeare's version.) The only surviving evidence of such a touring version is *Der Bestrafte Brudermord* (*Fratricide Punished*), derived from a now-lost manuscript dated 1710. The text may well have changed in the long interval between 1586 and 1710, but could still reflect features of the play as acted in Germany in the 1580s. One clue is that the Polonius figure is called Corambus, essentially the same name as the "Corambis" of the unauthorized first version of *Hamlet* published in London in 1603. "Corambus" or "Corambis" may mean "cabbage twice cooked," hence a dull dish; "*bis*" is Latin for "twice." Or perhaps "Coram" is the legal term of art meaning "in the presence of," alluding to the old counselor's windy love of clichés.

In any event, if the German text we have is anything like the lost *Hamlet* (and we should allow for the possibility that it reflects some details of Shakespeare's own play, since the 1710 date comes later), the resemblances point to materials that Shakespeare might well have used. In *Der bestrafte Brudermord*, as in Shakespeare's play, the ghost of Hamlet's father first appears to Francisco, Horatio, and others on watch at night. When Hamlet joins them, the Ghost comes again, laments to Hamlet the Queen's hasty re-marriage, describes his own murder by means of hebona poured in his ear, and urges revenge. The Ghost, now unseen, bids the men on guard to swear an oath as they move from place to place. Hamlet confides to Horatio the whole story of the murder. The King, a carouser and smooth deceiver, forbids his stepson to return to Wittenberg, even though permission has been granted for Leonhardus, son of Corambus, to return to France. Corambus, persuaded that Hamlet is suffering from love madness, arranges for himself and the King to overhear Hamlet's encounter with Ophelia and his urging her to go to a nunnery.

When players arrive from Germany, in *Der bestrafte Brudermord* as in Shakespeare's play, Hamlet instructs them in the natural style of acting and commissions them to put on a play before the King about the murder of King Pyrrus by his brother, again by means of poison poured in the ear. The King responds guiltily to his witnessing of the play-within-the-play. When Hamlet then finds the King alone at prayer, he postpones killing the King lest the man's soul be sent to heaven. Making his way to his mother's chambers, Hamlet stabs Corambus through a tapestry. Hamlet is sent to England with two unnamed courtiers. On his return to England, he engages in a duel with Leonhardus, who has conspired with the King to employ a poisoned dagger, with poisoned wine as a contingency plan. The deaths occur much as in Shakespeare's play. The dying Hamlet urges that the crown of Denmark be bestowed on his cousin, Duke Fortempras of Norway, of whom we have not heard earlier.

These correspondences are quite extensive, and include many circumstances not in Saxo or Belleforest. At the same time we find numerous differences, some of them amusing. The deranged Ophelia in *Der bestrafte Brudermord* imagines herself to be in love with a court butterfly named Phantasmo, a rough equivalent of *Hamlet*'s Osric. This court creature, whom Hamlet tauntingly addresses as "Signora Phantasmo," is involved in a comic action to help the clown Jens with a tax problem. Hamlet foils his unnamed escorts to England, who are under orders to kill him, by asking them to shoot him as he kneels between the two; at the critical moment, he ducks and they shoot each other. He finishes them off with their own swords and finds on their persons an incriminating letter requesting the English king to execute Hamlet if he is not already dead. The deadly wine cup intended for Hamlet in the final scene contains finely ground oriental diamond dust as its fatal ingredient. Ophelia is reported to have committed suicide by throwing herself off a hill. And so it goes. The clownish routines are not unlike those in the anonymous *King Leir*. One can perhaps catch a glimpse here of the kind of sorting out that Shakespeare must have employed in making use of sources that were simultaneously full of rich theatrical moments and goofy nonsense.

Why did Shakespeare choose to write a play on the Hamlet story at some point in the years 1599–1601? The reason may lie in the name of Shakespeare's hero. Surprisingly, this name Hamlet is not directly related etymologically to the Danish Amleth, despite the resemblance. The Danish name, appearing in various forms in Scandinavia and in Iceland, may mean something like "an imbecile, a weak person," though some etymologists suspect that the name could have taken on such a meaning from the ancient story itself (since Saxo's hero adopts the disguise of an imbecile to confuse his enemy). The name Hamlet, on the other hand, is not an uncommon proper name in England; it is sometimes varied to *Hamnet*. Now, that is really inter-esting. Shakespeare chose the name Hamnet for his only son, born as a twin to Judith and baptized in Holy Trinity Church, Stratford-upon-Avon, on 2 February 1585. (A first child of Shakespeare's marriage to Anne Hathaway, Susanna, had been born in late May, 1583, some six months after the couple had been married.) Both Hamnet and Judith appear to have been named after Shakespeare's friends and neighbors, Hamnet Sadler, a baker, and his wife, Judith. Hamnet Sadler is men-tioned in Shakespeare's last will and testament. Godparents frequently had a say in naming the newborn child in early modern England.

Did Shakespeare have the story of Hamlet in mind when he named his son Hamnet? That seems unlikely, even though, as we have seen, an anonymous play named *Hamlet* came in existence some time in the late 1580s. Why would Shakespeare choose the form "Hamnet" instead of "Hamlet," if that were his intent? More plausibly, he may have been attracted to the name and story of Hamlet in 1599–1601 because it put him in mind of his only son. Young Hamnet was dead by the time Shakespeare wrote his play. Hamnet died in August of 1596, at the age of eleven, and was buried in Stratford. We do not know from what causes Hamnet died, or where he is buried, or even if Shakespeare was able to be with his son on this sad occasion; Shakespeare was living in the London area, in Bishopsgate, near the playhouse called the Theatre where the acting company to which he belonged put on plays, while his family stayed in Stratford.

We do know that in that same year proceedings were instituted, presumably by Shakespeare himself, to enable his father, John Shakespeare, to bear arms as a gentleman. John Shakespeare had applied in his own person for this honor some twenty years earlier, but without success. The College of Heralds in London preserves two drafts of a coat of arms devised for John Shakespeare of Stratford and dated 20 October 1596. The resulting coat of arms translates the name "Shakespeare" into a rather obvious visual metaphor: a falcon brandishing or shaking a spear above a legend, in French: "*Non sans droict*," "Not without right." The grant of heraldic honors to John Shakespeare was confirmed by the College of Heralds in 1599, two years before John died in 1601. The play *Hamlet* is obsessed with a son's sense of obligation to honor and defend the memory of a dead father; Hamlet promises that he will remember his father "whiles memory holds a seat / In this distracted globe" (1.5.97–8). The *Henry IV* plays and *Henry V*, written in the years 1596 to 1599, are no less deeply concerned with a son's relationship to his father and the son's duty to be a worthy heir and successor to the man who sired him. Is *Hamlet* in part Shakespeare's artistic response to the death of his only son and to the father who would die not long after the play was written? Three or four years might seem a long time to come to terms thus with the death of a son, but the healing process can be slow, especially in dealing with such a traumatic loss. These, at any rate, are some reasons for wondering about the close resemblance between Shakespeare's title for *Hamlet* and the name of his dead son.

Whatever his feelings about Hamnet when he wrote *Hamlet* some time around the turn of the century, Shakespeare had other powerful reasons for taking up a story of fratricidal murder and its devastating consequences. He had, by this time, pretty much finished what he had to say in the vein of English history and romantic comedy: *Henry V*, in 1599, was the last English history play he would write until *Henry VIII* in 1613, while *Twelfth Night*, written about this same time, capped his career as comic dramatist even as he turned to problem plays like *Troilus and Cressida* and *Measure for Measure*. *Julius Caesar*, in 1599, with its powerful blend of Roman history and tragic event, also afforded Shakespeare a way of redirecting his course toward the writing of great tragedy. He must have known the lost old play of *Hamlet*, with its rich store of narrative that he could refashion as he had done in his *King John* and his *Henry IV–Henry V* sequence and was to do in *King Lear*. He had read Belleforest's *Histoires Tragiques* and must have known, at least indirectly, Saxo's account. He evidently saw in the narrative of the Danish Prince the rich opportunity for transforming that story into a tragedy that would make the world take note. It is to his play that we next turn, and to the way in which it appears to have been staged in 1599–1601 by the acting company to which he belonged.

2

Actions That a Man Might Play:
Hamlet on Stage in 1599–1601

In order to appreciate the extraordinary range of staging and film possibilities that have been employed over the centuries in producing *Hamlet*, we need to know first what the staging would have been like in 1599–1601, presumably at the Globe Theatre south of the River Thames and also at court or on tour. We cannot be sure that the unauthorized quarto of 1603 is entirely truthful in boasting that the play had been acted "in the city of London, as also in the two universities of Cambridge and Oxford, and elsewhere," but that this popular play went on tour at some point seems likely. We have already seen that the lost *Hamlet* may have been performed by English actors traveling in Germany in 1586 and then in 1626. To this can be added an odd note of stage history: on 5 September 1607, off the coast of Sierra Leone, a certain Captain Keeling, in command of an East India Company ship named the *Dragon*, arranged to have "the tragedy of *Hamlet*" acted on board twice as entertainment for the captain of another vessel—an activity which, the captain wrote, "I permit to keep my people from idleness and unlawful games or sleep." Whatever else this bizarre item may suggest about life on board a vessel of the East India Company in the early seventeenth century, it certainly testifies to the sense in which *Hamlet* had already become a household, or at least a shipboard, name.

The reasons for assuming a date of original performance in 1599–1601 are, briefly, these. The play must have been in existence by 26 July 1602, when it was entered for publication in the London Stationers' Register, a record of transactions of the official guild of stationers, that is, book printers, publishers, and sellers. Such a registration was the publisher's way of establishing what we would call copyright protection, prior to actual publication. At the earlier limit, *Hamlet* is not mentioned in the list of Shakespeare's plays in Francis Meres's *Palladis Tamia*, autumn, 1598, which is generally quite accurate and comprehensive. Gabriel Harvey, to be sure, attributes the "tragedy of Hamlet, Prince of Denmark" to Shakespeare in a marginal note in Harvey's copy of Speght's 1598 edition of Chaucer's works, but he could have scribbled this marginal note any time after that. *Hamlet* repeatedly alludes to the story of the assassination of Julius Caesar, which Shakespeare had dramatized in 1599, but we cannot be sure that these allusions necessarily followed hard upon the earlier play. So too with *Hamlet*'s close affinity at times to John Marston's *Antonio's Revenge*, registered on 24 October 1601, determining whether Shakespeare's work preceded or followed that of Marston is not easy to ascertain. *Hamlet*'s account, contained chiefly in the 1623 Folio text, of a professional rivalry between the adult players and the boy actors tends to confirm a date of 1599–1601, when the so-called War of the Theatres was at its height, but does not help much in narrowing the date. (See the next chapter for a more extensive discussion of this theatrical rivalry.)

The 1603 title page proclaims that *Hamlet* "hath been divers times acted by His Majesty's servants in the city of London." By "His Majesty's servants" is meant the acting company to which Shakespeare belonged, usually referred to as the King's Men. Beginning in 1594 as the Lord Chamberlain's Men, they had been renamed "His Majesty's servants" in 1603, shortly after King James VI of Scotland came to the English throne as James VI and I, succeeding his cousin Queen Elizabeth, who had reigned for nearly forty-six years. The honor of being named the King's company acknowledged in effect that they, as the Chamberlain's Men, were the leading company of adult actors in London's highly competitive theatrical marketplace. They beat out the Lord Admiral's Men, their chief rival among the public companies.

Richard Burbage was the lead actor of the Chamberlain's/King's Men; Edward Alleyn commanded the same position in the Admiral's Men. Burbage came from an influential family in the world of London's commercial theatre; his father, James Burbage, had built (as we have seen) in 1576 a theatrical building called simply the Theatre, presumably because there was no other such structure at that time designed expressly for public acting. A year or so later the Curtain went up nearby in Moorfields, north of London's city walls but close enough that customers could walk to either theatre from the city. The Rose was built on the south bank of the River Thames, a little to the west of London Bridge, in the late 1580s.

Shakespeare joined a new company in 1594 headed by Richard Burbage and his brother Cuthbert. Together the Burbages, including their father James, owned five "shares." Shakespeare bought one share (possibly with financial assistance from the young Earl of Southampton, to whom he had dedicated two early poems, *Venus and Adonis* and *The Rape of Lucrece* in 1593–4, and for whom he may have written some of his sonnets). Other single shares in what then became known as the Lord Chamberlain's Men were originally purchased by John Heminges, Thomas Pope, Augustine Phillips, and Will Kempe. The sharers jointly owned the company, ran its business, incurred its financial risks, and reaped such financial rewards as they could gather through charging admission to its shows, receiving payment for guest appearances at court, and the like. This particular company did very well; Shakespeare and his fellows became moderately wealthy. The Lord Chamberlain was a powerful man at court, able to provide the company with the protection it needed from the London authorities, who were perennially looking for excuses to close down the playhouses, and from laws against vagabondage. Henry Carey, first Baron Hunsdon, was Lord Chamberlain from 1583 until he died in July 1596; his son, George Carey, second Baron Hunsdon, succeeded him in March 1597. During the brief interval, when the office was held by Henry Brooke, Lord Cobham, the company was known as Lord Hunsdon's Men.

The roster of this company remained remarkably stable: Burbage stayed on as lead actor until his death in 1619, Pope until his death in 1603, Phillips until his death in 1605. Kempe left the company in 1598, but was replaced by Robert Armin, who then became another long-term regular. Henry Condell and Will Sly joined by 1598; Condell stayed on long enough to join with Heminges in editing the Folio collection of Shakespeare's plays in 1623. The Lord Chamberlain's Men acted at the Theatre in Moorfields, and then, in 1599, when they ran into difficulties with their landlord, moved to the south bank of the River Thames, having acted also at the Curtain playhouse in Moorfields during a period of transition. They used the timbers of the Theatre to build a similar structure on the Bankside, naming it the

Globe. The housing was presumably much like that of the Theatre, since the recycled timbers were hand-hewn and needed to be reassembled whenever possible into the exact same part of the building. Probably the company introduced some changes to the stage area on the basis of years of experience, but essentially the Globe was a reincarnation of the Theatre.

Shakespeare was an actor as well as playwright; we know this from casting lists for plays performed by the Chamberlain/King's company, especially those of Ben Jonson—though, unfortunately, not for any of Shakespeare's own. The evidence suggests that Shakespeare acted until 1603 at least, but thereafter may have been excused from performing because he was so extraordinarily valuable as a playwright. He produced roughly two plays a year over a twenty-year period. As an actor he seems to have taken relatively minor roles. Stage tradition, never entirely reliable, credits him with having played the old servant, Adam, in *As You Like It* in 1599 or thereabouts, and the Ghost in *Hamlet*. Stage lore speaks of him as having preferred the parts of kings and old men. Whatever the truth of this claim, we, in fact, know very little as to which roles he may have played.

With Burbage as lead actor playing such roles as Hamlet, Othello, King Lear, and presumably Macbeth, Antony, Coriolanus, and Prospero, the company then had about five to eight other "sharers," or full company members, to take on the important secondary roles. In *Hamlet*, this would probably mean Claudius, Polonius, Laertes, the Ghost (allegedly acted by Shakespeare), Horatio, Rosencrantz, Guildenstern, Fortinbras, the Player King, the First Clown or gravedigger, and Osric. Some doubling would have been possible, if needed: the Player King, for example, appears only in act 2, scene 2 and act 3, scene 2, so that his part could easily be doubled with that of Osric or Fortinbras. Either Rosencrantz or Guildenstern could double with Osric or Fortinbras, both of whom appear only in the final scenes after Rosencrantz and Guildenstern are reported dead.

The company may have been large enough by 1599–1601 not to have to double many parts, though actors were accustomed to doubling. The company probably distributed important secondary roles routinely, with little effort at specialization; these actors were professionals, ready to take on roles as required. Hired extras might have been used for parts such as Marcellus, Francisco, and Bernardo in the night watch, Voltimand and Cornelius as ambassadors to Norway,

Reynaldo as servant to Polonius (appearing only in act 2, scene 1), the players of the Prologue and of Lucianus in "The Murder of Gonzago," the Second Clown or gravedigger, a sailor, a priest, another ambassador, Fortinbras's "*army*" (4.4.0 SD), and various gentlemen, lords, and messengers with brief speaking parts. Actor sharers could have doubled some of these roles; the distinction between the smaller secondary roles and "bit" parts is not firm.

The company evidently had an actor who specialized in important clownish roles. Will Kempe, until his departure in 1598, seems to have played Bottom the Weaver in *A Midsummer Night's Dream* (*c.* 1595) and Dogberry in *Much Ado About Nothing* (1598–9). When Kempe was replaced by Robert Armin, we find comic roles of a new and more witty philosophical cast, including, evidently, Touchstone in *As You Like It* (*c.* 1599), Feste in *Twelfth Night* (1600–2), Lavatch in *All's Well That Ends Well* (*c.* 1601–5), and the Fool in *King Lear* (*c.* 1605–6). What Armin's role in *Hamlet* might have been is not clear, though the First Clown or gravedigger is one possibility.

Women's roles were assigned to boy actors, who could act thus until their voices changed, at sixteen or so—a late date by our standards, owing to the fact that the onset of puberty was generally delayed as a result of poor nutrition. The roles of Gertrude and Ophelia would go to the most highly trained and probably oldest boys. Evidently too the Player Queen in "The Murder of Gonzago" would be played by a boy. Hamlet jests with this boy when the acting company arrives at Elsinore, making a point of the lad's growing toward manhood with the prospect that his voice will soon deepen: "What, my young lady and mistress! By'r Lady, Your Ladyship is nearer to heaven than when I saw you last, by the altitude of a chopine. Pray God your voice, like a piece of uncurrent gold, be not cracked within the ring" (2.2.424–8). (A chopine is a thick-soled shoe of Italian fashion; coins cracked within the ring featuring the sovereign's head were not passable as legal currency.) The boys' acting skill was considerable, as Hamlet implies when he interrogates Rosencrantz and Guildenstern in a Folio-only passage, alluded to above, about the companies of boy actors in "the city" (implicitly London) that are giving the adult actors such worrisome competition (2.2.326–62).

Adult actors also were well trained. Among other matters, they studied fencing and other forms of hand-to-hand combat in order to be able to choreograph their fight scenes (as at the end of *Hamlet*) or battles with grace and skill. Some were musicians, able to sing and play on stage, though offstage music might be provided as well. Ophelia sings in her mad scene (4.5), and the First Clown has a comic ditty (marked as "*Song*" in the original stage directions) as he digs Ophelia's grave in act 5, scene 1.

Sound effects could be impressive. A *flourish* or fanfare of trumpets announces the arrival of Claudius and his queen on the occasions of his entrance to a state event or formal session of the court (1.2.0, 2.2.0, 3.2.88). A *flourish* sounds also when the King and his entourage exit from a state occasion, as at 1.2.128, when Hamlet is left alone on stage. The royal entry at 3.2.88 is led by "*trumpets and kettledrums.*" "*The trumpets sound*" to signal that the dumb show is about to begin at 3.2.133.

The entrance of the King and his court in the play's final scene is especially elaborate: "*A table prepared. [Enter] trumpets, drums, and officers with cushions; King, Queen, [Osric], and all the state; foils, daggers; and Laertes*" (5.2.222 SD). These preparations are needed when the King calls for kettledrum and trumpet and cannon to sound while he drinks a toast: "*Trumpets the while*" (276 SD). Then, as Hamlet scores his first hit in the fencing match with Laertes, "*Drum, trumpet, and shot. Flourish. A piece goes off*" (282 SD). The "*piece*" is a piece of artillery, a cannon. In act 1, scene 4, "*A flourish of trumpets and two pieces go off*" within (that is, off stage) as a means of informing Hamlet and his companions on the battlements, and us as audience, that Claudius is draining down draughts of Rhenish wine while "The kettledrum and trumpet thus bray out / The triumph of his pledge" (1.4.6–12). At 2.2.368, an offstage *flourish* signals the arrival of the itinerant players to Elsinore. When, on the other hand, the King enters more privately, to confer with Rosencrantz and Guildenstern or Polonius or Laertes, no trumpet signal is heard. Drums announce the arrival of Fortinbras and the English ambassadors at 5.2.363. In the play's very last moments, Fortinbras orders his soldiers to "shoot," meaning presumably that the final tragic procession off stage, with the bearing away of the dead bodies of the King, the Queen, Hamlet, and Laertes, is accompanied by the firing of a peal of ordnance. Other sound effects are heard, such as the crowing of a cock (1.1.142) to warn the Ghost that the time has come for him to return to his otherworldly abode.

The Elizabethan public stage had essentially no scenery. We have no contemporary picture of the interior of Shakespeare's Globe Theatre, unfortunately, though we do have a drawing of the Swan Theatre on the Bankside, made by the Dutch Van Buchell and seemingly based on a description and a sketch by Johannes De Witt, who visited London in 1596 (see Illustration 2). In addition, a contract for the building of the Fortune Theatre has survived, as do a few representations of stages on title pages of published books. Several illustrations show theatre buildings from the outside, in views of the Bankside and London. From these pieces of evidence, we can reconstruct a polygonal, round-shaped playhouse, inside of which was built a rectangular stage about forty-three feet wide and twenty-seven feet deep, raised about five feet above the ground. The yard, perhaps seventy feet in diameter, was open to the sky. It surrounded the raised stage on three sides. In this yard stood spectators that Hamlet disparagingly refers to as the "groundlings" (3.2.11), who ordinarily paid a penny for admission. Around them were arrayed the roof-covered galleries, with seats, on three levels, where more well-to-do spectators could sit and watch the play. These customers entered into the galleries from the yard by means of stairs, after paying an additional price for their seats. Some space was apparently reserved as a "lords' room" for especially prominent spectators. A sloping roof, supported by two pillars that rose up through the stage, covered much of the acting area. A hut above the rest of the structure provided room for machinery used in raising and lowering effects. A flag could be flown from a masthead here, presumably to announce a play in progress or about to begin.

The acting area of crucial concern is backstage, and here, regrettably, the Swan drawing raises questions as well as suggesting some answers as regards the Globe Theatre. We cannot, after all, assume that London's public theatres were identical to one another; indeed, we know that the Fortune was rectangular rather than polygonal in shape and that the Rose was smaller than the Globe. Most importantly, not all theatres seem to have had the same number of doors leading on stage from the enclosed space behind what was known as the "tiring house façade" or wall separating the main stage from the actors' dressing area. The Swan drawing shows two large doors in the façade, to the left and right of center. Nothing is shown between the doors other than a bare wall, whereas a number of Renaissance English plays seem to demand a central third door, or at least a "discovery space" that could be curtained off, allowing for scenes of hiding or the quick revealing of actors, as, for example, when

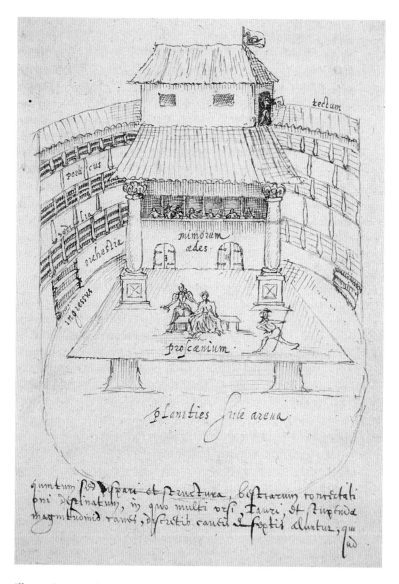

Illustration 2. The Swan Theatre, *c.* 1596, in a drawing by the Dutch Van Buchell and seemingly based on a description and a sketch by Johannes De Witt, who visited London in 1596. Courtesy of the Division of Special Collections, University Library, Leiden, The Netherlands, and University Library, Utrecht, Ms. 32, fol. 132r.

Prospero pulls back a curtain and *"discovers"* Ferdinand and Miranda playing chess in *The Tempest* (5.1.172).

No less intriguing is the space above the two doors and the tiring house wall. The Swan drawing shows a kind of gallery with six bays in which persons appear to be watching a play below them on the main stage. Such a gallery seems to have been a regular feature of the London public theatres, but was it really used for spectators? Some plays require acting "above"; Romeo and Juliet, in their first extended wooing, are to be imagined with Romeo on the main stage as though in the garden behind the Capulets' house and Juliet at her window above. Perhaps the gallery was used for seating of spectators when that space was not needed for the play, as seems to be the case with *Hamlet*. We can then imagine this play in the Globe Theatre with spectators literally on all sides, demanding of the actors that they perform "in the round" even more fully than would always be required of them in a theatre with an audience on three sides. The spectators in the gallery would presumably be well-to-do, like opera viewers in box seats near to the stage where the occupants can both see and be seen.

Although the Swan drawing shows no trap door in the main stage, a trap door was required in some Elizabethan plays, and *Hamlet* unquestionably makes use of it and of the space under the stage, as we shall see. On the underside of the roof over the stage, also not visible in the Swan drawing, were representations of heavenly bodies, probably including the sun, moon, planets, and zodiacal constellations. Hamlet will have occasion to refer to this world above his head when he discourses about "this brave o'erhanging firmament, this majestical roof fretted with golden fire" (2.2.301–3). We will come back to both these points.

Although scenery in our accepted sense of the term was not employed on the Elizabethan stage, the spectacle was designedly handsome. The building itself, with pillars and other ornaments painted to resemble marble, was itself an object of monumental beauty. Costuming was expensively made and generally gorgeous; some evidence suggests that the players might obtain rich garments from wealthy courtiers who would wish to have a new outfit for important court occasions and might therefore be ready to discard last season's clothes. Costumes are especially important on a stage devoid of ordinary scenery; they stand out in marked contrast to their surroundings and help to differentiate characters one from another. A priest is to be accoutered in clerical garb in Ophelia's funeral procession (5.1.216). Similarly appropriate attire are needed for the gravediggers, the Ghost, the ambassadors (2.2.57, 5.2.363), young maidens, aged counselors, soldiers on watch, captains, sailors, players, gentlemen, lords, and foppish courtiers like Osric.

Props too take on a heightened visual importance in a theatre of presentational rather than representational stage picture. Marcellus, one of the guards on watch, is armed with a "partisan" or long-handled spear (1.1.44); so too presumably are Bernardo and Francisco. Hamlet is armed, when he encounters his father's ghost, with a sword (1.5.155), upon which he obliges Horatio and the other to swear an oath of secrecy. Polonius must have money and papers about him which he hands to Reynaldo to be delivered to Laertes in Paris (2.1.1). Voltimand gives a paper to Claudius when Voltimand and Cornelius return from their successful diplomatic mission to Norway (2.2.76). Polonius has a letter, written by Hamlet to Ophelia, which Polonius reads to the King and Queen (2.2.109–19). Hamlet reads a book when Polonius attempts to find out what is troubling Hamlet (2.2.168); Ophelia pretends to be reading when she is placed as a decoy in Hamlet's path (3.1.56). She has love letters and other remembrances of Hamlet that she attempts to "redeliver" to him (94).

The dumb show preceding "The Murder of Gonzago" seemingly requires a bench or some means of representing *"a bank of flowers"* on which the Player King sleeps and is murdered by means of poison poured in his ear (3.2.133). In this same scene, Gertrude's request to her son to "sit by me" (107) indicates that she is sitting, as indeed she would be, at the side of her royal husband, in order to watch the play. Hamlet's sardonic offer to lie with his head in Ophelia's lap (3.2.112) would seem to require that she too is sitting. Presumably stagehands or extras have unobtrusively brought on cushions or chairs suitable for royalty, which are then quietly removed at the scene's end. Elizabethan plays regularly require such temporary bringing on of furnishings, which, in the absence of scenic background, take on an enhanced visual importance. Thrones were available, backstage, and could have been deployed on *Hamlet*'s most ceremonial occasions (1.2, 3.2, 5.2).

Props can lend visual focus to thematic ideas. The players are provided with recorders, or flute-like wind instruments, with which Hamlet insultingly teases Rosencrantz and Guildenstern (3.2.343–71).

The First Sailor hands a letter to Horatio (4.6.12). A Messenger arrives "*with letters*" for the King and Queen from Hamlet (4.7.35–7). The gravediggers have spades and mattocks; the spade is referred to repeatedly (5.1.29, 90, 94) and is also called a "dirty shovel" (102). Yorick's skull is an emblematic stage object in lines 172–216. Queen Gertrude has flowers with which to bestrew the gravesite of Ophelia (243). When the King and Queen enter to the dueling in 5.2, to considerable fanfare, a "*table*" must be "*prepared,*" that is, brought on stage, along with "*cushions,*" "*foils,*" "*daggers,*" and presumably wine in a cup (5.2.222). The cushions are evidently for sitting; the "*foils*" (rapiers), daggers, and wine are presumably brought in by servants and placed on the table. Hamlet and Laertes evidently fight not merely with rapiers, but with rapiers and daggers, one in each hand, in a style of fighting that was common. Military banners may herald the entrance of Fortinbras in act 4, scene 4 and in the play's final scene (5.2.363). All told, the list of props needed for a production of *Hamlet*, both large and small, is fairly extensive.

Gestures also take on an enlarged theatrical significance in presentational, non-scenic staging. The text of *Hamlet* is unusually attentive to gesture. The Ghost in scene 1 "stalks away," being "offended" by Horatio's attempt to question him (1.1.54). On its second visitation "*It spreads his arms*" and disappears when the soldiers strike at him (144). When Hamlet joins the watch, the Ghost "*beckons*" to him to follow to a more removed ground (1.4.57). When the soldiers attempt to restrain Hamlet from going, he breaks free. Hamlet writes, or seems to write, in the tablets of his memory to enshrine there what the Ghost has said to him (1.5.110–11); these "tables" may be actual writing materials in Hamlet's hands, or may signify a mental observation, or both, but in any case the gesture has thematic purport. He holds out his sword for the others to swear on it, and moves from place to place as the Ghost's sepulchral voice is heard beneath the staging moving "*hic et ubique,*" here and everywhere (155–89). Hamlet makes a point of exiting with the soldiers and Horatio together, rather than allowing them to yield him precedence, as a way of insisting on their brotherhood of secrecy (199).

Hamlet's erratic behavior in his pretended madness calls for gestures that are carefully calibrated, like props, for thematic effect. He behaves very oddly to Ophelia, in an offstage action described by her to her father: he appears to her in disordered dress, holds her at the length of

one arm, studies her face, and sighs piteously, all evidently with the
successful intent of convincing Ophelia and Polonius that he is mad
(2.1.79–102). His having no hat upon his head is a signifier to Elizabethan audiences of emotional distress, since gentlemen regularly wore
hats indoors as well as outdoors. In their next encounter he is very
rough with Ophelia, at least as acted in most modern versions
(3.1.120–52). He offers to lie in her lap at the play-within-the-play,
embarrassing her before the courtly assembly with his bawdy double
entendres (3.2.110–19). He calls for recorders and takes one in hand to
make his satirical point to Rosencrantz and Guildenstern that they are
"playing" with him (344–71). At 3.3.73-88, he draws his sword to kill
the kneeling and praying Claudius, but then, thinking of a better plan,
re-sheathes his weapon. In his mother's chambers (3.4), he stabs
Polonius through the arras, shows two likenesses of Hamlet senior
and Claudius to his terrified mother to force her to confront what she
has done in deserting the memory of her dead husband, and drags off
the dead body of Polonius as he leaves.

At Ophelia's gravesite he picks up a skull which turns out to be that
of Yorick, the old King's jester, and uses it as a *memento mori* to reflect
on death and forgetfulness, before throwing it to earth in revulsion at
its putrid smell (5.1.183–200). He conceals himself as the royal party
enters and then comes forward to grapple with Laertes at Ophelia's
grave (222–68). The final scene details his actions in the duel with
meaningful precision: he scores the first hits, he declines to drink from
the wine cup, he exchanges weapons with Laertes when he perceives
that Laertes's weapon is unbated (that is, not blunted with a button), he
stabs the King, he prevents Horatio from drinking from the poisoned
cup, and still more. These specified gestures are strikingly focused on
Hamlet himself. He is the action hero of his play.

Hamlet is fascinated by theatre, to such an extent that the play of
Hamlet invites us to be continually aware of its metatheatrical meanings—that is, its series of observations on the art of acting. Hamlet has
known the visiting players for some time, and greets them as old
friends (2.2). He is able to recite, for the First Player and his company,
some thirteen lines of tragic blank verse, with only a slight hesitation
at first, before turning over the rest of the speech to the First Player
(450–64). Polonius allows that Hamlet's recitation is "well spoken,
with good accent and good discretion" (466–7). Actually, Hamlet is
irritated at Polonius for boasting of his own experience as an actor and

posing as an expert; Polonius's later recollection of having enacted Julius Caesar and having been "killed i'th' Capitol" where "Brutus killed me" elicits from Hamlet a withering put-down: "It was a brute part of him to kill so capital a calf there" (3.2.101–4). Hamlet's impatience with Polonius's complacency is almost professional, as though acting is too fine a calling to be trivialized by such a claim of membership in its mystery. When Polonius complains of the First Player's recitation in act 2, scene 2 as "too long," Hamlet is no less acerbic: "It shall to the barber's with your beard" (498–9). Hamlet will brook no competition from this old fool. Hamlet is also a playwright of sorts, though amateur: he offers to set down "some dozen or sixteen lines" to be inserted into "The Murder of Gonzago" for the upcoming theatrical entertainment, and is gratified that the First Player agrees to this proposition.

Hamlet's advice to the players in the fine points of their calling sounds like a manifesto for Shakespeare's own acting company:

> Speak the speech, I pray you, as I pronounced it to you, trippingly on the tongue. But if you mouth it, as many of our players do, I had as lief the town crier spoke my lines. Nor do not saw the air too much with your hand, thus, but use all gently; for in the very torment, tempest, and, as I may say, whirlwind of your passion, you must acquire and beget a temperance that may give it smoothness. Oh, it offends me to the soul to hear a robustious periwig-pated fellow tear a passion to tatters, to very rags, to split the ears of the groundlings, who for the most part are capable of nothing but inexplicable dumb shows and noise. I would have such a fellow whipped for o'erdoing Termagant. It out-Herods Herod. Pray you, avoid it.
>
> (3.2.1–14)

Hamlet insists that the performers of his generation must reform the excesses of previous acting traditions and styles, which have tended too often to be bombastic. Good acting must convey real passion as intense as that of a tempest or whirlwind, but must do so with decorum and restraint of gesture. He deplores the tastes of many who stand in the yards of the public theatres, the "groundlings," who, by their craving for mindless and noisy spectacle, encourage actors to pander to what audiences ask for. This is an elitist gospel of theatre, and goes with what Hamlet has said earlier to the First Player concerning the passage about the death of Priam and the grief of Hecuba that they have recited between them. It was, Hamlet recalls, "never acted, or if it was, not above once, for the play, I remember, pleased not the million; 'twas caviar to the general. But it was—as I received it, and others, whose judgments in such matters cried in the top of mine—an excellent play, well digested in the scenes, set down with as much modesty as cunning." By avoiding spicy improprieties and affectation, the play has proved itself to be "honest," "as wholesome as sweet," well-proportioned, and not simply showy (2.2.434–45).

This is praise indeed, all the more so in that Hamlet uses these terms to describe a speech that strikes us today as studiously classical—Virgilian, Senecan, and virtually a closet drama, rather than something for the Elizabethan popular stage. Hamlet joins forces with highbrow critics who prefer such rarefied drama to anything cooked up to please the million. When elite drama of this sort is performed on the popular stage it is "caviar to the general," that is, choice fare served up to those who lack sophisticated taste and thus cannot appreciate true refinement. Hamlet refuses to cast pearls before swine.

These are remarkable things for Richard Burbage to be saying in the Globe Theatre, surrounded on three sides by the very "groundlings" that he professes to deplore. Are Hamlet and Shakespeare insulting the audience? If that seems unlikely, perhaps the answer is that both Hamlet and Shakespeare are appealing to those who aspire to good taste, implicitly asking all of the audience, including those who stand in the yard, to join with him and the acting company in preferring a drama of true elegance and beauty.

Hamlet (and no doubt Shakespeare) holds to a noble and ethical view of what drama can hope to accomplish. "The purpose of playing," Hamlet insists, "was and is to hold as 'twere the mirror up to nature, to show virtue her feature, scorn her own image, and the very age and body of the time his form and pressure" (3.2.20–4). Good drama can make a crucial difference in our lives by showing us our ideal selves and by assisting us to differentiate virtue from vice, so that we can cling to virtue. At its highest potential, drama performs an ethical function. That is why bad acting is so deplorable. All too easily an actor can make "the unskillful laugh," but in doing so he "cannot but make the judicious grieve, the censure of the which one must in your allowance o'erweigh a whole theatre of others" (24–8). Again we hear the appeal to the select few who have intellectual breeding and good taste. Any persons can join this company of the wise, so long as they agree not to applaud actors who strut and bellow.

The actors bear a heavy responsibility in this too, of course. Clowns in particular must learn to "speak no more than is set down for them." They must avoid ad-libbing and laughing at their own inanities in order to prompt "some quantity of barren spectators to laugh too, though in the meantime some necessary question of the play be then to be considered. That's villainous, and shows a most pitiful ambition in the fool that uses it" (3.2.39–45). Hamlet is uncompromising in his insistence on drama of the highest ethical and aesthetic standards. During the players' performance, Hamlet knows bad acting when he sees it: "Leave thy damnable faces and begin," he growls at the player enacting Lucianus as he is about to commit the murder in "The Murder of Gonzago" (251). Hamlet is also adept at parodying bad acting himself, as when he bursts in upon Ophelia in disarray, "his knees knocking each other, / And with a look so piteous in purport / As if he had been loosèd out of hell / To speak of horrors" (2.1.83–6), or when he plays mad to the easily duped Polonius (2.2.171–219).

If we look scene by scene at Shakespeare's dramaturgical method in *Hamlet*, we are bound to admire his skill in exploiting the resources of the Globe stage. The staging of the opening scene is remarkable, especially from our modern point of view. We may be accustomed today to presentational staging without scenery, but we are unacquainted with a total absence of artificial lighting. *Hamlet*, acted on the Bankside in a theatre open to the sky in the afternoon, had to begin in full daylight. How were the actors in this original production to convey a sense of night and of terror? They did so in good part by their nervous gestures and staccato exchanges of information. Probably they did not carry torches or lanterns, though such were common staging devices elsewhere in Shakespeare to convey as sense of nighttime. The audience knew only at this point that two actors, attired as soldiers and armed with long-handled spears, were frightened and nervous about something. The text specifies that Bernardo, the first to speak, asks "Who's there?" when it turns out that he is only now arriving on watch; it should be Francisco's business to make this demand of the newcomer. "Nay, answer *me*. Stand and unfold yourself," he bids Bernardo.

On the Elizabethan stage, in broad daylight, the actors needed to rely on gesture to convey what it is to be terrified by dark midnight and a dread of the unknown. From their gestures, an Elizabethan audience would gather that the soldiers on guard can barely see each other. The man who has been on watch, Francisco, is grateful to be relieved, because, as he confesses, "I am sick at heart." What is amiss? Soon others join them: another soldier named Marcellus, and a gentleman named Horatio. He is demonstrably a gentleman because he is dressed accordingly. He also appears to be a skeptic about a "dreaded sight" that has been "twice seen of us" (1.1.29), that is, by the soldiers on watch. Horatio has been asked to come along to verify what they have seen and to cope with it somehow in ways that learned gentlemen might understand better than common soldiers. Francisco, having been relieved of the watch by Bernardo, leaves.

The paradoxical advantage of staging such a midnight encounter in full daylight is that it calls upon the spectators, whether Elizabethan or modern, to use all their imaginative skills to conjure up in their minds a scene that is presented by the actors only through a kind of theatrical shorthand. London's new Globe Theatre, by offering matinee performances, can enable audiences today to experience what it must have been like for Elizabethan spectators to witness a ghost at two o'clock in the afternoon in an amphitheatre open to the sky. Theatre deals incessantly in symbolic representation, and the more it is employed the more the spectators are drawn in as partners in the enterprise of substantiating an illusion. When actors mime fearful surprise, the audience must supply what is missing, by tacitly entering into a contract of willing suspension of disbelief. The spectators know that the actors are actors and that the time is not literally nighttime. The spectators are comfortably aware that as spectators they are outside the circle of illusion. They assent to a dramatic fiction, and, by so doing, enter into the process of turning illusion into event. Perhaps a bell backstage has tolled midnight; the text specifies that the bell was "beating one" (1.1.43) when, on two previous nights, something unusual occurred. Not yet knowing what this unusual thing might have been adds to the spectators' involvement in the suspense.

How would Shakespeare's company have staged the Ghost, allegedly with the playwright himself in the role? Not by means of offstage sound effects or spooky lighting in a darkened theatre. The Ghost must stalk on stage, right in front of the terrified soldiers and the spectators. He must resemble "the King that's dead" (1.1.45), helmeted and with a grizzled beard, armed "from top to toe" (1.2.229), so that the audience can confirm with its own eyes the soldiers' detailed observation of his appearance. He seems remarkably real. At the same time, stage action must convey the sense in which this is an "illusion" (1.1.131). The effect is created by having the soldiers strike ineffectually at the Ghost with their long-handled spears. As Marcellus observes, when the Ghost has disappeared the second time, "it is as the air invulnerable" (151). Actors can easily convey the impression that the blows aimed in the Ghost's direction appear to go right through him. The Ghost's sudden entrances and exits must employ another *trompe l'oeil* device: the men on guard are talking earnestly, unaware of the actor who quietly enters through one of the doors and moves perhaps behind one of the stage pillars. Nothing in the text suggests that the trap door is to be employed at this point.

The opening of scene 2 employs a dramaturgic device that is characteristically Shakespearean: a sudden shift from a small scene of cold and isolation and terror to one of courtly splendor. The large cast required in this scene enters in full panoply. "*Flourish. Enter Claudius, King of Denmark, Gertrude the Queen, [the] Council, as Polonius and his son Laertes. Hamlet, cum aliis,*" that is, with others. This last note seems to call on the acting company to fill the stage with as many bodies as are available. They are there on a momentous state occasion. The order of entrance is significant: musicians leading the procession, then the King and Queen, followed by his counselors. Hamlet, tellingly, is mentioned last; as son of the dead king and of the living queen he deserves a place of honor, but he is out of step. The contrast in staging between scenes 1 and 2 could not be more bold, and is accentuated by the rapidity of scene change on the open Elizabethan stage. Horatio and his two soldierly companions leave the stage with the intent of finding Hamlet, now that morning has arrived, and immediately the entrance for scene 2 begins. Chairs, perhaps thrones, may be brought on for the King and Queen.

Every visual sign is one of ceremonial splendor, albeit under conditions of some constraint. After all, the previous king has died very recently, and custom would require members of his family, especially his widow, to "do obsequious sorrow" for "some term" (1.2.1–4, 87–92), usually at least a year. The new king has some explaining to do. Are the courtiers expected to wear mourning, or bright costumes in celebration of the new regime, or something of both? Claudius's words seem to call for a tactful blend or compromise, enabling the royal couple to celebrate their marriage publicly "With an auspicious and a dropping eye, / With mirth in funeral and with dirge in marriage, / In equal scale weighing delight and dole" (11–13). These oxymorons might encourage the court to dress accordingly, perhaps in full regalia but with a black armband or sash of mourning. An Elizabethan audience would have found the scene visually familiar, since the courtiers are dressed in contemporary costume.

Hamlet is vividly distinguished from the others. He is dressed in "inky cloak" and "customary suits of solemn black" (77–8). These outward shows cannot convey adequately his inner grief, but they are at least a way of paying due respect to a king whom the rest of the courtiers seem ready to forget. Costuming assumes a highly symbolic role in depicting how the court is to negotiate the conflicting strategies of mourning and celebration. Special effects are no less important, as Claudius and his entourage exit to the sound of trumpets and to Claudius's promise that the toasts he plans to offer on this celebratory day will be greeted by the thunder of cannon (126–7). This departure once more provides a quick transition from a full stage to one of quiet and isolation, first of Hamlet in soliloquy and then in intense conversation with Horatio and the soldiers who can tell him what to expect that night.

When the play returns to the guard platform at midnight, after another private scene (1.3) in which Laertes bids farewell to his sister Ophelia and their father, Shakespeare provides his audience with another juxtaposition of lonely nighttime darkness and festive, fully lighted celebration. Horatio and Marcellus resume the watch, this time with Hamlet. From their conversation, and also by their gestures and the way they are dressed, the audience learns that "it is very cold" and in the middle of the night: it has struck twelve (1.4.1–4). Again, the sense of time and weather must be conveyed, on the Elizabethan stage in the full light of the afternoon, by costumed actors and their gestures. The rhythms of repetition carry the audience back to scene 1. The time "draws near the season / Wherein the spirit held his wont to walk" (5–6). Meanwhile, offstage noises must create the impression of a celebration going on within the castle. "*A flourish of trumpets, and two pieces go off.*" Hamlet explains to the others that the King "doth wake tonight and takes his rouse," that is, reveling and carousing late into the evening. A wild German dance, the "swaggering upspring," is in process, and, as the King "drains his draughts of Rhenish down, / The kettledrum and trumpet thus bray out / The triumph of his pledge" (8–12). Drum and trumpet sound each time Claudius drinks his wine in one continuous pouring down his throat. The contrast between cold and warm, dark and light, outside and inside is both visual and auditory, conveyed by musical effects, while Hamlet provides a running gloss. When the Ghost returns, he enters presumably as before, stealthily and frighteningly, but with stage effects that are meaningfully varied. First, he "*beckons*" Hamlet to go with him to some other location; Hamlet understands that the Ghost wants to speak with him alone. Hence Hamlet breaks away from his companions' attempts to restrain him and follows the Ghost off stage, presumably both exiting through the same door, whereupon the others follow, also through the same stage door. A scene break has occurred. But, whereas later actor-managers will respond to a felt need to alter the scenery, since the location has changed, the non-scenic presentational stage of the Elizabethan theatre provides an easier means of shift. "*Enter Ghost and Hamlet*," presumably in that order, at the start of act 1, scene 5, and presumably through the other main stage door. This is standard procedure. The five lines of dialogue at the end of scene 4 among Horatio and the others, after the Ghost and Hamlet have left, provide a perfectly satisfactory interval of time to allow the audience to imagine the Ghost and Hamlet having moved to some new spot where they can be alone.

Once the Ghost leaves, having informed Hamlet of the horrible details of the murder and having instructed him in his duty of revenge, Hamlet is joined by the others, who presumably enter through the second stage door used by the Ghost and Hamlet to arrive at their new location. Soon the Ghost's voice is heard crying out from a striking new location "*under the stage*" (1.5.158) to underscore Hamlet's adjuration to his companions that they swear secrecy upon the sword that he holds out to them. "Swear," cries the Ghost. "Come on," says Hamlet, sardonically amused, "you hear this fellow in the cellerage. / Consent to swear" (158–61). Hamlet understands that the Ghost is calling to them from some other world, in or below the earth. The Ghost has just explained his reasons for hasty departure: he has scented the morning air, and has seen from the pale ineffectual fire of the glow worm that the dawn was near (59, 90–1), just as, in scene 1, he also vanished at the approach of dawn as signaled by the crowing of the cock.

Why is the Ghost so apprehensive about the approach of dawn? The play, for its own purposes, adopts the folk belief that ghosts and other spirits can visit earth only at night (as also in A *Midsummer Night's*

Dream, 3.2.378–87). Hamlet's father's ghost is thus "Doomed for a certain term to walk the night" (1.5.11). Now he is *under the stage*, repeatedly bidding the awed Horatio and Marcellus to shift ground and swear thrice. Something about the number three makes it magical. The audience assents to a theatrical convention: in the imaginary world of the Globe, Purgatory and hell lie below, while the main stage represents the earth on which human actions take place.

The celestial world above the actors' heads, meanwhile, is represented on the Elizabethan stage by the "heavens" depicted on the underside of the roof over the stage. Hamlet alludes directly to the heavenly bodies depicted there when he describes to Rosencrantz and Guildenstern how he has lost all his mirth, to such an extent that

this goodly frame, the earth, seems to me a sterile promontory; this most excellent canopy, the air, look you, this brave o'erhanging firmament, this majestical roof fretted with golden fire, why, it appeareth nothing to me but a foul and pestilent congregation of vapors. (2.2.297–304)

Evidently Hamlet gestures deictically towards the representations of sun, moon, and constellations in the "heavens" above him to make his point. His phrasing, "this brave o'erhanging firmament," aptly describes the small roof that is depicted in the Swan drawing jutting out over the Elizabethan stage; the "majestical roof fretted with golden fire" is again architecturally precise in describing what he and the audience can see as they look upward. The Globe Theatre, with its symbolic name representing not just the earth but the cosmos in which, according to legend, Hercules held up the earth on his shoulders, contains within itself a depiction of the world standing both physically and metaphorically between heaven and hell. Such was the standard iconography of the cosmos encapsulated in medieval Corpus Christi drama and in countless artistic realizations of God's creation. If, as seems likely, the Globe logo showed a globe perched on Hercules's shoulders, Hamlet's discussion of a "firmament" and a "majestical roof" would have been perceived as self-referential: the Globe offers itself in this play as the habitation of mankind, where the story of Hamlet unfolds in the sight of heaven above and hell beneath. Hamlet's own reference to "Hercules and his load too" at 2.2.361–2 further reinforces the connection. Hamlet, in fact, has compared himself invidiously to Hercules: Claudius is no more like Hamlet senior, says Hamlet, "Than I to Hercules" (1.2.152–3).

When Ophelia, obedient to her father's command, returns to Hamlet the love letters he has written her, and is repeatedly and angrily told to "Get thee to a nunnery" (3.1.94–138), in what way does Elizabethan staging represent the overhearing of their conversation by the King and Polonius? Presumably the audience can see these two, hiding backstage or behind a pillar or otherwise complying with Polonius's instruction to the King, "Let's withdraw, my lord" (56). We are thus continually aware of their presence. Is Hamlet also aware, and if so, when? Have they betrayed their snooping by making a noise or being briefly seen by Hamlet? The question especially is much debated in critical scholarship and subjected to varying interpretations on stage. Hamlet may well seem to know at some point, if not from the start, that he is being overheard. At the end of his bitter disquisition to Ophelia about betaking herself to a nunnery, he suddenly asks, "Where's your father?" When she replies, "At home, my lord," no doubt awkwardly, since she is not a practiced liar, he shoots back, "Let the doors be shut upon him, that he may play the fool nowhere but in's own house" (3.1.131–4). Hamlet knows well enough that the King has been using secret means and agents (especially Rosencrantz and Guildenstern) to keep track of his unpredictable stepson, and Hamlet is well acquainted too with Polonius's fatuous pride in his own ability as master spy: as the old man has boasted to the King and Queen, "If circumstances lead me, I will find / Where truth is hid, though it were hid indeed / Within the centre" (2.2.157–9; see also 1.3.91–2 and 2.1.1–69). Suspecting, then, that Ophelia's father is listening, Hamlet might have reason to suppose that the King is in hiding too. Elizabethan staging conventions of gesture and speech would have given the actors ample means to suggest such an interpretation.

Hamlet's parting shot in this scene appears to be one of defiance to his uncle. "I say we shall have no more marriage," he declares. "Those that are married already—all but one—shall live" (3.1.149–51). To Claudius, Hamlet's reference to one married person who shall not live can only mean Claudius himself. The point is an important one in interpreting Hamlet's character and motive, for it suggests that he wishes to throw down the gauntlet to Claudius. He puts his opponent on guard. Hamlet desires revenge; he also wishes, as a gentleman, to fight fair.

Whether the King and Polonius need to give away their secret presence in an Elizabethan production by making some noise is a question often asked by critics like John Dover Wilson, but the seeming problem may be one that has been created by post-Shakespearean staging concepts. Wherever Claudius and Polonius conceal themselves on the Elizabethan stage, the audience must be aware of their presence; they are "unseen" by Hamlet, but the audience can "see" everything. Presentational staging provides the acting company with an opportunity for ironic visual juxtaposition. Because the audience knows that Claudius and Polonius are there, it can interpret Hamlet's remarks as prompted by the presence of the overhearers. Presentational staging obviates a problem that a "realistic" set can make difficult.

The staging of "The Murder of Gonzago" before the Danish court raises questions that again bear on critical interpretation. How is the dumb show to be presented on the Elizabethan stage, and why does it not trigger a guilty response from Claudius? As the lengthy stage direction at 3.2.133 in the second quarto indicates, the dumb show visually reports the whole story of the murder: the King and Queen's loving fondness for each other, her "*show of protestation*" that she loves only him, his lying down to sleep "*on a bank of flowers,*" her leaving him, the arrival on stage of the murderer, his taking off the King's crown and kissing it as token of the murderer's ambition to rule, the pouring of poison into the sleeping King's ears (plural in the second quarto and Folio stage directions), the Queen's return to find the King dead, her "*passionate action,*" the Poisoner's arrival with "*some three or four*" to "*condole with her,*" the carrying off of the King's dead body, the Poisoner's wooing of the Queen "*with gifts,*" her initial reluctance, and her final acceptance of the Poisoner's love. The dumb show thus dramatizes in pantomime the whole story, considerably more than is subsequently shown in the spoken play before the King arises and storms out of the room. Most of the onstage audience cannot know at first what to make of this dumb show, but Claudius is in a position to comprehend every detail. Why does he wait?

Interpretation may depend on staging. Perhaps the players of the dumb show in the Elizabethan theatre are to perform downstage, with the onstage audience upstage and facing out into the theatre auditorium so that we can savor their conversations and their responses. The King and others, engaged in quiet conversation among themselves, may be partly inattentive to the dumb show. The King has been speaking with Hamlet and listening to Polonius (3.2.91–5, 109).

Ophelia's question to Hamlet after the presentation of the dumb show, "What means this, my lord?" (134), plainly indicates that she doesn't know what it all means. "Belike this show imports the argument of the play," she decides, and then, when the Prologue enters, she asks "Will 'a tell us what this show meant?" (137–41). If she is thus in the dark, perhaps the King sees (even if he has been paying attention to the dumb show) that he can afford to wait; no dangerous disclosure has manifested itself yet. More simply, a Renaissance English audience would perhaps understand intuitively that they too are to wait for the spoken text and not rush to conclusions. Other Renaissance plays, notably *The Spanish Tragedy*, seem to observe a similar convention: although no dumb show precedes the play-within-the-play at the end of this revenge tragedy, the Duke of Castile is handed an "argument" or summary of the plot, and yet takes no alarm. The stage convention may simply be that a dumb show is a kind of entertaining riddle to which a Renaissance audience gives a provisional response while awaiting the spoken text.

The mistaken slaying of Polonius in act 3, scene 4 vividly illustrates the use on the Elizabethan stage of the curtained discovery space. A curtain hung in front of the discovery space would provide room for Polonius to hide himself there without detection until he cries out and is stabbed. Evidently Polonius then falls forward through the curtains (called "the arras" at 2.2.163, 3.3.28, and 4.1.9), or else Hamlet pulls back the curtains and finds him there, at which point Hamlet addresses the body in a mocking eulogy. The discovery space, opening as it seems to have done into the actors' dressing area or "tiring house" backstage, might also provide a convenient means for Hamlet to exit when he drags the dead body off stage at the scene's end. Meantime, the corpse has been visible throughout Hamlet's painful interview with his mother and, more briefly, with his father's ghost. Hamlet gestures toward the dead Polonius when he says to his mother, "For this same lord, / I do repent" (3.4.179–80). The body is there throughout most of the scene as a baleful and vivid reminder that scores are yet to be settled.

The gravedigging scene in act 5, scene 1 makes capital use of the trap door. The First Clown or gravedigger sings as he digs. He throws up a skull as Hamlet and Horatio watch from a distance, and then another. Presumably he is in the grave, that is, in the trap but with head and shoulders visible to the audience. Hamlet and Horatio come to the grave's edge, then hide as an elaborate funeral procession enters; as earlier in act 3, scene 1, the stage pillars or the discovery space afford opportunities for hiding. The Elizabethan spectators are able to see the hidden figures and hear their *sotto voce* conversation as the funeral procession nears the gravesite; as in the earlier overhearing scene, Elizabethan presentational staging bestows on the audience an omniscience that none of the characters on stage can fully share. The mourners, including the King, the Queen, Laertes, a Priest, and various lords, follow the dead body, and with "maimèd rites" (5.1.219), that is, with certain standard forms of ritual observation left out because of the questionable nature of Ophelia's death. An Elizabethan audience would presumably be able to detect these symbolically meaningful omissions, since those lapses in ceremony are immediately evident to Hamlet. He knows too, in the semiotics of worship, that the truncated effects signal a presumption of suicide. Laertes makes plain his distress at the unwillingness of the Church to honor the dead Ophelia with full rites.

When all are gathered at the gravesite, Laertes melodramatically asks that the grave attendants "Hold off the earth awhile, / Till I have caught her once more in mine arms." Seemingly then he jumps down into the grave, exclaiming, "Now pile your dust upon the quick and dead" (5.1.249–51). Hamlet comes forward and grapples with Laertes so violently that the two have to be parted. Does Hamlet jump down into the grave or trap also, and if so is there room for two men fighting over the dead body of Ophelia? (The gravedigger will presumably have lifted himself up out of the grave well before this, as the burial ceremony is about to begin.) Some contemporary evidence suggests that Hamlet did indeed jump in. "Oft have I seen him jump into the grave," observes an anonymous funeral elegy for Richard Burbage in 1619, a remark usually taken to refer to Burbage's performances in *Hamlet*. The unauthorized quarto of 1603, though often unreliable textually, can be helpful with visual effects, and is perhaps so in this instance: "*Leartes leaps into the grave*," reads a stage direction, followed almost immediately with "*Hamlet leaps in after Laertes.*" Possibly the two men clamber out of the trap as they struggle. In any event, the staging seems designed to highlight the sense in which Hamlet and Laertes are foils to each other. Presumably the boy playing Ophelia can manage his exit under the stage in time to allow room for Hamlet and Laertes to grapple there; Laertes does express a wish, as he jumps in the grave, to catch Ophelia once more in his arms (250), but that action need not be visually presented.

The staging of the play's final scene is busy and suspenseful. Once a table has been brought in for weapons and wine, and the royal audience has been seated, the dueling begins. Laertes exchanges his rapier for another, presumably to arm himself with the poisoned weapon, though the trusting Hamlet discerns nothing amiss. Trumpets sound. Hamlet does so well in the fencing that Laertes evidently deserts his gentlemanly code of honor by stabbing Hamlet with his poisoned rapier between rounds, while Hamlet's guard is down. Again, the 1603 quarto is more helpful than the other early texts in providing visual evidence of what happens next: "*They [Hamlet and Laertes] catch at one another's rapiers and both are wounded. Laertes falls down. The Queen falls down.*" Hamlet, in other words, perceiving that Laertes's weapon was unbated, forces an exchange of weapons and charges furiously on Laertes, wounding him fatally with a rapier thrust. Hamlet does not yet know of the poison.

The means of the Queen's death provides us with another staging challenge. She and Hamlet appear to have come to a reconciliation. Earlier, Hamlet has been disgusted with his mother's overhasty marriage to such a brute as Claudius, and has even wondered if she knew of the murder of her husband beforehand (3.4.29–30); after all, the Gurutha of Saxo's Scandinavian account is reported to have been adulterously involved with Feng. Hamlet has satisfied himself that his mother was not guilty to such an extent as that, but he does arraign her of unseemly lechery and of unforgivable disloyalty to the memory of Hamlet's dead father. (Part of "The Murder of Gonzago," perhaps indeed the portion that Hamlet offered to write and insert into the players' script, seems at least as intent on exposing his mother's perfidy as that of Claudius.) Hamlet's purpose seemingly is to expose his mother to "those thorns that in her bosom lodge" (1.5.88), as the Ghost had instructed, even though the Ghost's visit to the Queen's chambers in 3.4 seems prompted by a worry that Hamlet is going too far. Hamlet has vowed, in soliloquy, that he will "speak daggers" to the Queen, "but use none" (3.2.395–6). His intents are thus not physically threatening; he is concerned with the welfare of his mother's eternal soul.

Gertrude, resistant at first to Hamlet's arraignment of her, breaks down in tears and promises to do what Hamlet earnestly asks her to do:

stay out of Claudius's bed, and preserve Hamlet's secret that his madness is only a pretense. Gertrude obeys this latter injunction by lying to her husband when Claudius finds her alone. "Mad as the sea and wind when both contend / Which is the mightier," she exclaims, as her way of accounting for Hamlet's "mad" behavior in killing Polonius (4.1.7–8). Now, in the final scene, Gertrude chooses to declare her loyalty to her son by disobeying her husband. "Gertrude, do not drink!" he orders her. Wives are supposed to obey their husbands. Gertrude does not. "I will, my lord, I pray you pardon me," she replies as she drinks the poisoned wine (5.2.293–4).

Directors have a choice here as to whether Gertrude drinks not suspecting the wine itself, or takes what she surmises to be poisoned wine as an act of expiation. By now, to be sure, she could be suspicious of her husband's capacity for evil plotting by means of poisoned wine, but the text probably supports the unsuspecting interpretation. "The Queen carouses to thy fortune, Hamlet," she has just announced (5.2.291). Her wish is to make a public demonstration of pride in her son, and if to do so means disobeying her husband, so be it. Claudius meantime is unable to stop her from drinking the wine, since the reason he has for wishing to prevent her is something that he dares not utter. And so Claudius goes to his death having managed, by his own cleverness in devising a backup plan for the death of Hamlet, to bring about the death instead of Queen Gertrude. Claudius killed his brother to obtain Gertrude and the Danish throne; now, by his own undoing, he will have neither. This is another striking example of a recurrent motif in *Hamlet*, that of the inventor of war weaponry who is blown up by his own devices. Purposes mistook have justly fallen on the inventors' heads (386–7).

The entry of Fortinbras at the very end is replete with irony. He is, as his name implies, strong in arms. He has bided his time well throughout the play, agreeing to attack Poland instead of Denmark so long as the Danes are determined to resist his invasion of their country. Now that Claudius, Gertrude, and Hamlet lie dead, not to mention the others who are dead also, Denmark lacks a royal family. Hamlet's last verbal act is to "prophesy" that "th'election lights / On Fortinbras" (5.2.357–8). The very eventuality that Hamlet senior and Claudius have striven to prevent, the incorporation of Denmark into Norway, seems about to occur. Yet Hamlet has long admired Fortinbras, albeit quizzically, for his ability to get a job done. He is the play's most successful model of forthright action producing the desired result. He does not hesitate to use violence. As putative successor to the Danish throne, he is given the statesman's privilege of pronouncing a eulogy over the fallen hero. Yet Fortinbras's accomplishment must be seen finally in a deeply ironic context, of Laertes's fatal mistaking through forthright action, of Horatio's sardonic and existential view of history, and Hamlet's own puzzled strivings to discover some truth in the paradox of action and passivity. When all is said, Fortinbras's political and military success can be seen as just that: a triumph in a materialistic world that cannot fathom the complexity of Hamlet's tragedy. Worldly success has only itself as a reward.

Hamlet, with his keen interest in the acting profession and in distinguishing good acting from bad, wishes above all to be a good actor in his own play. The models offered in other Elizabethan revenge tragedies, like Hieronimo in *The Spanish Tragedy* or Lucianus in "The Murder of Gonzago," or Amleth in Saxo Grammaticus's *Danish History*, are not entirely reassuring. The traditional revenger is bloody, bold, driven to extremes of violence, and justified finally only by the colossal evil of his adversary. Hamlet does not wish to be like that. He has his chance to kill in cold blood when he happens across Claudius at prayer. What would we think of *Hamlet* if it ended with the death of Claudius in this way? Such an act would terminate the life of one who is guilty of a "foul and most unnatural murder" (1.5.27). Yet we, and presumably an Elizabethan audience as well, would have trouble sympathizing with such a revenge other than as the embodiment of a fierce code of an eye for an eye.

The ending that Shakespeare has devised for his hero is unlike that of any other revenge play. By enabling Hamlet to kill Claudius in a nearly unpremeditated and just reprisal, after Hamlet has accepted his role as instrument of the will of heaven, the play removes from this revenger the stigma of his calling. Hamlet dies not as a homicidal killer but as victim of the huge injustice he has sought to remedy. Hamlet's death is a sacrifice. Only in such a play could Horatio say, as farewell his dear friend, "Good night, sweet prince, / And flights of angels sing thee to thy rest!" (5.2.361–2). By submitting to the will of providence, Hamlet has found out the perfect role for himself.

3

The Play's the Thing: Ideological Contexts of *Hamlet* in 1599–1601

To visualize *Hamlet* on stage in 1599–1601, as the previous chapter has attempted to do, is to raise further questions of interpretation. This book's overall aim is to study the varying ways that audiences, critics, and readers of *Hamlet* down through the centuries have looked at this remarkable play in relation to their own cultural, philosophical, religious, and political preoccupations. Can we discern what Shakespeare's audiences in 1599–1601 made of the play in their own terms? We have few critical responses to the play (or to other plays) during Shakespeare's lifetime. Francis Meres, to be sure, compares Shakespeare to Ovid. Ben Jonson praises Shakespeare as England's best poet and the greatest comic dramatist of all time. John Weever speaks of Shakespeare as "honey-tongued." But these tributes tend to be brief and laudatory, without much analytical insight. Can a staging interpretation of the play in its own time enable us to discern what cultural significance the play may have had for contemporary spectators and readers?

A first consideration is to ask what we mean by the play *Hamlet*, since it exists as a text in three early forms. These have been briefly alluded to already. How did *Hamlet* come into being as a script for performance and as a printed text in three markedly different versions?

The first printed text of *Hamlet* appeared in 1603, advertising itself as having been "diuerse times acted by his Highnesse seruants in the Cittie of London: as also in the two Vniuersities of Cambridge and Oxford, and else-where." Although "A booke called the Revenge of Hamlett Prince Denmarke as yt was latelie Acted by the Lord Chamberlayne his seruantes" had been registered for publication in 1602 to the publisher James Roberts, the 1603 text was instead published by

Nicholas Ling and John Trumbell, and evidently without the authorization of Shakespeare's acting company. This text is notably shorter and seemingly more flawed than an authorized version that appeared the next year, in 1604, published by James Roberts and pointedly advertising itself on its title page as "*Newly corrected, augmented, and amended.*" Some existing copies bear the date 1605. Somehow, Ling and Trumbell had got hold of an imperfect text of this immensely popular play, perhaps with the connivance of some bit players in the Lord Chamberlain's company, and rushed it into print to steal the march on Roberts. The abbreviated 1603 text may also reflect a shortening for performance. Both the 1603 and 1604–5 versions appeared in quarto format, that is, in a book roughly 7 x 5 inches in size for which each large printing sheet, with four pages of text on each side, had been folded twice. (A folio text folds its printing sheet only once, with only two 14 x 9 pages on each side.) The 1604–5 quarto appears to be a reliable text, based seemingly on Shakespeare's papers with some markings for stage performance. (A third quarto of 1611 was a reprint of Q2; the undated Q4 was a reprint of Q3; Q5 of 1637 was a reprint of Q4. None of these reprints had any independent authority for their readings, though Q4 may have been consulted by the Folio compositors, as indicated in the following paragraph.)

The 1604–5 text, the so-called second quarto (Q2), is the version preferred by most modern editors, although a growing body of opinion insists cogently that each text has its own integrity and rationale. The text of *Hamlet* in the first collected edition of Shakespeare's plays, *Mr William Shakespeare's Comedies, Histories, and Tragedies*, the so-called First Folio of 1623, appears to have been set from a transcription of a Shakespearean draft, copied (somewhat carelessly) to provide legible copy for the printers. The printers may also have consulted an undated fourth quarto at points when the manuscript seemed unclear, but not very often. This Folio text contains some authorial revisions and some new dialogue that are unquestionably authentic. It also incorporates some questionable readings, owing perhaps to the careless copying, or to new printer's errors, and some cuts of about two hundred lines. Many of these cuts may represent a shortening for performance; *Hamlet* is a very long play, and may well have been too long for ordinary performance. The cuts are especially notable in act 4 and in the long final scene of act 5, as though the acting company found that it could move the story along more swiftly at this point without losing

the thread of the narrative. Conversely, the 1623 additions are relatively few in number; the longest and most lively, alluding to a threat
to the adult actors posed by the juvenile acting companies, with their
penchant for satire of the contemporary scene (2.2.326–62), seems to
have been inspired by a sense of crisis in the world of the London
theatre (alluded to briefly in the previous chapter). Other Folio additions are, for the most part, brief.

The 1623 text (F1) certainly provides valuable new material not in
the 1604–5 quarto and some corrected readings. The 1603 unauthorized quarto (Q1) is also on occasions a useful witness, especially for
visual effects as reported in the stage directions, as when we learn in Q1
that the ghost of Hamlet's father enters to Hamlet and his mother in
her private chambers "*in his night gowne*" (3.4), not in full armor as in
act 1. If this text was put together in part by hired actors, or possibly by
means of someone furtively taking down what he had heard and seen
in performance, the result might well be a mangled text leaving out
much dialogue, but nonetheless visually observant in describing stage
business. Overall, the 1604–5 quarto seems closest to something that
Shakespeare wrote, since the 1603 quarto is manifestly corrupt and the
1623 Folio text depends on an indirect chain of transmission. Still, the
differences in the three texts need to be kept in mind whenever we
encounter disputed readings or material present in one text and not in
the others, most notably in the Folio-only depiction of the so-called
War of the Theatres in act 2, scene 2.

These textual questions are hotly debated today. The first quarto has
its champions as an authentic early Shakespearean version. Some
editors see more authorial intent in the Folio revisions than my
account here supposes, as is true also in the contested case of *King
Lear*. Even if the second quarto of *Hamlet* is arguably closer to a
Shakespearean original than the first quarto or the Folio, what is
undoubtedly true is that the three texts of *Hamlet* provide us with
multiple states of a play that evolved over time. The 1603 quarto, for all
its defects, represents one stage of creation and change. The play
evolved, and continues to evolve, in Shakespeare's manuscript or
manuscripts, in the theatre, in the copying labors of various scribes,
in more than one publisher's shop and printing house, in the editorial
work of many editors since 1623, and in the manifold critical interpretations of scholars and critics up to the present. The three texts of
Hamlet deserve recognition as distinct entities. They can be consulted

and compared in the two-volume Arden 3 edition of the play by Ann Thompson and Neil Taylor (2006), or in *The Three-Text "Hamlet": Parallel Texts of the First and Second Quartos and First Folio*, edited by Bernice W. Kliman and Paul Bertram in old spelling (1991). Forthcoming is my online three-text edition for Internet Shakespeare Editions (ISE).

What philosophical and religious questions might have seemed uppermost to audiences watching *Hamlet* in 1599–1601? An Elizabethan audience looking for a bloody revenge tragedy in the vein of Thomas Kyd's *The Spanish Tragedy* and the lost *Hamlet* (see chapter 1) would presumably not have been disappointed with what they saw. "Haste me to know it," exclaims Hamlet, as he waits breathlessly to learn from his father's ghost the details of the "foul and most unnatural murder," "that I, with wings as swift / As meditation or the thoughts of love, / May sweep to my revenge" (1.5.26–32). The Ghost's plea to his son is unambiguous: the son is to "Revenge." Hamlet understands this, and responds viscerally to the pagan ethic of an eye for an eye: in a revenge culture like that of ancient Scandinavia, a son has a sacred duty to kill the murderer of his father. The code demanding revenge would apply to the murder of any close relative, but the murder of a father has a special urgency. The murderer of Hamlet's father is, moreover, a regicide: the brother he has slain was King of Denmark. Claudius is a usurper and a murderer.

To the crimes of brother-murder and regicide are added those of incest and adultery. Today we would probably not regard the marriage of a man with his deceased brother's wife as incest, nor would we find a man guilty of adultery for sleeping with a once-married woman who is now a widow, but to Hamlet and his dead father, and presumably to an Elizabethan audience, the crimes are precisely these. In the Ghost's estimate, Claudius is "that incestuous, that adulterate [i.e., adulterous] beast" (1.5.41). "Bear it not," he enjoins his son. "Let not the royal bed of Denmark be / A couch for luxury [i.e., lechery] and damnèd incest" (82–4). Lechery and incest are thus not only crimes, they are sins, endangering the immortal soul of the perpetrator—and, in this case, also threatening the spiritual welfare of the man's spouse. "Leave her to heaven," the Ghost instructs his son regarding his mother the Queen, "And to those thorns that in her bosom lodge, / To prick and sting her" (87–9). Hamlet, for his part, has already expressed his dismay and revulsion at his mother's "most wicked speed, to post / With such dexterity to incestuous sheets" (1.2.156–7). Later, as he considers the fittest way to kill his uncle, Hamlet determines to do the deed "When he is drunk asleep, or in his rage, / Or in th'incestuous pleasure of his bed" (3.3.89–90). And finally, when he does in fact complete the revenge by stabbing the King and then forcing the poisoned wine down his throat, Hamlet sums up the case against Claudius with "Here, thou incestuous, murderous, damnèd Dane, / Drink off this potion" (5.2.327–8). All in all, Claudius stands condemned of sinful crimes that strike at the very heart of Elizabethan culture: at ties of blood kinship in the family, at marriage, at the state, and at no less than three of the sacred Ten Commandments (thou shalt not kill, thou shalt not commit adultery, thou shalt not covet thy neighbor's wife).

We can well imagine, then, that an Elizabethan audience would understand and sympathize with Hamlet's urgent feeling that he must act. Nor does he have any moral compulsions against killing a murderer like Claudius. Clearly, Hamlet cannot hope to have legal recourse against the Danish monarch; he never considers such an option. Having received his father's dread command, Hamlet musters up his resolve for the deed. "Hold, hold, my heart," he says to himself, "And you, my sinews, grow not instant old, / But bear me stiffly up" (1.5.94–6). He vows to wipe away from the "table" or tablet of his memory all trivial considerations, so that the Ghost's commandment "all alone shall live / Within the book and volume of my brain, / Unmixed with baser matter" (103–5). He enjoins Horatio and the night watch to keep his secret so that he may proceed with the business. He does indeed regard it as a "cursèd spite" that he was born to set right the time that is so "out of joint" (197–8), but this is not because he is squeamish at the thought of blood.

When necessity requires, Hamlet sends Rosencrantz and Guildenstern to their deaths at the hands of the English King with no appearance of remorse. He seems rather proud of having outwitted his two escorts at their own game; as he says earlier to his mother, anticipating how he will deal with the two of them, "'tis the sport to have the enginer / Hoist with his own petard, and't shall go hard / But I will delve one yard below their mines / And blow them at the moon" (3.4.213–16). His metaphor is from the digging of countermines under enemy fortifications in order to blow them up by means of an explosive mechanism called a petard. The "enginer" or maker of military contrivances must bear constantly in mind the danger of being blown up by his own devices. Hamlet's contest with Claudius and his agents is a war, with no room for sentimentality. "Why, man, they did make love to this employment," Hamlet tells Horatio. "They are not near my conscience. Their defeat / Does by their own insinuation grow" (5.2.57–9). That is, Rosencrantz and Guildenstern deserve what they have gotten for sticking their noses into Hamlet's business.

Hamlet's animus toward Rosencrantz and Guildenstern may stem from a suspicion that they have been aware of Claudius's full villainy. An Elizabethan audience, on the other hand, might have been inclined to exonerate them of evil intent, since the play gives no indication otherwise. The result is a fine irony: these two young men are no doubt ambitiously eager to be of service to a powerful man who has promised to reward them for their services, but they also are motivated by a desire to protect the monarch. "The cess of majesty / Dies not alone, but like a gulf doth draw / What's near it with it," declares Rosencrantz, enunciating what an Elizabethan audience would have recognized as a paraphrase of the often-cited and politically orthodox "Homily Against Disobedience and Willful Rebellion." "Never alone / Did the King sigh, but with a general groan," Rosencrantz concludes (3.3.15–23). The King's life is sacred and must be preserved at all costs. Yet to Hamlet these erstwhile companions of his youth are enemies serving a monstrous tyrant and usurper. He calculatedly makes plans to finish them off before they can bring about his death. His causing their deaths is thus both premeditated and, from his own point of view, a justifiable act of self-defense.

If Hamlet is matter-of-fact about his deadly proceedings against Rosencrantz and Guildenstern, he is even more cold-blooded in contemplating the killing of Claudius. The hated uncle is, as Hamlet tells his mother, "A murderer and a villain," "a vice of kings, / A cutpurse of the empire and the rule, / That from a shelf the precious diadem stole / And put it in his pocket" (3.4.99–104). Such a man does not deserve to live. When Hamlet comes upon Claudius on his knees at prayer, he is at first ready to act on the instant: "Now might I do it pat, now 'a is a praying; / And now I'll do't" (3.3.73–4). Hamlet draws his sword. He then hesitates, but not out of scruples about homicide; quite the contrary. His Christian upbringing teaches him at this moment only that if he were to kill Claudius at prayer, the man's soul might go to heaven. This would be "hire and salary, not revenge"

(79). Claudius's murderous act demands reciprocity. A better plan, as Hamlet sees it, will be to slay Claudius

> When he is drunk asleep, or in his rage,
> Or in th'incestuous pleasure of his bed,
> At game, a-swearing, or about some act
> That has no relish of salvation in't—
> Then trip him, that his heels may kick at heaven,
> And that his soul may be as damned and black
> As hell, whereto it goes. (3.3.89–95)

Hamlet not only premeditates the killing of Claudius, he does so in a vengeful manner worthy of Hamlet's literary ancestor, Saxo's Amleth. Nineteenth-century readers and audiences, as we shall see, had great difficulty accepting this bloodthirstiness on Hamlet's part, since that later age preferred to think of him as an upright moral character who would be revulsed by the prospect of homicide, but the play text strongly suggests that for Elizabethan spectators the potential for violence in Hamlet was not inconsistent with the man or with his story.

Hamlet has other blood on his hands; indeed, he is responsible for more deaths by far than anyone else in the play. The killing of Polonius is a serious miscalculation. Hamlet plausibly supposes the man's voice behind the arras in his mother's "closet" (3.3.27) or private chambers to be that of her new husband, and so he stabs (see Illustration 3). The moment seems at first to have provided the very sort of occasion that Hamlet has wished for: a moment of "incestuous" intimacy between Claudius and his sister-in-law-wife. The act is thus a deliberate attempt to fulfill the Ghost's instructions by sudden, violent, and contrived homicide. Hamlet acts in full accord with the code of vengeance urged on him by his father's spirit. Yet his attempt has seemed somehow destined to "turn awry, / And lose the name of action" (3.1.88–9).

Polonius, to be sure, has put himself in a place where he might be mistaken for Claudius. Hamlet experiences no personal sorrow at the death of this man, whom he has regarded as a tiresome busybody. Like Rosencrantz and Guildenstern, in Hamlet's view, Polonius deserves what he gets for snooping into the affairs of others, especially those of Hamlet. "Thou wretched, rash, intruding fool, farewell!" is all the eulogy Hamlet is willing to expend on the man whose blood is now staining the floor of his mother's chamber. "I took thee for thy better. Take thy fortune. / Thou find'st to be too busy is some danger"

Illustration 3. John Philip Kemble, in the role of Hamlet, *c.* 1790, points to the dead body of Polonius, whom Hamlet has stabbed through the arras (3.4). Courtesy of the Harvard Theatre Collection, Houghton Library, Harvard University.

(3.4.32–4). This brusque judgment expresses the ethical view of the revenge plot that those who are (however unwittingly) the instruments of King Claudius can expect to be hoisted on their own petard. Yet Hamlet also has reason to be concerned about the consequences of a seemingly tragic error. He has killed the wrong man and senses that he will have to pay for it, just as Polonius has paid his dues for being a snoop. The Hamlet that Shakespeare presents to his Elizabethan spectators is viscerally responsive to the demands of the revenge code but also able to perceive the problems it poses for ethical and religious thought.

Ophelia is another victim of Hamlet's vengeful acts, if only indirectly. Her madness is brought on by her father's death and perhaps too by what she perceives as Hamlet's cruel treatment of her; her mad snatches of song dwell distractedly on a white-haired old man who is "dead and gone" and on young men who "will do't, if they come to't," promising to wed in order to "tumble" gullible young ladies in bed (4.5.23–64). We learn a bit later from Queen Gertrude that Ophelia has drowned, perhaps innocently in her madness, though the coroner finds it a suicide. (Coroners in Shakespeare's day were instructed to issue a finding of suicide in such dubious cases, partly because swimming was regarded as reckless self-endangerment and thus virtually a suicidal act, but more importantly because the estate of the deceased would then go to the Crown.) Hamlet may show his regret when he proclaims to the assembled court at Ophelia's graveside, "I loved Ophelia. Forty thousand brothers / Could not with all their quantity of love / Make up my sum" (5.1.272–4). Whatever his feelings may be, Ophelia can be added to the growing list of those who have died as a result of Hamlet's actions. Like her father, though with less intent, she has had the misfortune to be in the wrong place at the wrong time.

Hamlet's last acts are to kill Laertes and Claudius. About Laertes's death Hamlet is truly sorry, and is fully ready to exchange forgiveness with Laertes as they both approach their deaths. Laertes's regret is that he has been fatally misled by Claudius and has conspired to murder Hamlet by underhanded means of secret poison, in a way that a true gentlemen would never countenance. Hamlet has freely acknowledged Laertes to be "a very noble youth" (5.1.224). He tells Horatio that he is "sorry . . . That to Laertes I forgot myself" (5.2.75–6) when the two of them grappled at Ophelia's grave. Hamlet offers an interesting reason for his regret at having wronged Laertes: "by the image of my cause," he says to Horatio, "I see / The portraiture of his" (77–8). That is, Hamlet perceives a parallel in the lives of himself and Laertes. Both are sons of slain fathers, and hence both feel bound by sacred obligations of revenge. Hamlet understands that Laertes's vengeful fury is directed against Hamlet himself, for he did kill Polonius. Hamlet may allude to this parallelism as he and Laertes are about to duel in the final scene, when Hamlet says, "I'll be your foil, Laertes" (5.2.253). "Foil" can mean anything that serves by contrast to set off something else to advantage. It can also mean a repulse or baffling check, as in dueling; Hamlet is playing with words, as he so often does. Originally, a foil is a leaf or, by extension, a thin leaf of metal placed behind or under a precious stone to set off its brilliancy. Metaphorically, the word nicely describes paired relationships like those of Laertes and Hamlet (and Fortinbras), whose similar situations invite reflections on their differing responses to their fates. *Hamlet* is structured to a significant extent by such foil relationships.

To understand, from an Elizabethan perspective, the justification of Hamlet's last act of homicide, his killing of Claudius, we need to go back into earlier parts of the play to examine more closely the nature of the Ghost's dire commission to his son: "Revenge my foul and most unnatural murder."

The Ghost manifestly comes out of a pagan revenge tradition that is pan-European and presumably universal, from the Scandinavian north of Saxo Grammaticus and from the Roman south of Seneca. Both worlds were pagan, and both valorized an ethical code of an eye for an eye that was (and is) inimical to Christian teaching. The idea was also anathema to Queen Elizabeth's government because it consigned into private hands the settlement of disputes that ought to be handled by the state. Sir Francis Bacon was one among many who, in his essay "Of Revenge," argued that revenge was "a kind of wild justice." It did constitute indeed an ethical code of justice in that it offered satisfaction for wrongs done to an individual or family or social group. Its rules were clear. The trouble, of course, was that private feuding might never stop: the revenging of a crime would require the relatives or social partners of the victim of this revenge to reciprocate, and so on potentially to the end of time. Punishment for homicide was far safer when vested in the presumably impartial authority of the state. A wronged party could then be satisfied by seeing the offending party punished, but without committing an act of revenge that would invite retaliation. Elizabeth's government often cited the biblical text, "Vengeance is mine, saith the Lord" (see Hebrews 10.30, Psalm 94.1, Romans 12.19), as a religious commandment that posited a deep analogy between earthly and divine justice.

Although the ghost of Hamlet's father instructs his son to revenge in language that accords with the pagan code of vengeance so plentifully deployed in Saxo and Belleforest, the Ghost also speaks in terms that are recognizably those of the Roman Catholic liturgy. Apparently, he has come from Purgatory. He does not use the term; Shakespeare

employs it only twice in all his plays, once when Romeo laments that
being banished from Verona and his Juliet is "purgatory, torture, hell
itself" (*Romeo and Juliet*, 3.3.18) and again when Emilia, in *Othello*, says
jocosely to Desdemona that she would "venture purgatory" by committing adultery if the reward were great enough (4.3.80). These are
casual and offhand allusions. The Ghost's depiction of his afterlife is, on
the other hand, detailed and graphic:

> I am thy father's spirit,
> Doomed for a certain term to walk the night,
> And for the day confined to fast in fires,
> Till the foul crimes done in my days of nature
> Are burnt and purged away. But that I am forbid
> To tell the secrets of my prison house,
> I could a tale unfold whose lightest word
> Would harrow up thy soul, freeze thy young blood,
> Make thy two eyes like stars start from their spheres,
> Thy knotted and combinèd locks to part,
> And each particular hair to stand on end
> Like quills upon the fretful porcupine. (1.5.10–21)

This picture would be familiar to Shakespeare's audience as a description of Purgatory: a place of purging and purification in which,
according to Roman Catholic belief, "souls who depart this life in
the grace of God suffer for a time, because they still need to be
cleansed from venial sins, or have still to pay the temporal punishment
due to mortal sins, the guilt and the eternal punishment of which have
been remitted" (*The Catholic Dictionary*). During Shakespeare's lifetime, the issue divided Catholics from Protestants, who generally
rejected the concept of Purgatory along with saint worship and all
but two of the seven Holy Sacraments as Catholic dogma needing to
be reformed away.

Is Shakespeare's familiarity with the concept of Purgatory in *Hamlet*
a sign that he himself entertained Catholic sympathies? The case has
been urged recently by a number of scholars, who point to other
possible indications. The Ghost describes in these terms the unima-
ginable horror of his having been murdered:

> Thus was I, sleeping, by a brother's hand
> Of life, of crown, of queen at once dispatched,
> Cut off even in the blossoms of my sin,
> Unhousled, disappointed, unaneled,

No reckoning made, but sent to my account
With all my imperfections on my head.
Oh, horrible! Oh, horrible, most horrible! (1.5.75–81)

The terms here, "Unhousled, disappointed, unaneled," have precise technical meanings in Catholic theology. To die "unhousled" is to die not having received the Eucharist in the sacrament of Last Rites or Extreme Unction. This sacrament requires an anointing by the priest of a person in danger of death, accompanied by a set form of words, aimed at ensuring the eternal health of the soul. To be "disappointed" is to be inadequately furnished for one's journey into death. "Unaneled" again means to have died without receiving Extreme Unction. Shakespeare does indeed show here his familiarity with Catholic practice.

Whether this passage reveals anything about his own religious preferences is a matter of debate. A backward look of only a few years or decades into Shakespeare's family history would, of course, discover evidence of Catholic faith, since the English Reformation had begun in 1534, some thirty years before Shakespeare was born, and conversion of the English countryside to the new religion proceeded only slowly in the regions, like Warwickshire, not close to London. England had reverted to Catholicism under Queen Mary in the years 1553–1558, but then had returned to Protestantism under Mary's half-sister, Elizabeth, some six years before Shakespeare was born. On the whole, nonetheless, the consensus view probably is that we cannot know about Shakespeare's personal religious persuasions. He may well have been a communicant of the Established Church, as were most of his countrymen, but even that would tell us little. In his writings he does not dwell in a dogmatic way on the assurances of an eternal life.

Hamlet appears to be a believing Christian. He has studied at Wittenberg, a fact that might commend him to Protestant and reforming members of Shakespeare's audience. Wittenberg is where Martin Luther had posted his celebrated 95 theses to the church door in 1517 and where he had met William Tyndale in 1524; it was also the base for Philipp Melanchthon, a German scholar and key Protestant theologian. Many of Hamlet's utterances are distinctly Christian, even if not always identifiably Protestant in emphasis. "Angels and ministers of grace defend us!" he exclaims when he first sees his father's ghost

(1.4.39). Longing for death in his great unhappiness over his father's death and his mother's overhasty marriage, Hamlet might contemplate suicide were it not that "the Everlasting" has "fixed / His canon 'gainst self-slaughter" (1.2.131–2). In his famous soliloquy on "To be or not to be," he again yearns for release from life's tribulations, by means of a "bare bodkin" or unsheathed dagger if necessary, were it not that "in that sleep of death what dreams may come, / When we have shuffled off this mortal coil, / Must give us pause. There's the respect / That makes calamity of so long life" (3.1.67–77). He swears "by Saint Patrick" (1.5.142), who, among his other saintly roles, was thought to be the keeper of Purgatory. To his dear friend Horatio, when they have seen the Ghost, Hamlet insists that "There are more things in heaven and earth, Horatio, / Than are dreamt of in your philosophy" (1.5.175–6)—that is to say, than are to be found in the subject called "natural philosophy" or "science" that you skeptical thinkers like to talk about. (Some scholars prefer the Folio reading, "our philosophy.") Hamlet takes it for granted that the devil actively pursues the souls of mortals, and, being able "T'assume a pleasing shape," may wish to entrap Hamlet himself; perhaps the devil "Abuses me to damn me," he ponders (2.2.599–604).

Hamlet is deeply persuaded of the innate depravity of the human race, in ways that Elizabethan spectators would have recognized as integral to the Christian theology they were taught in church. "Get thee to a nunnery," he says to Ophelia.

Why wouldst thou be a breeder of sinners? I am myself indifferent honest, but yet I could accuse me of such things that it were better my mother had never borne me: I am very proud, vengeful, ambitious, with more offenses at my beck than I have thoughts to put them in, imagination to give them shape, or time to act them in. What should such fellows as I do crawling between earth and heaven? We are arrant knaves all; believe none of us. (3.1.122–30)

If Hamlet, being "indifferent honest," that is, about as virtuous as ordinary decent people, finds himself to be such an inveterate practitioner of the Seven Deadly Sins, what hope is there for humanity generally? Earlier, when Polonius has said that he will provide hospitality for the visiting players "according to their desert," Hamlet has a sharp reply: "God's bodikin, man, much better. Use every man after his desert, and who shall scape whipping?" (2.2.527–30). These are central tenets of medieval and Renaissance Christianity of all persuasions, from Saint Augustine down to Luther and Calvin; indeed, both Luther and Calvin used these ideas to reinforce their insistence that human beings cannot hope to save themselves by their own merits, since they have essentially none; grace is a great and mysterious gift of God, all the more wondrous in being so utterly undeserved. "We are arrant knaves all."

This Christian emphasis on the innate sinfulness of the human condition would help Elizabethan audiences understand why the Ghost of Hamlet's father has had to spend time in Purgatory, even if some members of that audience would no doubt regard the idea of Purgatory as Catholic superstition. When the Ghost refers to "the foul crimes done in my days of nature" and to his having been cut off by death "even in the blossoms of my sin" (1.5.13, 77), an Elizabethan audience would naturally wish to consider what those crimes and sins might have been. Some readers today, as we shall see, look for evidence of reprehensible behavior. Was it that the old king lived by the sword? Horatio relates how Hamlet senior, "When he the ambitious Norway combated . . . in an angry parle . . . smote the sledded Polacks on the ice" (1.1.65–7). But Horatio says this admiringly of a ruler who was esteemed by "this side of our known world" as "valiant Hamlet" (88–9). Elizabethan audiences presumably would have recognized in old Hamlet a type of chivalry, daring to fight old King Fortinbras of Norway according to the conditions of "a sealed compact / Well ratified by law and heraldry" (90–1). Was old Hamlet covetous of power? Was he a patriarch who domineered in his marriage? Not as the play sees him, largely through Hamlet's eyes, to be sure; he appears to have been a caring, even uxorious husband, so loving of his wife "That he might not beteem the winds of heaven / Visit her face too roughly" (1.2.140–2).

Elizabethans, whether hostile toward the Catholic doctrine of Purgatory or not, probably would have understood that the play offers a more plausible reason for old Hamlet's having to endure torment for a time after death: when he was alive on this earth, old Hamlet inevitably shared the common lot of humanity in being prone to sinfulness. To wake up in the morning is to think proud thoughts, to be occasionally angry, to covet possessions and wealth, to be indolent, to lust for food and sexual pleasure. All Christian faiths in the Renaissance held to this view as formulated in the Scriptures, in the epistles of Saint Paul particularly, and in the writings of Saint Augustine. The Catholic

Church added an important further factor: unless one received Extreme
Unction at the time of death, one was destined to be sent to one's final
account with all one's imperfections on one's head (1.5.79–80). In
Catholic theology, this meant Purgatory "for a certain term" (11). A
person who was suddenly and violently murdered would, of course,
have no opportunity for receiving Last Rites. The Anglican Church of
the sixteenth century had removed Extreme Unction from the traditional list of the seven sacraments, and had rejected the idea of Purgatory, but still took seriously the idea that a sinner at the time of death
needed to prepare for divine judgment by being deeply penitent for all
sins and crimes that he or she had committed.

Stephen Greenblatt, in his *Hamlet in Purgatory* (2001), offers a number of useful confirmations here. Elizabethans were indeed vividly
aware of the doctrine of Purgatory, argues Greenblatt, but they had
to find other ways to remember the dead, since the doctrine was no
longer allowed by the Anglican Church. Theatre, of which *Hamlet* is a
striking instance, provided one important path of remembrance.
Medieval accounts, such as the French fourteenth-century *The Gast
of Gy* (a tale still in circulation two centuries later), strongly fortified
the common belief that ghosts could return from Purgatory to visit
loved ones in the hope of obtaining their prayers or "suffrages" aimed
at reducing the agony of punishment for sins in Purgatory. A great fear
for many Christians in late-medieval Europe was that of dying without
receiving Last Rites, since even venial sins, like taking too much
pleasure in the marriage bed, would then require a "certain term" of
retributive punishment in Purgatory. Only the very rich could afford
the exorbitant fees demanded by the church for the singing of prayers
and masses for the dead. Henry VII had spent stupendous sums
ensuring the perpetual singing of masses for his soul; ordinary Christians had to do with far less, but still experienced a deeply felt need,
even in Protestant times, for some means of providing consolation for
the dead. Greenblatt proposes that *Hamlet* imaginatively re-enacts an
encounter between Shakespeare and his father, who may have pro-
fessed himself a Catholic when he died in 1601; Hamlet, trained
at Wittenberg and perhaps sympathetic to the Protestant view that
Purgatory is more a work of poetic imagination than a dogmatic
truth, understands the need of his Catholic father's ghost for remembrance but must respond to that need in his own way. *Hamlet in
Purgatory* also helps make clear that Hamlet's delay in seeking revenge

is well motivated in a genuine anxiety as to whether visitations from the realm of the dead might be diabolically intended to deceive the living; Greenblatt's ghost stories offer numerous examples of profound worry on this score.

Another possible interpretation from an Elizabethan point of view of Hamlet's encounter with his father's ghost is to posit that Shakespeare has superimposed on each other two incommensurate worlds, one of pagan Scandinavia committed in a straightforward way to an ethic of revenge, as in Saxo, and the other a Christian world of central Europe, with its promise of rewards or punishments in the afterlife. Denmark is nicely positioned geographically between these two realms: it is part of Scandinavia, with the realms of Sweden and Norway stretching northeastward, but it is also neighbor to Germany (including Wittenberg) on its southern border, with access to France and Poland. To the southwest lies Paris, a place of cultural values that are sharply contrasted with those of Fortinbras's Norway. How are these worlds to coexist? How should Hamlet, a Christian, steer his path between them as he seeks to fulfill his father's dread command? As we have seen, Hamlet entertains no scruples against killing when no other solution offers itself in dealing with a remorseless and canny adversary. Hamlet is not a pacifist. He does not appeal to Christian teaching as a reason for not using force against Claudius. Indeed, his hope is to kill Claudius in such a way as to send the man's soul to eternal torment. He moves quickly when the time seems ripe for action, and, as we have seen, sheds more blood than anyone else in the play. Hamlet's reasons for caution and delay are motivated by very different considerations, ones that, for Elizabethan viewers and for ourselves, may have much to do with the innately problematic nature of action.

After his first impulse to act "with wings as swift / As meditation or the thoughts of love" so that he may "sweep" to his revenge (1.5.30–1), Hamlet soon realizes that choosing the path to take is not as simple as all that. Claudius, he perceives, is canny, secretive, and ruthless. No persons in Denmark, other than Hamlet and Horatio and perhaps the soldiers on watch, ever know what Claudius has done until the final scene of revelation. The new king has won the support of key courtiers, like Polonius, in the electoral process of choosing him king. Denmark being an elective monarchy, and the crown prince away at Wittenberg when the old king suddenly and inexplicably dies, Claudius has known how to insinuate himself into the electoral process; he has, as Hamlet later puts it, "popped in between th'election and my hopes" (5.2.65). Claudius is a past master in the political art of collecting IOU's by doing benefits for important people in the expectation of their returning the favor when most needed. Polonius mistrusts young Hamlet, and so perhaps do other electors—those highly placed oligarchs who, like the cardinals of the Catholic Church, "elect" a new leader when the post falls vacant.

In his first public appearance (1.2), Claudius brilliantly displays the political skills that would have been evident to any Elizabethan viewer. He smoothly justifies his hasty marriage to his widowed sister-in-law on the grounds of a national emergency, ingratiates himself with those like Polonius who have elected him king, addresses Laertes by name no fewer than five times in the business of authorizing Laertes to return to Paris (42–62), and sets in motion a diplomatic gambit aimed at forestalling an impending Norwegian invasion. This gambit, we learn later at 2.2.58–80, succeeds remarkably well; young Fortinbras agrees to attack Poland instead of Denmark, in return for the granting of safe passage for him and his troops across the Danish peninsula. Claudius is a capable ruler, and in a style of administration quite unlike that of his dead brother. Claudius prefers tough, prudent negotiation. One can hardly imagine him smoting the sledded Polacks on the ice or taking up the King of Norway's challenge to a personal duel.

Facing such a skillful and powerful opponent whose crime is unknown to almost everyone, Hamlet adopts a guise of madness, as did Amleth in Saxo and Belleforest. He enjoins Horatio and the soldiers on watch not to give away his secret in this; later, he asks the same boon of his mother (3.4). He will, as he puts it, "put an antic disposition on" and bear himself in ways that will seem "strange" and "odd" (1.5.179–81). Whether he is ever truly mad is a question much discussed, as we shall see, though the text gives little if any support for the notion that he really is so. Ophelia, when she goes mad, does not recognize people, and seems totally disconnected from what is going on around her. The same is true of King Lear in his mad scenes in that play. Madness was a stage convention in the Elizabethan theatre, and Hamlet does not display its characteristics. He is, to be sure, depressed and melancholic at times, deeply anxious and worried and disgusted by what he sees around him, but this is not the same as true madness. To quote Polonius's splendidly self-referential definition, "to define true madness, / What is't but to be nothing else but mad?" (2.2.93–4).

Polonius does think that Hamlet is mad—"Mad let us grant him, then" (100)—but Polonius is easily misled. Claudius is of quite another opinion: having overheard Hamlet berate Ophelia, the King offers his firm opinion that "what he spake, though it lacked form a little, / Was not like madness" (3.1.166–7). Hamlet is anxious to impress on his mother the same truth when she supposes that he is madly hallucinating his father's ghost: "Mother," he urges, "Lay not that flattering unction to your soul / That not your trespass but my madness speaks" (3.4.143–53). The mad behavior, as in Saxo, is best understood theatrically on the Elizabethan stage as a device of concealment. And it does keep Claudius guessing, even if the King is plainly skeptical.

No one is more impatient than is Hamlet with the delays that seem forced upon him. In one of his finest soliloquies, having been moved by the visiting First Player's recitation of a Virgilian set piece about the grisly death of King Priam and the mournful cries of Queen Hecuba at the fall of Troy to the Greeks, Hamlet excoriates himself for not being stirred to action when the Player can weep for a Hecuba who is only a character in his tragic speech. "What's Hecuba to him, or he to Hecuba, / That he should weep for her? What would he do / Had he the motive and the cue for passion / That I have?" (2.2.559–62). Yet the question prompts Hamlet to postpone any immediate attempt at homicide in favor of commissioning the visiting players to stage "something like the murder of my father" in Claudius's presence. Such an event, Hamlet feels sure, will allow him to observe the King's looks to see if Claudius will "blench" or flinch. "Murder, though it have no tongue, will speak / With most miraculous organ" (594–6). Claudius will be "struck so to the soul" by a dramatic representation of his crime that he will reveal, by his involuntary responses, any guiltiness that he may feel.

Hamlet's stratagem at this point has struck some readers (including Sigmund Freud, as we shall see) as stalling for time, and that is, of course, possible; but his own plausible explanation is that he feels a strong need for verification of the Ghost's instructions to him. "The spirit that I have seen / May be the devil," he reflects, "and the devil hath power / T'assume a pleasing shape; yea, and perhaps, / Out of my weakness and my melancholy, / As he is very potent with such spirits, / Abuses me to damn me" (2.2.599–604). This too could be a rationalization on Hamlet's part for delay, but historically we need to remember that many or most people of Shakespeare's generation did believe in spirits and devils. Not to believe in the devil's skill in deception and persuasiveness was to doubt the Church's position on the subject. And in a stage play like *Hamlet*, a ghost takes on tangible reality. The ghost of Hamlet's father is described for us in detail. He resembles "the King that's dead" (1.1.45). Horatio is converted from skepticism to belief: "Before my God, I might not this believe / Without the sensible and true avouch / Of mine own eyes" (1.1.60–2). Later, when the Ghost appears to Hamlet in Gertrude's chambers, he is accoutered "in his habit as he lived" (3.4.141). The Ghost, then, is very "real" in Elizabethan stage terms. Moreover, Church wisdom and popular lore alike confirm Hamlet's fear that the Ghost may be the devil in disguise, tempting Hamlet into rash and even damnable behavior.

Once the visiting players' play called "The Murder of Gonzago" has been acted before Claudius and the court with the wished-for result of demonstrating to Hamlet and Horatio the King's guilt, Hamlet no longer hesitates. "I'll take the Ghost's word for a thousand pound," he crows excitedly to Horatio (3.2.284–5). Horatio agrees that the King's response confirms all their suspicions. Summoned thereupon by Rosencrantz and Guildenstern to visit his mother in her chambers before he goes to bed, Hamlet proceeds there at once. On the way, he happens upon Claudius at prayer and determines, as we have seen, to postpone the killing not out of moral scruples about homicide but because another time will be better suited to sending the King's soul straight to hell (3.3.89–9). Immediately thereafter Hamlet arrives at his mother's chambers, hears a man's voice behind the arras, stabs, and realizes he has killed the wrong person. Hamlet has acted resolutely, as he has longed to do. He has found the opportune moment, it seems, to kill Claudius when he is about to be "in th'incestuous pleasure of his bed" (3.3.90). Hamlet's assumption that a man concealed in his mother's chambers could only be Claudius must have seemed entirely reasonable to Elizabethan audiences. Yet it all goes wrong.

Hamlet appears to derive two insights from this miscarriage of his plans. One is that swift, resolute action is not the uncomplicated solution one might have hoped. The other is that he, Hamlet, will have to pay for this killing of Polonius, just as Polonius has paid the price of his meddling. Heaven will have it thus. "Heaven hath pleased it so / To punish me with this, and this with me, / That I must be their scourge and minister" (3.4.180–2), Hamlet tells his mother. These terms are quite precise and in accord with Elizabethan terminology. A "scourge," literally a whip, is here both an instrument of divine punishment and a cruel bringer-on of disaster, destroying many lives (*Oxford English Dictionary*). A person fulfilling the role of scourge may be ironically unaware that his or her cruelty is fulfilling a divine purpose; though intending evil, like Richard III, the scourge figure ultimately and unintentionally rids a corrupted world of those whom God wishes to chastise. A "minister" in Elizabethan terms is more simply one who carries out the wishes of a higher authority. Hamlet's Christian belief comes to his assistance at this crucial moment, convincing him that heaven has somehow had a hand in the mistaken killing of Polonius, and that heaven will direct Hamlet's future course in ways that he himself cannot fathom or predict.

The subsequent course of the play seems to confirm Hamlet in his faith that heaven is in charge of all that happens. The death of Polonius has at least two consequences: Ophelia goes mad, and her brother Laertes returns from Paris in a furious determination to revenge his father's death. As a means of pursuing this aim, Laertes unwittingly becomes an instrument of Claudius's fervent wish to bring about the death of Hamlet. Laertes is right in thinking that Hamlet is the slayer of Polonius. Laertes is, however, fatally misled by the cunning Claudius, whose guilt of a worse crime is unknown to all but Hamlet and Horatio. Unaware of what Claudius is up to, Laertes agrees to a plot of a poisoned rapier and wine cup. He does so with misgivings, since these are not the means used by an honorable gentleman seeking to settle scores. More significantly here, Laertes's misjudgment demonstrates the dangerous logic of rash and sudden action when it is insufficiently informed by all that the would-be doer needs to know. As he dies, Laertes realizes that he has acted wrongly, not only by employing unethical means but by not considering what Claudius's motives might have been for seeking the death of his nephew. "The King, the King's to blame" are Laertes's last words (5.2.323). At last he knows, but too late. He serves as a perfect example, for Elizabethan audiences as for ourselves, of the potentially disastrous results of swift, imperfectly considered action.

Hamlet thinks a lot about this crucial matter of when and how to act, of how to sort out the rival claims of sudden action and passive reflection. He meditates on this philosophical problem when he encounters a captain serving under the command of Fortinbras, the

Norwegian prince who is now marching across Denmark to attack Poland. Hamlet is curious to know what the campaign is supposed to accomplish. The captain is quite frank and disillusioning. The territory they hope to conquer is only "a little patch of ground / That hath in it no profit but the name" (4.4.19–20), he says. The captain would not pay five ducats for it, or choose to farm it. Well, then, replies Hamlet, the Polish general will not bother to defend it. Oh, yes, is the answer, "it is already garrisoned." Hamlet is amazed at the apparent futility of this imminent military engagement, predictably at huge expense and with a staggering cost of human lives. "Two thousand souls and twenty thousand ducats / Will not debate the question of this straw," he concludes (24–7).

Left to himself (in a soliloquy cut from the 1623 Folio text), Hamlet pursues the matter further by applying it to his own situation. Here he is, not yet having carried out the solemn command of his father to revenge. Hamlet sees that "Examples gross as earth" exhort him, especially now in this instance of an army ready to expose "what is mortal and unsure / To all that fortune, death, and danger dare, / Even for an eggshell" (47–54). Hamlet envies Fortinbras's unflinching resolution to engage in battle, but he also sees what is absurd about the cause. He feels upbraided in his inactivity by the example of twenty thousand men

> That for a fantasy and trick of fame
> Go to their graves like beds, fight for a plot
> Whereon the numbers cannot try the cause,
> Which is not tomb enough and continent
> To hide the slain. (4.4.61–6)

Yet even as he berates himself for cowardice, he sees the absurdity of the result. He perceives in himself a mixture of "one part wisdom" and "three parts coward" (43–4). He is dismayed to seem cowardly, but acknowledges that one part of wisdom which must not be forgotten. How is one to choose when to act resolutely and when to hold back in wise reflection?

In his conversations with Horatio, Hamlet loves to debate this philosophical problem of action and passivity. As Hamlet perceives, Horatio is a stoic. Hamlet admires and loves Horatio for his remarkable ability to be "As one, in suffering all, that suffers nothing, / A man that Fortune's buffets and rewards / Hast ta'en with equal thanks" (3.2.65–7). Hamlet offers here a crisp, thumbnail definition of stoicism. As understood in Shakespeare's time, it is a philosophical view counseling repression of emotion, indifference to pleasure or pain, and patient endurance. The true stoic is not merely one who can endure misfortune with equanimity; he must equally resist the blandishments of Fortune, on the grounds that if one eschews a desire for good luck or wealth, one cannot be disappointed when fickle Fortune turns the other way. The true stoic must be truly indifferent to Fortune's buffets *and* rewards. Horatio is like that, in Hamlet's estimate. Part of Hamlet longs to be like that also, for it would relieve him of much unhappiness about the way things have turned out so badly. But how is one to reconcile this sort of philosophical passivity with the Ghost's command that Hamlet do something to remedy the crime of murder?

The problem returns as a point of philosophical debate in Hamlet's conversation with Horatio after Hamlet has returned from England. He senses, as do we, that accounts must somehow be squared between him and Claudius, and soon. The King is aware that Hamlet has returned, not having been executed in England as the King has hoped and requested. As Horatio observes, "It must be shortly known to him [Claudius] from England, / What is the issue of the business there." Hamlet concurs. "It will be short," he says, adding, "The interim is mine" (5.2.71–3). This passage occurs in the Folio text only, not in the earlier quartos, as though Shakespeare added a revision to make the point entirely clear. Hamlet knows that he has only a little time in which to act. He has not forgotten his reasons for needing and wanting to kill the man "that hath killed my king and whored my mother, / Popped in between th'election and my hopes, / Thrown out his angle for my proper life, / And with such cozenage." Is it not "perfect conscience," he asks Horatio, "To quit him with this arm? And is't not to be damned / To let this canker of our nature come / In further evil?" (63–70). And yet Hamlet's mood is more nearly one of resignation. He appears to have no plan.

Instead, Hamlet now seems to be waiting for heaven to assist and direct his course. He is by now fully aware that rash action can have a proper place in human conduct. "Rashly," he says to Horatio, "And praised be rashness for it—let us know / Our indiscretion sometimes serves us well / When our deep plots do pall" (5.2.6–9). Yet Hamlet has no rash action in mind to serve the present moment. He speaks disparagingly of "our deep plots," which are too likely to create disaster. Apparently, then, the best sort of "rash" action may be that which is provided for us by some beneficent higher power. Contemplation of the futility of our "deep plots," says Hamlet, "should learn us / There's a divinity that shapes our ends, / Rough-hew them how we will" (9–11). Hamlet sees providence at work in his account to Horatio of his sea voyage, when he discovered that he had with him his father's "signet" or great seal with which to seal up the commission to the English king now ordering the deaths of Rosencrantz and Guildenstern instead of himself: "Why, even in that was heaven ordinant" (48). When Osric arrives at this point to propose a duel between Hamlet and Laertes, Hamlet wonders if this is perhaps the way in which heaven will offer an opportunity for "rash" action. Urged by Horatio to decline the offer of a duel if his mind misgives him, Hamlet frames his answer as a defense of passivity:

Not a whit, we defy augury. There is special providence in the fall of a sparrow. If it be now, 'tis not to come; if it be not to come, it will be now; if it be not now, yet it will come. The readiness is all. (5.2.217–20)

In his appeal to "special providence," Hamlet speaks the language of an Elizabethan Protestant Christian steeped in the teachings of John Calvin. "Special providence" here signifies a heavenly and foresighted management of human affairs that is intended for some unique occasion or purpose. Hamlet is prepared to place himself in the hands of providence. Accepting that he must act when heaven chooses and only then, Hamlet surrenders to the will of heavenly necessity. He will be heaven's minister in some way that he cannot foresee, and need not foresee. Heaven will take care of everything and will give him his cue when it is his turn to act. Hamlet's language is purposefully metatheatrical here; he is aware that he is performing a role in a drama scripted by supernal powers.

And so it turns out, as Hamlet interprets his own story. The duel provides him the occasion to exchange swords once he has been unfairly wounded by Laertes's unbated and poison-tipped rapier. The text suggests that Laertes dies not by a fatal thrust from Hamlet, but from the poison; as Laertes says, dying, "I am justly killed with mine own treachery" (5.2.309). Hamlet thus sees himself as fulfilling exactly the role he has wished to fulfill: he has become the instrument of some higher intelligence directing his actions in ways that he could not have predicted or shaped for himself. Hamlet knows nothing of the poison until the deed is done. Similarly, Hamlet kills Claudius in a way that he has not planned, and under circumstances that amount to something close to justifiable self-defense: Claudius has shown his intent to kill Hamlet, and now Hamlet acts first. The deed is as nearly unpremeditated as can be, granted that Hamlet has wished all along to fulfill his father's command. He has not plotted this final homicide. To the contrary, he has been the victim of a sinister plot against him. He also dies, as he has repeatedly wished, yet without committing suicide. Providence, in his view, has done well, far better than he could have devised.

Elizabethan spectators, then, were given good reason to conclude, if they chose to agree, that Hamlet's story ends justly and providentially. The great weight of tragic event is ameliorated by the audience's perceptions that things have fallen out as they should. But what is that audience to make of the paradoxical fact that Hamlet, having been instructed to revenge a foul and most unnatural murder by slaying Claudius, discovers his true path at last by resolving to do nothing and to place himself at the disposal of providence? This is a puzzle indeed, one that strikes at the heart of Hamlet's great philosophical problem of adjudicating the disputed claims of action and passivity.

One way to explore the paradox is to note that the Ghost's instruction to kill Claudius is in accord with the pagan code of revenge found in its most uncomplicated form in Saxo Grammaticus, whereas Hamlet's calm resolution at the end to place himself at the will of heavenly providence is in accord with Hamlet's growing belief in Christian teaching. Such a gospel, of accepting that "The readiness is all" and that one must learn to "Let be" (5.2.220–2), is also wedded (as it frequently was in medieval thought) to classical stoicism. Hamlet is satisfied with this resolution of his difficulties, and does not complain that the Ghost's pagan command seems to have led him down a garden path, and yet the inconsistency remains. It can perhaps be attributed to Shakespeare's widely divergent sources: on the one hand, a Scandinavian saga of bloody revenge, and on the other a Christian tradition of late-medieval Europe in which the spirit of revenge is seen as anything but uncomplicated. Shakespeare sets these two worlds uneasily side by side and finds wonderful drama in the indeterminacy of the debate. Drama thrives on conflict and uncertainty, and *Hamlet* is preeminently a play in which questions are asked but not fully answered.

One indication of the way in which *Hamlet* indeed refuses to tidy up the debate for its Elizabethan audience is to be found in Horatio's last comments on the tragic tale that he and the audience have witnessed. Horatio, though broken-hearted at the loss of his dear friend, has always differed from Hamlet on philosophical issues. He does so still, implicitly at least, at the end of the play. Horatio's view of history, and of this story, is anything but providential. He promises to reveal to the others a saga

> Of carnal, bloody, and unnatural acts,
> Of accidental judgments, casual slaughters,
> Of deaths put on by cunning and forced cause,
> And, in this upshot, purposes mistook
> Fall'n on th'inventors' heads. (5.2.383–7)

Horatio's is a secular view of history, in which events occur accidentally, casually, or as a result of human violence. A sense of reciprocity informs this view, as though somehow violence punishes itself, but it does not do so through providential guidance. Horatio's interpretation of history is more nearly existential, despite his calling at times on God as a witness and protector (see, for example, 1.1.60 and 1.4.91). He is a skeptic and a rationalist, willing to believe what he can see with "the sensible and true avouch" of his own eyes (1.1.60–2). His skepticism is dramatically useful, in that an Elizabethan audience is likely to be persuaded of those wondrous things Horatio comes to believe: the reality of the Ghost, the murder of Hamlet senior, the romantic account of Hamlet's escape from pirates. Horatio is a reliable witness. Still, his interpretation of Hamlet's story is finally at variance with Hamlet's own. Elizabethan and modern spectators alike are left, at the end of the play, with a deep uncertainty as to how they should interpret the role of the heavens, if any, in human affairs.

Hamlet in 1599-1601, then, shows a keen awareness of religious and philosophical controversies that were of particular interest to Elizabethan audiences. What about the political controversies of those years? Queen Elizabeth was aging and childless, leaving unsettled the question of her successor and whether that inheritor of the throne would be Protestant or Catholic. She was also a female monarch, arousing in her subjects both adulation and misogynist anxieties about what the Scottish Presbyterian clergyman John Knox called "the monstrous regiment of women" (*The First Blast of the Trumpet*

Against the Monstrous Regiment of Women, Geneva, 1558). Steven Mullaney detects in this bifurcated royal image a parallel to *Hamlet*, where Hamlet's mourning for his dead father "is displaced or at least overlaid and complicated by misogyny toward a queen who is too vital, whose sexuality transgresses both her age and her brief tenure as a widow." Peter Erickson similarly argues that "the latent cultural fantasy in *Hamlet* is that Gertrude functions as a degraded figure of Queen Elizabeth" (see Further Reading for citations). Did Elizabethan viewers catch glimpses of their own queen in Shakespeare's portrayal of a woman whose sexuality is such a source of dismay and revulsion to her son? If the comparison did suggest itself to some members at least of Shakespeare's audience, would they have viewed the idea as potentially dangerous or even treasonous? Evidently, Shakespeare's company was never asked to explain itself on this matter. Is the thesis too speculative? Or does it invite us to wonder how the play resonated in the world of *fin de siècle* politics as Queen Elizabeth neared the end of her life? If the analogy works, it must be at the level of unconscious psychological suggestion.

Elizabeth's fondnesss for, and then her bitter disillusionment with, Robert Devereux, second Earl of Essex, offers itself as another potential focus of political interpretation of *Hamlet*. Essex was a constant focus of a disaffection that culminated, in 1601, in an abortive uprising by his followers against the Queen's ministers. It was put down and Essex was executed, but not before the specter of civil conflict had alarmed everyone. Some scholars have wondered if Rosencrantz's allusion in the 1604–5 quarto to an "inhibition" that "comes by the means of the late innovation," thereby causing "the tragedians of the city" to travel on tour rather remaining in town (2.2.329–33), might refer to the Essex rebellion, in which case the passage would have to have been written in 1601 or later. Essex was much admired by playwrights and their audiences, at least until the failure of the rebellion attempt. Shakespeare, in the Chorus to Act 5 of *Henry V*, 1599, praises "the General of our gracious Empress / As in good time he may, from Ireland coming, / Bringing rebellion broachèd on his sword." Most commentators agree that the Chorus refers to Essex, who had been dispatched to Ireland in March of 1599 to put down the insurgency of the Earl of Tyrone; he returned to England in late September of that year, unsuccessful and under a cloud, but in the interim he was widely regarded as a hero stoutly resisting the commands of his queen. In February, 1601, on the eve of the Essex rebellion, Shakespeare's acting company was called upon to perform a play—almost surely Shakespeare's *Richard II*—about King Richard II, presumably as a means of arousing feelings of resentment against Queen Elizabeth; defamatory analogies between her rule and that of Richard II were legion and notorious. The Lord Chamberlain's Men were exonerated, but only after having been severely examined on the event. *Julius Caesar*, 1599, is filled with disillusionment about political conflict. *Troilus and Cressida* (probably late 1601, after the Essex rebellion had ended in failure), seems preoccupied with historical accounts of great men having betrayed their best selves. The controversy stirred up by the impetuous Essex was thus very much in the news when *Hamlet* was written and produced. Did it leave its mark upon that great play?

James Shapiro, in his *1599: A Year in the Life of William Shakespeare* (2005), pursues a possible *Hamlet* connection to Essex by noting the existence in late 1599 of a secret plot on the part of Essex and his followers to negotiate with James VI of Scotland, offering guarantees of support for James's claim to the English throne, by force if necessary, in return for the rehabilitation of Essex, who by this time was in disgrace for the failure of his Irish expedition. When James proved unwilling to commit himself to such a risky enterprise, some of Essex's followers, notably Lord Mountjoy (who had succeeded Essex as Lord Lieutenant in Ireland), also refused to make a commitment, saying that the plan now savored too much of Essex's own private ambitions. Shapiro concedes that few in England could have known of this treasonous conspiracy, and that a resemblance in the Essex story to two situations especially in *Hamlet*—namely, an abortive coup attempt by Laertes's faction, and the intent of a neighboring prince (young Fortinbras of Norway) to invade Denmark—can only be "sheer coincidence"; even so, argues Shapiro, these were times "when such things could be imagined—and by some even plotted." This argument is speculative. Yet Shapiro's idea may have suggestive force when stated by him in more general terms: "*Hamlet*, composed during these months, feels indelibly stamped by the deeply unsettling mood of the time" (p. 281). Essex was no Prince Hamlet, nor was meant to be, but even so Shakespeare's stirring tragedy of a young man paying the ultimate sacrifice in his struggle with a powerful and corrupt court may well have resonated with some audience members for whom the fall of Essex (in 1599 and then more tragically still in 1601) was a living instance of what Hamlet calls "the insolence of office." The purported connection between the Essex episode and *Hamlet*, then, is speculative, especially so since the text of the play affords only one glancing and ambiguous reference to what might or might not be the Essex affair in the years 1599–1601: the "late innovation." Even here, Rosencrantz says that this "late innovation" has led to an "inhibition," with the result that the "tragedians" or players "of the city" have been obliged to tour the countryside. Might this not refer instead to an order of the Privy Council on 22 June 1600 restricting the number of playhouses and performances? Hamlet and Rosencrantz seem particularly interested in a theatrical rivalry between the adult players and the boy companies. As Rosencrantz reports the matter to Hamlet, the adult players no longer "hold the same estimation" they previously enjoyed (2.2.328–35). This phrase appears in the 1604–5 quarto; the 1623 Folio version gives a much more detailed account of a rivalry between the adult acting companies and "an aerie [nest] of children, little eyases [young hawks], that cry out on the top of question and are most tyrannically clapped for't," all of which might suggest a reference to the so-called War of the Theatres in which the audacious success of the boy actors in the "private" theatres (i.e., indoors acting locations designed for well-to-do and courtly audiences) was giving Shakespeare and his adult colleagues at the "public" theatres a serious run for their money. This "war" was at its height in 1599–1601. The "late innovation" to which Guildenstern refers could then point to the renewal of acting by the boy companies in 1600 after nearly a decade of governmental suppression because of their penchant for topical satire.

Why then was the long passage describing this controversy cut from the 1604–5 quarto, to appear only in the 1623 Folio (2.2.337–62)? It could have been added in the Folio rather than having been cut from the second quarto, but then the 1603 first quarto also refers to the stage quarrel; as "Gilderstone" explains in that text, "the public audience that came to them [the adult players] are turned to private plays, and to the humour of children" (7.266–73), suggesting that the story was part of the play as Shakespeare originally wrote it. Perhaps it was excised from the 1604–5 quarto because the matter was stale news by then; it would have been even more so in 1623, but may have been part of an uncut text to which the 1623 editors had access. Or it may have been cut from the 1604–5 quarto because the publisher and Shakespeare's company did not wish to offend Queen Anne, consort of King James VI and I. Shortly after the coronation in 1603, she had become the sponsor and royal protector of the boys' acting company known formerly as the Children of the Chapel Royal and now renamed as the Children of the Queen's Revels.

Here then was a topical quarrel that may have seemed particularly lively in 1599–1601, especially to the author of *Hamlet*, with his mind so much on theatre and acting. The controversy was enlivened by a clash of personalities, notably between Ben Jonson (author of *Cynthia's Revels*, 1600, and *Poetaster*, 1601) and his attackers, John Marston and Thomas Dekker; their *Satiromastix* (1601) contained a thinly veiled satirical portrait of Jonson that had been replied to in kind by Jonson in *Poetaster*. In an anonymous Cambridge play of 1601–2 called *The Return from Parnassus*, Shakespeare is credited with having put them all down, especially that "pestilent fellow," Jonson, to whom Shakespeare has allegedly given a "purge." The notoriety of this exchange is of less interest to us today than the larger issue of an ideological and commercial competition between the adult companies and the boys' companies; Jonson wrote *Cynthia's Revels* and *Poetaster* for the Chapel Children. The elitist drama of the boy companies was polemically and culturally at odds with the more publicly oriented drama of the adult actors. Shakespeare's account, in the Folio passage of *Hamlet*, though measured and judicious, does seem to regard the runaway success of the boys' companies, with their penchant for irreverent and even scurrilous satire, as a threat to the adult companies, and particularly to the Lord Chamberlain's company for whom Shakespeare wrote and acted.

If such is the nature of *Hamlet's* engagement with politics at court and in the city of London, we are left with something of a puzzle. Why are not the ominous issues of regime change and rebellion more evident in the play? Why is the Earl of Essex, so much on the scene in *Henry V, Julius Caesar,* and *Troilus and Cressida*—all of them written pretty much at the same time as *Hamlet*—so shadowy a figure in this play if his presence is really felt at all? In short, how politically topical was *Hamlet* in its own time? Polonius is sometimes seen as a caricature of Lord Burghley, Elizabeth's chief minister—those who claim the seventeenth Earl of Oxford as author of Shakespeare's plays argue that Oxford would have been in a particularly advantageous position to study the mannerisms of his father-in-law, Burghley—but the satirical sketch of a busybody and spy is too generic to require topical particularity, and Burghley had died in 1598, before *Hamlet* was written. *Measure for Measure, King Lear, Macbeth,* and other Shakespearean plays of the early Jacobean years lend themselves readily enough to topical political interpretation. *Hamlet* seems less inclined that way. The puzzle is all the more intriguing in that, as we shall see in the final two chapters of this book, *Hamlet* was to become in modern times a potent vehicle for expressing political dissent and disillusionment. As in so many things, *Hamlet* raises more questions than it answers.

Hamlet is a play of timeless appeal; its many ideas are stirringly universal. Nevertheless, as we set about to examine its rich history down to the present day, we would do well to reflect, as this chapter has attempted to do, on the many ways in which *Hamlet* participates in and reflects its Elizabethan cultural background. As a revenge play in a popular theatrical genre, *Hamlet* asks its audience to judge the play's protagonist by ethical standards, but it does so in conflicting ways. Hamlet is a revenge hero with a just cause and with many deaths on his account, like other protagonists in tales of revenge. At the same time, he is a Christian. His father's ghost comes to him from Purgatory, having committed sins that require spiritual cleansing since he died suddenly without receiving Last Rites. Many Elizabethans would have taken for granted that ghosts are real and able to appear to some persons and not to others. Hamlet's final determination is to leave matters in the hands of Providence, trusting that he can then be an agent of divine will. Yet even this resolution is complicated by Horatio's secular and existential view of history that implicitly denies providentiality. The play may embody topical resonances to the unhappy saga of Queen Elizabeth's troubled relationship with the Earl of Essex.

All these intriguing propositions and interpretations will be reviewed, interrogated, and upended in the story lying ahead of the play's reception down through the four centuries and a little more that have elapsed since the play was first written and performed.

4

The Mirror Up to Nature: *Hamlet* in the Seventeenth and Eighteenth Centuries

Hamlet was performed at court in 1619 by the King's Men and again in 1637, probably with Joseph Taylor, Richard Burbage's successor as leading man, in the lead role. Burbage died in 1619, having played the part over a number of years since its premier performances in 1599–1601. We do not have a record of how often it was revived in the early seventeenth century, but the popularity of the play in print, demanding no less than eight editions by 1637, with five quartos before the Folio edition of 1623, would seem to suggest that it was popular on stage also—more so in its day than any other play by Shakespeare except (in descending order) *1 Henry IV, Richard III*, and *Pericles*. The funerary tribute in 1619 to Burbage, "Oft have I seen him jump into the grave," similarly points to repeated performances. Another tribute to Burbage on that funerary occasion laments, "No more young Hamlet, though but scant of breath, / Shall cry, 'Revenge!' for his dear father's death." Other than these scattered hints, together with the bizarre record of a shipboard performance in 1607 and some evidence of the play's touring in Germany in 1626 (see chapter 2), we have no records of performance down to the closing of the theatres by the Puritans in 1642. Nor is the play much talked about in contemporary gossip or critical observation.

During the mid-century years of civil conflict between Puritans and Royalists, performance of Shakespeare was only barely kept alive in an informal and anemic way. This happened not in any public theatres, since they had all been closed in 1642, but informally and surreptitiously, in the occasional presentation of skits or "drolls" limited to a few scenes and to certain favorite comic characters. *A Midsummer Night's Dream* took the form of "The Merry Conceited Humours of Bottom the Weaver." *Henry IV, Part I* was transformed into "The Bouncing Knight," centered on the antics of Falstaff. *Hamlet* was reduced to "The Gravemakers," focusing on act 5, scene 1, with no doubt an enhancement of the clownish humor. The genre of the "droll" continued on into the Restoration years as well, notably in John Lacy's *Sauny the Scot*, produced at the Drury Lane Theatre in 1667, with a parodic treatment of Petruchio (in *The Taming of the Shrew*) as a brute and with a big role for his servant, now cast as a Scottish clown.

The theatre that returned to London with the Restoration of the Stuart monarchy in 1660 differed substantially from that of Shakespeare's heyday. By Restoration times, theatre audiences, who even in Shakespeare's later years were already inclining more and more toward courtly and sophisticated taste, were virtually limited to a self-selected group of courtiers and gentry. The plays they saw, both new and revived, were mounted in indoor theatre spaces that were mostly new, some of them elegant. At the beginning of the Restoration, royal patents for acting companies were limited to two. The company of Sir William Davenant, the Duke of York's players, began performing in 1660 at the old theatre in Salisbury Court. (James, the Duke of York, was the younger brother of King Charles II and next in line to the throne; his succession in 1685 was to cause such a furor because of his Catholicism that James would be replaced by William of Orange, William III, and James's daughter Mary, in the so-called "Glorious Revolution" of 1688.) In 1661 this company moved to a new theatre in Lincoln's Inn Fields, and then in 1671 to Dorset Gardens. All of these locations were in what is now called the West End, westward of London's ancient town walls. A second company under the management of Thomas Killegrew, the King's company, moved in 1660 from the Red Bull to a theatre built on Gibbons's Tennis Court in Vere Street and thence to a theatre on Bridges Street, Drury Lane, in 1663. When this first so-called Theatre Royal was destroyed by fire in 1672, Killegrew's company set up temporarily in Lincoln's Inn Fields, and then moved to the magnificent second Drury Lane Theatre, designed by Christopher Wren, in 1674.

The rights to perform *Hamlet* passed in the early 1660s from Shakespeare's old and no longer operating company, the King's Men, to

William Davenant and the Duke of York's company. Stage tradition credits Davenant with having coached Thomas Betterton as Hamlet and Betterton's wife Mary Saunderson as Ophelia in the acting style that Davenant recollected from the performances of Joseph Taylor and his colleagues prior to 1642, but in truth Davenant's *Hamlet* bore only a partial resemblance to the Shakespearean original. Performed at intervals from 1661 to 1709 with Betterton in the lead role, the new *Hamlet* was shortened by some 841 lines, leaving out most of the Fortinbras story (though retaining his appearance in act 5), Polonius's advice to Laertes and to Reynaldo, most of Laertes's advice to Ophelia, the roles of Voltimand and Cornelius, much of Rosencrantz's and Guildenstern's parts, Hamlet's advice to the players, the last thirty-eight lines of Hamlet's highly emotional interview with his mother in act 3, scene 4, Hamlet's encounter with the captain in Fortinbras's army, and parts of Hamlet's soliloquies throughout other than "To be or not to be." These cuts were incorporated in published quartos in 1676 and 1695, along with a notice that "This play being too long to be conveniently acted, such places as might be least prejudicial to the plot or sense are left out upon the stage." To be sure, some of these cuts may have been inherited from productions before 1642, since the play probably was always too long for full presentation. Davenant also refined the language in accordance with Restoration taste. Overall, nonetheless, *Hamlet* was less altered than were some other Shakespeare plays, such as *King Lear, Macbeth, Measure for Measure, Much Ado About Nothing, The Taming of the Shrew*, and *The Tempest*. The text of *Hamlet* in the Restoration and early eighteenth century was substantially shortened but not extensively adapted.

Restoration theatres increasingly made use of elaborate scenic effects that, in Shakespeare's day, had been used chiefly in the presentation of masques at court. Most were imported from continental stage practice; King Charles II and his courtiers had become acclimatized to such theatrical devices during their enforced sojourn abroad during the Civil War. The proscenium arch was introduced, allowing a curtain to close off the stage area behind it, although action could still be placed on the apron or outer stage. Because scenic effects could now be introduced, productions of Shakespeare moved toward the visual and operatic. Artificial lighting was needed for indoor performance. Changes of these sorts moved Restoration theatre away from the fluidity and flexibility of the Elizabethan open-

air presentational stage, devoid of scenery, towards something closer
to scenic verisimilitude.

Hamlet was in fact the first Shakespeare play to be performed with
the use of perspective scenery, at the Lincoln's Inn Fields theatre,
designed in such a way as to create the illusion of deepening space
toward the back of the set. The effect would have been accomplished
by means of painted flats behind the proscenium arch, some of them
moved onto the stage from both wings along grooves in the stage
floor. The flats were done up to resemble the battlements of a castle in
act 1, scene 1 and scenes 4 and 5, a room in the palace for state
occasions in act 1, scene 2 and elsewhere, an unspecified outdoor
setting for Hamlet's encounter with Fortinbras's captain in act 4,
scene 4, and the like. The sets were not overly elaborate and were
designed for quick placement and removal; a generic set representing a
castle interior could serve for a number of occasions. These sets were
not very "realistic" by later standards; they were "stock" scenes
intended for repeated deployment. Still, the move toward scenic
representation was underway. Divisions between scenes could now
be marked by the lowering and raising of the curtain; scenes were thus
visually discrete. The moving of the Ghost and Hamlet from one guard
platform to another in act 1, scene 4 and then scene 5 would perhaps
no longer be accomplished simply by an exit and re-entrance a few
moments later.

Acting styles were affected by changes in stage and theatre management. Perhaps the most significant development was the emergence of
the actor-manager, who had a major financial investment in the
company. He managed or co-managed its affairs, provided some
direction of individual productions, and starred as lead actor. This
sort of prominence was new, despite Shakespeare's having been able
to rely on Richard Burbage for leading roles. Although the Burbage
family did own a controlling share of the King's Men while Shakespeare belonged to that group, the actor-sharers divided acting responsibility more or less equally, apportioning the important secondary
roles among themselves in a practical way. Those men were expected
to be versatile in the sharing of acting assignments. The companies of
the Restoration and eighteenth century, on the other hand, gave a
new prominence to actor-managers like Thomas Betterton and David
Garrick.

This structural shift in the acting company placed new demands on the script. It encouraged the curtailment of secondary roles to allow more room for the lead actors. Shakespeare's plays with large roles for the protagonist, like *Hamlet* and *Macbeth*, rose to prominence in the theatre repertory, whereas others lacking such a focus, such as *The Comedy of Errors* or *Love's Labour's Lost*, were less often seen. Women's roles underwent a similar change of emphasis as the companies, following continental example, moved from the employment of boy actors in female roles to the employment of mature (and at times notorious) women. The new actresses, like the leading men, demanded plays and parts suited to their talents. Shakespeare's scripts were accordingly revised to meet these needs.

Not surprisingly, then, contemporary notices of *Hamlet* in the Restoration theatre tend to focus on Betterton as the star performer. His commanding presence is ably rendered in the portrait that Sir Geoffrey Kneller painted of him in about 1690. Colley Cibber, who was to be an actor-manager for the united acting companies at the Theatre Royal in 1690, has recorded for posterity his admiration of Betterton in the role of Hamlet, especially in his scene with his father's ghost on the castle battlements. Instead of bellowing in a brazen attempt to dazzle audiences, Cibber reports, Betterton chose, by "straining vociferation requisite to express rage and fury," to convey "an almost breathless astonishment, or an impatience, limited by filial reverence." He "opened with a pause of mute amazement; then, rising slowly to a solemn, trembling voice, he made the Ghost equally terrible to the spectator as to himself" (*An Apology for the Life of Colley Cibber... Written by Himself*, London, 1740). Restoration audiences were evidently inclined to luxuriate in sensational moments of this sort at the expense of textual completeness or accuracy.

An illustration from Nicholas Rowe's 1709 edition of the plays depicts the moment when the Ghost suddenly appears to Hamlet and the Queen in her chambers (3.4; see Illustration 4). A high-ceilinged room is lit by a candelabra. Two pictures adorn the wall-papered walls. Hamlet, stage right, raises his left arm in astonishment at what he sees; the Ghost, stage left, makes remonstrating gestures. The Queen, seated further backstage between the two opposing figures, reacts in consternation. A chair is thrown to the ground, in a stage gesture David Garrick would later adopt as his own. The Ghost is in armor; Hamlet and the Queen are dressed in Restoration courtly garb.

Illustration 4. Thomas Betterton as Hamlet, confronting his father's ghost in his mother's chambers as Gertrude looks on in amazement and dismay, 3.4. The portraits on the wall, one partly concealed by a curtain, are of the dead King Hamlet and his brother, Claudius, now king. The overturned chair visualizes the emotional intensity and disarray of the scene. From an illustration in Nicholas Rowe's edition of 1709. Courtesy of Special Collections, Regenstein Library, University of Chicago.

Hamlet is bewigged; the Queen wears a full-bodied low-cut gown. Restoration actors costumed themselves thus for the most part, in order to bring Shakespeare's plays as much as possible into alignment with contemporary mores and customs. A picture hanging in the Garrick Club in London shows Betterton as Hamlet in a clerical neckcloth and ministerial outfit, with Elizabeth Barry as Gertrude in a crimson velvet robe over a white satin underskirt. This was to be the style generally of dressing for *Hamlet* down to the time of David Garrick. Social indelicacies, such as Hamlet's remark to Ophelia about lying in her lap and practicing "country matters" between maids' legs (3.2.110–19), tended to be dropped.

Meanwhile, the two acting companies, having moved in successive steps to more elegant quarters in the more fashionable district to the west of the old City, united in 1682. Audiences were too small to support both. Thereafter the combined company performed usually in the Drury Lane Theatre, the smaller of the two houses. This single company was the sole source of legitimate drama in London until 1695, when the restiveness of some underpaid actors led to the establishment of a newly patented acting company in Lincoln's Inn Fields. The new company enlisted some impressive talent, notably Thomas Betterton, Elizabeth Barry, and Anne Bracegirdle. Despite such a powerful beginning, and a new theatre building in the Haymarket in 1705 designed by Sir John Vanbrugh, the project dwindled and eventually failed, leaving the field to Colley Cibber at Drury Lane in 1717 and afterwards. All the actors united again in one company. Haymarket was turned into an opera house.

Increasingly in the seventeenth century, critical appraisals of *Hamlet* demanded more elegance and refinement of style than had been expected in the Elizabethan age. In his own day, Shakespeare was lauded as poet and dramatist by Frances Meres (*Palladis Tamia*, 1598), John Weever (*Epigrams in the Oldest Cut and Newest Fashion*, 1599), Gabriel Harvey (in his marginal notes in a copy of Speght's *Chaucer*, 1598–1601), Anthony Scoloker (in his prefatory epistle to *Diaphantus, or The Passions of Love*, 1604), William Camden (*Remains of a Greater Work Concerning Britain,* 1605), and others, a number of whom offered special praise to *Hamlet*. Harvey noted in his copy of Speght's *Chaucer*, mentioned in chapter 2, that "The younger sort takes much delight in Shakespeare's *Venus and Adonis*, but his *Lucrece* and his tragedy of *Hamlet, Prince of Denmark* have it in them to please the wiser sort."

Yet even in the early years Shakespeare was criticized for his lack of classical sophistication and polish. Robert Greene, addressing fellow dramatists in his *Groatsworth of Wit*, 1592, lashed out at an "upstart crow, beautified with our feathers," who "supposes he is as well able to bombast out a blank verse as the best of you." The offending "Shake-scene" is clearly meant to signify Shakespeare, since Greene paraphrases a line from Shakespeare's *3 Henry VI*. Greene enviously sees the young dramatist as a plagiarist of no taste or originality.

Ben Jonson's appraisal of Shakespeare is decidedly mixed. On the one hand, writes Jonson in his tribute "To the memory of my beloved, the author Mr. William Shakespeare" published in the 1623 Folio, Shakespeare is the "soul of the age, / The applause, delight, and wonder of our stage," a "monument without a tomb" whose art will endure "while thy book doth live." Shakespeare deserves to be honorably remembered with Chaucer, Spenser, and Francis Beaumont. He outshines Lyly, Kyd, and Marlowe in the theatre, and indeed is worthy of comparison as a tragic writer with Aeschylus, Euripides, and Sophocles. As for comedy, Shakespeare has no peer in "insolent Greece or haughty Rome," or in any writer since. This is high praise indeed. Yet even in this commemorative poem Jonson cannot resist digging at Shakespeare for having only "small Latin and less Greek."

Elsewhere, too, Jonson complains of Shakespeare's lack of neoclassical sophistication. In a conversation with William Drummond of Hawthornden (1619) he objects that Shakespeare "wanted art" because in a play (*The Winter's Tale*) he "brought in a number of men saying they had suffered shipwreck in Bohemia, where there is no sea near by some hundred miles." In *Timber, or Discoveries*, Jonson chides Shakespeare for his unrestrained facility in writing. "The players have often mentioned it as an honor to Shakespeare that, in his writing, whatsoever he penned he never blotted out [a] line. My answer hath been, would he had blotted a thousand." In a prologue to his own *Every Man in His Humour* (1616 Folio text), Jonson satirizes English history plays (and implicitly, most of all, Shakespeare's sequence of three *Henry VI* plays and *Richard III*) in which, "with three rusty swords, / And help of some few foot-and-half-foot words," the actors "Fight over York and Lancaster's long jars, / And in the tiring-house bring wounds to scars." Jonson is impatient with plays (implicitly including Shakespeare's late romances) that flout the classical unities of time and space by dramatizing the lives of characters who grow up from childhood to old age in the course of a single play or are wafted "o'er the seas" by an obliging chorus (as in *Henry V*).

Jonson would presumably have disapproved of *Hamlet*'s extensive disregard for the classical unities of time and place, especially in the interval needed for Hamlet's journey to England and back to Denmark. Jonson might have protested against the insertion into a great tragedy of comic dialogue, notably in Hamlet's duel of wits with Polonius (see 2.2.171–219), in the bantering about death and burial in Ophelia's graveyard (5.1.1–216), and in the delicious satire of Osric as a court butterfly (5.2.81–193). If Jonson also frowned at Hamlet's inveterate punning, he would have been anticipating the critical lament of Dr Samuel Johnson, in the later eighteenth century (see below), who regarded Shakespeare's fondness for wordplay as the "fatal Cleopatra" of an otherwise brilliant poet and dramatist.

Jonson's criticisms are of a piece, and they continue on into the Restoration period, where indeed Ben Jonson, often performed on stage, was widely regarded as a more pleasingly correct dramatist than Shakespeare. John Dryden's critical estimate of Shakespeare, like Ben Jonson's, is mixed. Though Dryden freely allows that Shakespeare has many times "written better than any poet, in any language," with "the largest and most comprehensive soul," yet Shakespeare is "the very Janus of poets" in that he "wears almost everywhere two faces; and you have scarcely begun to admire the one, ere you despise the other" (*Essay of Dramatic Poesy*, 1665). Like other Elizabethans, in Dryden's view, Shakespeare often indulges in "low" style by failing to produce graciously elegant dialogue of the sort one might hear in Restoration courtly society. Dryden cites an instance of inappropriate language in *Hamlet* in the First Player's Virgilian speech about the slaughter of Priam (2.2.452–518), which Dryden regards as written in a "blown puffy style" and hence something that one would prefer to ascribe to some other author ("The Grounds of Criticism in Tragedy," prefaced to Dryden's 1679 adaptation of *Troilus and Cressida*). "I may venture to maintain," writes Dryden, "that the fury of his fancy often transported him beyond the bounds of judgment, either in the coining of new words and phrases, or racking words which were in use into the violence of a cathresis [i.e., catachresis, the misuse of words]."

John Dennis's *Essay on the Genius and Writing of Shakespeare* (1712) similarly expresses a regret, shared by many of his generation, that Shakespeare, "one of the greatest geniuses that the world e'er saw for the tragic stage," could not have "joined to so happy a genius learning and the poetical art." By "poetical art" Dennis means the classical unities and other rules of literary decorum. Alexander Pope joins the chorus of those who regard Shakespeare's faults as comparable in magnitude to the greatness of his genius, adding that Shakespeare's ill-educated audience is chiefly to blame (preface to Pope's edition of *The Works of Shakespear*, 1725).

The truncated and refined version of *Hamlet* that Restoration play-goers saw on stage, with Betterton as Hamlet, seems not to have pleased everyone. John Evelyn noted in his *Diary* for 16 November 1661, "I saw *Hamlet, Prince of Denmark*, played, but now the old plays begin to disgust this refined age, since His Majesty's being so long abroad." On the other hand, Samuel Pepys, that indefatigable playgoer and diarist who seems to have known everyone that counted, was so struck with Hamlet's "To be or not to be" soliloquy that he commissioned a musical rendition of it. (Hamlet's letter to Ophelia inspired no less than nine metrical and musical adaptations between 1786 and 1861.) Pepys bought an edition of Shakespeare's plays on 4 December 1661. He saw *Hamlet* acted by the Duke's company at the playhouse identified by Pepys as "the Opera" in Salisbury Court, on 24 August 1661, "done with scenes very well, but above all, Betterton did the prince's part beyond imagination." On 27 November in that same year, *Hamlet* was again "very well done" at "the Theatre" in Lincoln's Inn Fields, and still again on 5 December at "the Opera." By 28 May 1663, when Pepys again "saw *Hamlet* done, giving us fresh reason never to think enough of Betterton," Davenant's company had settled in at "the Duke's House," that is, their new theatre in Lincoln's Inn Fields. Pepys's last recorded visit to the play was on 31 August 1668, at the same Duke of York's playhouse. There Pepys "saw *Hamlet*, which we have not seen this year before, or more; and mightily pleased with it; but, above all, with Betterton, the best part, I believe, that ever man acted."

Betterton's extensive longevity in the role of Hamlet, from 1661 until 1709, when he was seventy-four, yielded at length to the succession of Robert Wilks, joint manager with Barton Booth at the Drury Lane Theatre from 1709 onwards. (Colley Cibber was an important actor who shared in the management of Drury Lane for a time around 1717, but was not a great success as a tragedian, preferring as he did to specialize in eccentric roles.) Wilks played Hamlet until 1732. He also excelled as Macduff in *Macbeth* and the Prince of Wales in *Henry IV, Part I*. He went further than had Betterton in shortening the text of *Hamlet* by pruning Fortinbras from act 5 entirely, thus allowing the play to end on a tragic high note with Horatio's tearful farewell and eulogy to his sweet prince. This ending was to be the only one seen on stage from 1732 until 1897, and has been adopted as well in more recent times; Laurence Olivier's 1948 film is an example. An operatic *Hamlet* at the Haymarket in 1712 took its inspiration chiefly from Saxo Grammaticus's *Historia Danica*.

The Restoration and early eighteenth century was thus a time, for *Hamlet* and other Shakespearean plays, of several intertwined developments: the emergence of the actor-manager with his powerful control over his company and the texts that they acted, the narrowing down of theatre performances in Restoration London to two and sometimes one acting company, a focus on leading roles like that of Hamlet at the expense of secondary parts, indoor performances before select audiences with strong connections at court, movable stock scenic effects, artificial lighting, and women instead of boy actors in female roles. Concurrently, a sophisticated preference for refinement of taste and classical rules of decorum steered both productions and published texts toward correctness and elegance. Regarding Shakespeare as an untutored "natural genius" who wrote for unrefined audiences in an ignorant time, Restoration spectators and readers of Shakespeare generally applauded "improvements" to his text designed to elevate him to the high poetic status he deserved. Actors and editors alike excised secondary characters, unified action according to the classical unities, and attempted to render *Hamlet* and other plays more symmetrical and spectacular by the incorporation of scenic effects. The ideal of "poetic justice" mandated just punishment for the guilty in the struggle of vice and virtue. Hamlet was refashioned as exemplary hero.

A notable example of this approach in *Hamlet* criticism is to be found in *Characteristic Advice to an Author* (1710) by Anthony Ashley Cooper, third Earl of Shaftesbury, in which Shakespeare is praised for encouraging the disposition of the English people "towards the moral and instructive way." Despite Shakespeare's "natural rudeness, his unpolished style, his antiquated phrase and wit, his want of method and coherence, and his deficiency in almost all the graces and ornaments of this kind of writings," says Shaftesbury, "yet by the justness of his moral, the aptness of many of his descriptions, and the plain and natural turn of several of his characters, he pleases his audience and often gains their ear without a single bribe from luxury or vice." *Hamlet* in particular is the play "which appears to have most affected English hearts, and has perhaps been oftenest acted of any which have come upon our stage." The play "is almost one continued moral, a series of deep reflections, drawn from one mouth upon the subject of one single accident and calamity, naturally fitted to move horror and compassion."

Thomas Hanmer similarly finds instructive universality and compliance with the demands of poetic justice in Shakespeare's decision not to have the Ghost speak to his former wife in act 3, scene 4: "we could hardly suppose that a woman, and a guilty one especially, could be able to bear so terrible a sight without the loss of reason" (*Some Remarks on the Tragedy of Hamlet, Prince of Denmark*, 1736).

The early eighteenth century is also the era in which scholarly editing of Shakespeare's texts began. Four folio editions had been published in the seventeenth century, beginning with the great First Folio of 1623, followed then by editions in 1632, 1663 (with a second issue in 1664), and 1685. Each edition after 1623 simply reprinted its predecessor, with occasional corrections of errors that are sometimes of use to modern editors as shrewd guesses but that have no independent authority; that is, they show no signs of having been based on something that Shakespeare actually wrote. New errors turn up as well.

The publisher who took up the challenge and opportunity of offering new editions of Shakespeare for eighteenth-century Great Britain was Jacob Tonson. A supporter of the Copyright Act of 1709–10 that offered new legal protections of literary property, Tonson was eager to promote his own investments. These included the works of Shakespeare, along with Milton's *Paradise Lost* and the writings of Edmund Spenser, Francis Beaumont and John Fletcher, Edmund Waller, John Dryden, William Congreve, and still others. Tonson published a remarkable succession of editions of Shakespeare's plays in the years from 1709 to 1768, choosing as his editors Nicholas Rowe, Alexander Pope, Lewis Theobald, William Warburton, Samuel Johnson, and Edward Capell. These men were well known and respected as dramatists, poets, and scholars. Tonson saw to it that their editions, each "improving" on the previous one, presented

Shakespeare as Great Britain's greatest and most distinctive literary artist. The publishing venture was, in this sense, a kind of political statement. Tonson himself was a member of the politically influential Whig organization known as the Kit-Cat Club.

The first edition of Shakespeare to appear in this culturally momentous enterprise was Nicholas Rowe's six-volume edition in 1709, re-edited in eight volumes in 1714. Rowe was himself a writer of tragedies. He based his text of Shakespeare on the 1685 Fourth Folio, but he also introduced lists of *dramatis personae* on a systematic basis. (A few such lists are to be found in the earlier folios, but only sporadically.) Rowe marked entrances and exits with more care than had earlier editions, thereby dividing the play-texts into more scenes than had previously been enumerated, and he identified the locale of most scenes.

These "improvements" were a mixed blessing. Rowe adhered to the neoclassical dictum that a serious play like *Hamlet* should have five acts. The original quartos of *Hamlet* in 1603 and 1604–5, as well as other quartos published before 1623, had no act-scene divisions at all. The 1623 Folio started to provide such markings for *Hamlet* but did so in haphazard fashion, only for the first three scenes of act 1 and the two scenes of act 2. Actually, Rowe needed to do little to "improve" the text of *Hamlet* in this regard, since markings for acts 3, 4, and 5 had already been inserted into a quarto edition of 1676 based on the stage production at the Duke of York's Theatre. Because Rowe cared chiefly about marking the act divisions, he left the rest of the scene markings, other than act five, scene 2, to Alexander Pope (4.2 through 4.5) in 1723–5 and to Edward Capell (1.4, 1.5, 3.2 through 3.4, 4.6, and 4.7) in 1768. Rowe provided the scene numbering for act five, scene 2. This more or less systematic introduction of the five-act structure is symptomatic of the age's craving for neoclassical regularity.

Similarly, the providing of an indication of location for individual scenes clearly reflects neoclassical stage practice, and may in turn have influenced actor-managers to think visually in terms of specific locales. To indicate a shift from "*Elsinore. A guard platform before the castle*" (Theobald) in scene 1 to "*A room of state in the castle*" (Capell, substantially) in scene 2 can be helpful to readers, but at the same time it invites and feeds upon a "realistic" visual representation of the scene on stage. When, at the start of act 1, scene 5, an editorially added stage direction informs us that we are now in "*another part of the platform*"

(Capell again), theatre managers attuned to this language may feel the need for a set change. Rowe did not go this far in 1709, but he started things in that direction. He did not consult the early texts of 1603 or 1604–5, though he did propose a number of textual emendations. He also modernized spelling and punctuation in accord with early eighteenth-century practice.

Alexander Pope, in his six-volume edition of 1723–5 (second edition in eight volumes, 1728), marking up a copy of Rowe for his printer's copy, carried forward Rowe's task of providing regular divisions into acts and scenes. In fact, Pope employed the so-called "continental" system of scene division and numbering, grouping in a massed entry at the head of each scene the names of all the characters who are to take part in the scene in question, including those already on stage as the scene begins. This continental system also sometimes marked a new scene when a major character entered in what we would call midscene; that is, without waiting for the interval of a bare stage. This continental style of scene marking was standard practice among classical scholars editing the texts of ancient writers, and thus had a kind of cachet at the expense of theatrical practicality. Entrances and exits were often omitted; the text was to be read as a literary poem. Ben Jonson had employed this method when many of his plays were published.

More intrusively, Pope regularized a good deal of verse in *Hamlet* and other plays, in accord with his own presumably sophisticated literary taste. The implication was that Shakespeare's untutored genius would benefit from the refined polish of one of the apostles of the Age of Enlightenment. Pope relined as verse many passages that had been typeset as prose, often to good advantage but sometimes not. He substituted words that he preferred to the original, as when Ophelia returns some remembrances to Hamlet "That I have longèd long to redeliver"; Pope, bothered by the repetition in "longèd long," changed the phrase to read "longèd much" (3.1.95). Pope did not go back to the early quartos in any systematic attempt to see if they could be properly used in place of suspect Folio readings; that would be a project for later editors. Instead, he subjectively and sporadically made use of early quarto readings whenever such readings appealed to his poetic sensibilities as more felicitous than what he had found in Rowe's Folio text. As a major poet in his own right, Pope seems to have regarded the editing of Shakespeare as an opportunity to correct and improve Shakespeare's occasionally uncultivated phraseology. Some of Pope's "improvements," indeed, have won acceptance, as when he proposed "bourn" for "borne" in Hamlet's "The undiscovered country from whose bourn / No traveller returns" (3.1.80–1). At other times Pope seems too arbitrary or rigid, as when he drops the "Why" in Hamlet's "To feed and clothe thee? Why should the poor be flattered?" (3.2.58), apparently on the grounds that the iambic pentameter rhythm is more smooth without the "Why." Pope objects to Hamlet's "Nor do not saw the air too much with your hand" (3.2.4–5), presumably regarding the double negative of "Nor do not" as a grammatical error. Pope changes "Nor" to "And." Many of Pope's interventions now seem gratuitously dictated by eighteenth-century standards of well-bred taste.

Fortunately, by following overall the text of Rowe and his predecessors, Pope gave his readers a more or less complete version of the 1623 Folio *Hamlet*, which was, to be sure, a shortened version of the play. Lewis Theobald, editing the plays in 1733 and in subsequent editions, attempted to remedy some of Pope's interventions by going back to the early quartos and folios, and deserves credit for some brilliant emendations, but he too prepared his text for the printer by annotating a copy of a preceding edition, in this case Pope's, and thus perpetuated more errors than he managed to correct. Theobald's reward for daring to contradict Pope was to be crowned the King of Dullness in a version of Pope's *The Dunciad* (before 1742).

When we move on to the second half of the eighteenth century, we come to what is generally known in theatrical terms as the Age of Garrick, and deservedly so. David Garrick was the great actor-manager of the era and the star in his own productions. He achieved early fame in 1741–2 as Richard III at an unlicensed and short-lived theatre in Goodman's Fields. Following a great success in *Hamlet* (and *The Recruiting Officer*) at Dublin in 1742, Garrick moved to Drury Lane in that same year. His inability to get along there with actor and fellow manager Charles Macklin helped persuade Garrick that he needed to run his own show. He set about securing a patent for a new acting company in 1743. In 1746 he and James Quin collaborated in a memorable joint engagement at Covent Garden, where the actors had been offering stiff competition to Drury Lane since Covent Garden opened in 1732. But Garrick soon returned to Drury Lane, entering there into a co-directorship with James Lacy that inaugurated one of the most successful periods of English stage history down to the time of Garrick's retirement in 1776. The Covent Garden playhouse was refurbished and enlarged early in their regime, both exterior and interior, and then was enlarged again in 1763 to a capacity of about one thousand. Hamlet quickly became a favorite role for Garrick, and thus the play was centrally featured in the company's stock repertoire. Among his many accomplishments, Garrick improved the lighting system by increasing the number of footlights and mounting reflector lights on moving poles in the wings, making special effects more possible than before.

Garrick proudly believed that the theatre offered the only true interpretation of the dramatist's text; without performance, the text itself was lifeless and inert. Edmund Burke agreed, proclaiming that Garrick "had raised his profession to the rank of a liberal art." Garrick helped bring some aura of respectability to the theatrical world of London that was too often marred by rowdyism among the spectators, notoriety in the private lives of some performers, and complacent tolerance of trafficking in prostitution. His own private life was morally exemplary, and he was not reluctant that this should be widely known. His cult of Shakespeare was central to his design of commemorating Shakespeare as England's great literary genius and national treasure, with Garrick as the Bard's custodian and interpreter. In 1769, in Stratford-upon-Avon, Garrick was the presiding genius of a great three-day Shakespeare Jubilee created to celebrate and indeed venerate Shakespeare as England's greatest poet and dramatist. Although no Shakespeare plays were performed on that occasion, the festivities were splendid enough to designate Stratford for all time as a pilgrimage site for Bard enthusiasts. The high point appears to have been Garrick's recitation of his "Ode Upon Dedicating the Town Hall, and Erecting a Statue to Shakespeare."

For a time, Garrick used the version of *Hamlet* that had been handed down from Davenant, Betterton, and Wilks. From that already abbreviated text, Garrick further excised Hamlet's "Now might I do it pat" soliloquy as Hamlet happens upon his uncle at prayer (3.3.73–96), along with all mention of Hamlet's voyage to England. These alterations were calculated to improve the moral stature of Hamlet by taking away his bloodthirsty thoughts of wishing to send Claudius's soul to hell and his responsibility for the deaths of Rosencrantz and Guildenstern. Otherwise, Garrick seems to have been wary of adapting *Hamlet*, as his predecessors had also been.

In the role of Hamlet, Garrick was famous for the new gestures and stage business he brought to the interpretation of highly emotional moments. From the very first performances in 1742, Garrick thrilled the spectators as he followed his father's ghost from place to place on the battlements (see Illustration 5). A specially made wig gave the impression of his hair standing on end. When the Ghost appeared to him in his mother's chambers (3.4), a trick chair fell over to express Garrick's surprise and agitation. Grief for his father's death was the

Illustration 5. David Garrick as Hamlet, encountering his father's ghost on the battlements (1.5), in a painting by Benjamin Wilson. Garrick was renowned for the expressive eloquence of his gestures. Courtesy of ArenaPAL, London.

emotion that governed his behavior throughout. Some of this was no doubt inherited from Betterton, whose face had turned white as his shirt at the Ghost's appearance (the overturned chair, too, turns up in Illustration 4 of the scene in Nicholas Rowe's 1709 edition of the plays), and from Wilks, but Garrick made the role his own.

Garrick seemed amazingly convincing in the part, as though he was mourning the death of his own father. Henry Fielding's *Tom Jones* (1749) offers a wry tribute to this verisimilitude when the naive Partridge, having accompanied Tom to a staging of Garrick's *Hamlet*, is dismissive of the acting skill needed to produce a naturalistic effect. "Why, I could act as well as he myself," Partridge insists. "I am sure if I had seen a ghost, I should have looked in the very same manner and done just as he did." Partridge is more impressed by the highfalutin rhetoric of the actor playing the King. He "speaks all his words distinctly, half as loud again as the other," says Partridge in wondering admiration. "Anybody may see he is an actor" (book 16, chapter 5).

Partridge's recollection, though satirized by Fielding, is reinforced by the testimony of a German scientist, Georg Lichtenberg, in a letter written during a visit to England in 1775 (*Works*, 1817 ed., 3.214), describing Hamlet's first encounter with the Ghost. At Horatio's warning, "Look, my lord, it comes!" (1.4.38), writes Lichtenberg,

Garrick turns suddenly about, at the same instant starting with trembling knees two or three steps backward; his hat falls off; his arms, especially the left, are extended straight out, the left hand as high as his head. The right arm is more bent, and the hand lower; the fingers are spread far apart, and the mouth open. Thus he stands, one foot far advanced before the other, in a graceful attitude, as if petrified, supported by his friends, who, from having seen the apparition before, are less unprepared for it, and who fear that he will fall to the ground.

Lichtenberg adds a note about his own reaction to the scene: "so expressive of horror is his mien that a shudder seized me again and again even before he began to speak."

Not content with his huge success in the role over some twenty-five years, Garrick, in 1772, at the age of fifty-five, ventured to strike off more daringly on his own. At first he exulted in his success. "I must tell you," he wrote Pierre-Antoine Laplace, "that I have ventured to alter *Hamlet*, and have greatly succeeded. I have destroyed the Grave Diggers (those favorites of the people) and almost all of the fifth act. It was a bold deed, but the event has answered my most sanguine expectations." Soon, however, he came to regard his renovation of *Hamlet* as the most imprudent thing he had ever done. In this version of *Hamlet*, Garrick managed to rewrite the one great Shakespearean tragedy that had heretofore escaped major revision. What is left of the fifth act is now still further pared away. Hamlet never embarks for England at all. Laertes similarly never makes it to France because of a shipwreck. Laertes is without blame throughout, having never conspired with Claudius to kill Hamlet by means of a poisoned sword or poisoned cup. As the two young men duel in the final scene, the King steps between them and is slain by Hamlet, who, thereupon impaled by Laertes's sword in the scuffle, falls to the ground, exchanging forgiveness with Laertes. Horatio, in a fury at Hamlet's death, attempts to seek revenge on Laertes, but is persuaded instead by the dying Hamlet to bow to the will of heaven and rule jointly in Denmark with Laertes. Fortinbras is written out of the ending, nor do we hear anything of the executions of Rosencrantz and Guildenstern. No gravediggers are needed, since the burial of Ophelia is omitted entirely. Gertrude does not die of poison; instead, we learn that she has fallen into a trance and is on the verge of remorseful madness.

Garrick's intent in these changes seems to have been that of continuing still further a process already begun in his pre-1772 text, of exculpating Hamlet from any semblance of blame. Hamlet dies in a fair duel with an honorable and worthy opponent. The slaying of Claudius is virtually accidental, an unintended casualty of Hamlet's duel with Laertes. The deaths of Rosencrantz and Guildenstern are conveniently forgotten and in any case cannot be charged to Hamlet's account. Classical decorum is served by doing away with long gaps of time in the narrative and with travel into a foreign land. The death of the innocent Ophelia, so inconsistent with neoclassical ideas of poetic justice, is downplayed by the deletion of her burial scene. Gertrude does not die, evidently because poetic justice and just plain sentimentality would prefer not to see Hamlet's mother perish, but she is punished for her faithlessness to the memory of her first husband by a suitable emotional distress. The removal of the gravediggers eliminates the intrusion into a high tragedy of the low comic business that some neoclassical critics had found objectionable. Yet Garrick's desperate attempt in this *Hamlet* to please Enlightenment tastes did not succeed. Perhaps the times were changing by 1772. No doubt too audiences were aware of a fuller printed text of *Hamlet*, readily available for them to read.

Garrick retired in 1776, at the age of fifty-nine, and died some three years later, having managed to acquire a larger fortune than any other actor in English history up to that time, with the exception of Edward Alleyn in Shakespeare's day. Garrick was buried in Westminster Abbey. Joshua Reynolds, William Hogarth, Benjamin Wilson, and Thomas Gainsborough all painted his portrait. He enjoyed a truly remarkable success. Yet darker days were to come to the London stage after his departure. For all his theatrical genius, Garrick was a child of his time in his predilection for adapting Shakespeare to the presumed tastes of eighteenth-century spectators. *Hamlet* was becoming a philosophical text that appreciators of Shakespeare loved to study. A stage version brought to England at the end of the century by German actors provided the play with a happy ending; in it Hamlet is warned in time by the Queen's illness and manages to kill Claudius without dying himself. Perhaps this version contributed to a sense of malaise among some critics as they looked at what seemed to them a low state of Shakespearean performance.

The English-born actor and theatre director, Lewis Hallam, Jr, is believed to have been the first to perform the role of Hamlet in colonial North America. Having emigrated with his theatrical parents to the new world in 1752, he acted first in *The Merchant of Venice* in Williamsburg, Virginia, at the age of 12. Next year he and his family made their way to New York, where he subsequently founded, with his now-widowed mother and her new husband, David Douglass, a troupe that came to be known as the American Company. Performances of *Hamlet* took place in Philadelphia on July 1759 with young Hallam in the lead role and then in 1761 in the theatre on Nassau Street in New York that Lewis Hallam Sr had built in 1753. These productions restored the Gravediggers' scene, which had traditionally be curtailed or cut entirely, and made some attempt at period costuming. In 1796, the nineteen-year-old Thomas Abthorpe Cooper performed *Hamlet* at the Chestnut Street Theatre in Philadelphia, and then at the Park Street Theatre in New York. The scenery in the New York production was executed with some care and expense, in a conscious attempt to emulate the splendor of the London stage. Cooper soon became the young nation's most celebrated tragedian.

Meanwhile, in St Petersburg, Russia, in 1748, Alexander Sumaro-
kov produced an adaptation of *Hamlet* that, while following the
original quite closely, envisaged Hamlet as a figure of heroic resistance
against the tyranny of Claudius, thereby anticipating the way in which
the play would be used in Eastern Europe by the Hungarian author
Ferenc Kazinczy in 1790, by the Russian tragedian Pavel Mochalov in
1837, and as a protest against totalitarianism in the twentieth century
by Grigori Kozintsev and others.[1]

An Irish production of 1793 offers a wryly amusing glimpse into the
vexed state of affairs of British theatre at the end of the century. It was
advertised as follows in a newspaper and subsequently reprinted in
Anthony Hecht's *On the Laws of the Poetic Art* (Princeton: Princeton
University Press, 1995) and in John Julius Norwich's *A Christmas
Cracker* of 2005:

THEATRE ROYAL, KILKENNY, IRELAND (Irish players). On Saturday,
May 4, will be performed by command of several respectable persons in the
learned metropolis, for the benefit of Mr Kearns, the tragedy of HAMLET,
originally written and composed by the celebrated DAN HAYES of
LIMERICK, and inserted into Shakespeare's works. HAMLET by Mr Kearns
(being his first appearance in that character) who, between the acts, will
perform several solos on the potent bag-pipes, which play two tunes at the
same time. OPHELIA by Mrs Prior, who will introduce several familiar airs in
character, particularly THE LASS OF RICHMOND HILL and WE'LL ALL
BE HAPPY TOGETHER from the Rev. Mr Dibdin's ODDITIES. The
parts of the KING and QUEEN, by direction of the Rev. Mr O'Callagan,
will be omitted, as too immoral for any stage. POLONIUS, the comical
politician, by a Young Gentleman, being his first appearance in public.
THE GHOST, THE GRAVEDIGGER and LAERTES, by Mr Sampson,
the great London comedian. The characters will be dressed in Roman shapes.
     To which will be added an interlude of sleight of hand tricks, by
the celebrated surveyor, Mr Hunt. The whole to conclude with a farce,
MAHOMET THE IMPOSTOR, Mahomet by Mr Kearns.
     Tickets to be had of Mr Kearns at the sign of the Goat's Beard, in Castle
Street. The value of the tickets to be taken (if required) in candles, butter,
cheese, soap, etc., as Mr Kearns wishes in every particular to accommodate the
public. No persons will be admitted to the boxes without shoes or stockings.

Probably no adaptation of *Hamlet* in the late eighteenth century went
quite as far as this Irish production of 1793, but at the very least it
suggests how Shakespeare, and especially *Hamlet*, had achieved a kind

of wide popularity that bore only a tangential relationship to the play as it had been performed by Shakespeare and his original acting company.

If the late eighteenth century is the Age of Garrick in theatrical terms, it might be called the Age of Johnson in terms of literary criticism—Dr Samuel Johnson, that is, not Ben Jonson (who also sometimes spelled his name "Johnson"). Garrick and Johnson came from the same hometown, Lichfield, where Garrick was in fact Johnson's first pupil. The two of them went up to London at the same time in 1734, but subsequently fell out; now both lie buried in Westminster Abbey. Johnson was awarded the LLD at Dublin in 1765 and Oxford in 1775, though he rarely styled himself "Dr." His long-delayed edition of Shakespeare's plays appeared in eight volumes in 1765. Johnson defended Shakespeare's right to transcend the classical "rules" of time, place, and action and his mixing of comedy and tragedy, as in the gravediggers' scene in act 5, scene 1 of *Hamlet*, the pretended madness of Hamlet, and the foppishness of Osric, to which some other neoclassicists like Thomas Hanmer (1736) had objected.

Overall, Johnson's idea of Shakespeare is of one whose "just representation of general nature" has stood the test of time because of its universality of truth about the human condition. He praises *Hamlet* for its variety, its numerous incidents, and its interchangeable diversification of merriment and solemnity "that includes judicious and instructive observations." Johnson thus sees Shakespeare as a great moralist. To be sure, he objects to Hamlet's harsh treatment of Ophelia, and he deplores the haphazard nature of the catastrophe in the final scene. Especially worrisome to him are Hamlet's disingenuous apology to Laertes (5.2) and the death of "the young, the beautiful, the harmless, and the pious" Ophelia. Still, Johnson argues that Shakespeare is not guilty overall of having violated the dictates of poetic justice.

Other late-eighteenth-century critics apply similar standards, insisting on neoclassical decorum and moral value. In 1765 Oliver Goldsmith (*Works*, ed. James Prior, New York, 1854), feeling that the writings of "an author so universally held in veneration" should have its many errors examined, argues that the "To be or not to be soliloquy" is "a heap of absurdities." Elizabeth Montagu applies the test of dramatic propriety to the Ghost's appearances in *Hamlet*, finding them

to be highly successful by virtue of their avoiding idle frivolity and thus
adhering to what an eighteenth-century audience would expect in a
representation of the superstitious belief of an earlier age (*Essays on the
Writings and Genius of Shakespeare*, 1769). Henry Mackenzie (*The
Mirror*, no. 99, 18 April 1780) describes both Hamlet's virtues and
weaknesses "as our own; we see a man who in other circumstances
would have exercised all the moral and social virtues, placed in a
situation in which even the amiable qualities of his mind serve but to
aggravate his distress and to perplex his conduct. Our compassion for
the first, and our anxiety for the latter, are excited in the strongest
manner."

Joseph Ritson (*Remarks, Critical and Illustrative, on the Text and Notes
of the Last Edition of Shakespeare*, London, 1783) defends Hamlet's
apology to Laertes for the death of Polonius (5.2.224–42) from the
accusation of Dr Johnson that it is a "dishonest fallacy"; though it
might outwardly seem so, Ritson appeals to "better, because more
natural, judges" who will reflect that Hamlet has injured Laertes only
unintentionally. The speech to Laertes is, viewed thus, "a most gentle
and pathetic address." For William Richardson, in his *Essays on Some of
Shakespeare's Dramatic Characters*, 1784, Hamlet is "moved by finer
principles, by an exquisite sense of virtue, of moral beauty and turpitude." His utter dismay at the impropriety and depravity of his mother
is "the principle and spring of all his actions." Richardson ventures to
suggest that the sentiments Hamlet expresses on finding Claudius at
prayer are not his real sentiments, since a person of so sensitive
refinement would never give vent to "such savage enormity." Shakespeare has thus not "been guilty of any departure from nature, or any
infringement of poetical justice." All these critics feel it their duty to
offer moral judgments of Hamlet according to the codes of decorum,
propriety, and poetic justice.

On the Continent, the neoclassical spirit of the Age of Enlightenment generates something close to a consensus view of Shakespeare as
a genius beset by the misfortune of writing for a barbarous age. To be
sure, French intellectuals do lean heavily on the negative side of this
equation, affording David Garrick an opportunity to wrap himself
in the British flag as the champion of Great Britain's national poet
against the supercilious and rules-bound foreigners across the English
Channel. Voltaire (*Théâtre Complet*, 1768, 2.201) regards *Hamlet* "as a
vulgar and barbarous drama, which would not be tolerated by the

vilest populace of France or Italy," despite the fact that amid all the "vulgar irregularities" are to be found "some sublime passages, worthy of the greatest genius." The ghost of Hamlet's father "has a most striking theatrical effect." Viscount de Chateaubriand is even more negative in his *Sketches of English Literature* (1837), calling *Hamlet* a tragedy of maniacs in which all the characters are either crazy or criminal. More tolerantly though still condescendingly, the German critic G. E. Lessing, like Mrs Montagu, maintains that dramatic poets of an earlier age such as Shakespeare have a right to avail themselves of a widespread belief in ghosts at the time he wrote, even if Enlightenment thinkers and readers have disabused themselves of such superstitions. In this sense, the Ghost in *Hamlet* is a valid representation of a truth, since the Ghost "comes really from the other world" (*Hamburgische Dramaturgie*, 1767).

The editing of *Hamlet* and other Shakespeare plays in the mid-eighteenth century continued apace at the publishing house of Jacob Tonson, who, as we have seen, owned the copyright to Shakespeare's works and was, like David Garrick, intent on promoting that author as Great Britain's greatest cultural icon. Booksellers like Tonson were eager to promote multi-volume editions of standard authors, Shakespeare most of all. Encouraged by this commercial impetus, editing during this era made considerable advances in providing readers with more accurate texts. The Age of Enlightenment proved to be a fruitful time for analytical scholarship, to such an extent that textual advances came to be more and more at odds with the truncated and adapted versions of *Hamlet* seen on stage. For a time, to be sure, Shakespeare editors continued to mark up the text of their immediate predecessors, thereby perpetuating the editorial habits of the past. Thomas Hanmer in 1743–4 (published in Oxford, not by Tonson) and William Warburton in 1747 both did so, albeit offering some occasional emendations of merit. Even Samuel Johnson chose to mark up a copy of Lewis Theobald's 1757 text, with the result that many of Johnson's editorial efforts are a disappointment when compared with his brilliantly insightful essay written by way of prolegomenon. Johnson's notes are often valuable; his editing of Shakespeare's texts, including that of *Hamlet*, is generally not, suggesting that the great man tired of the assignment.

With Edward Capell, on the other hand, we arrive at an editor who saw the virtue and necessity of studying the early quartos and folios—

not, as in Pope's case, for the verbal felicities they might offer by way of alternative readings to those of the Folio text, but as versions that might bear the imprint of being closer to what Shakespeare had written. Capell's predecessors, including Johnson, had generally held to the view that the quartos were of inferior quality because they represented theatrical versions of the play. Capell saw that some quartos might have been printed from Shakespeare's own drafts. Capell's procedural method was overly eclectic from a modern point of view, but it was certainly a start, and it exerted a beneficial influence on George Stevens's 1773 revision of Johnson's edition. Capell was the last of Tonson's Shakespeare editors.

Edmund Malone, with a new publisher (J. Rivington), went still further in his ten-volume edition of 1790, by bringing to his editorial task a substantial knowledge of Elizabethan archival documents, including the Stationers' Register, Philip Henslowe's *Diary*, and the records of the Master of the Revels at court. Malone used as his textual authority for each play the earliest printed version. His knowledge of dating of such materials was imprecise, and earliest-first was not always the wisest choice, but at least Malone was working with a coherent textual theory. When he left unfinished at his death a Variorum edition of Shakespeare—that is, one that records systematically all textual variants in the early printed texts and in subsequent scholarly editions—the work was completed in 1821 by James Boswell, the son of Johnson's biographer. This became known as the Third Variorum. Earlier editions in 1803 and 1813 by Isaac Reed, based on Johnson/Malone, had called themselves the First and Second Variorums. Beginning in 1871, H. H. Furness would continue this tradition in what was entitled *The New Variorum Shakespeare*. That work is carried on today under the direction of a committee of the Modern Language Association of America.

Hamlet criticism and editing in the eighteenth century, then, is generally neoclassical in tone and method, preferring classical regularity and decorum, albeit with some large exceptions made for Shakespeare's genius. Criticism of this period manifests an abiding interest in character more than in plot or theme. It seeks to appraise and understand the moral purpose of the protagonist, and to measure the validity of the play's denouement by the standards of poetic justice. At the same time, the late years of the century exhibit signs of change. The Romantic movement begins not precisely in 1800, of course. Earlier indications are increasingly plentiful in appeals to the picturesque and the sublime. Character criticism, long practiced as a staple of interpretation, focuses in the Romantic period on Hamlet as one who possesses a delicate poetic sensitivity through which he is attuned to the great mystery of things. William Richardson, in 1784, anticipates the new critical fascination when he speaks of Hamlet as "moved by finer principles, by an exquisite sense of virtue, of moral beauty and turpitude." The Romantic insight into Hamlet's character is our next subject.

5

The Very Torrent, Tempest, and Whirlwind of Your Passion: *Hamlet* in the Nineteenth Century

In the late eighteenth and early nineteenth centuries, literary critics in England and on the Continent began to find in Shakespeare's art a potentially limitless repository of sublimity, poetic sensitivity, and mystery. Yet the decades after David Garrick were not flourishing ones for Shakespearean theatre, and perhaps especially so for *Hamlet*. William Hazlitt famously observed, in his *Characters of Shakespear's Plays*, 1817:

We do not like to see our author's plays acted, and least of all, *Hamlet*. There is no play that suffers so much in being transferred to the stage. Hamlet himself seems hardly capable of being acted. Mr Kemble unavoidably fails in this character from a want of ease and variety. The character of Hamlet is made up of undulating lines; it has the yielding flexibility of 'a wave o'th' sea'. Mr Kemble plays it like a man in armor, with a determined inveteracy of purpose, in one undeviating straight line, which is as remote from the natural grace and refined susceptibility of the character as the sharp angles and abrupt starts which Mr Kean introduces into the part. Mr Kean's Hamlet is as much too splenetic and rash as Mr Kemble's is too deliberate and formal. His manner is too strong and pointed. He throws a severity approaching to virulence into the common observations and answers. There is nothing of this in Hamlet. He is, as it were, wrapped up in his reflections, and only *thinks aloud*. There should therefore be no attempt to impress what he says upon others by a studied exaggeration of emphasis or manner; no *talking at* his hearers. There should be as much of the gentleman and scholar as possible infused into the part, and as little of the actor. A pensive air of sadness should sit reluctantly upon his brow, but no appearance of fixed and sullen gloom. He is full of weakness and melancholy, but there is no harshness in his nature. He is the most amiable of misanthropes.

Hazlitt's lament depicts a huge and seemingly impassable gulf between the stage and the literary study. To be sure, he lays a significant portion of the blame onto the acting of John Philip Kemble, who gained considerable fame in the role of Hamlet (and also King Lear and Othello) at Drury Lane from 1783 to 1802 and then at Covent Garden, and of Edmund Kean, whose roles at Drury Lane around 1814–1820 included Hamlet, Othello, Iago, and Shylock. Still, the disappointment of the Romantic critic with *Hamlet* in the theatre is all-embracing. Hamlet should be, according to the new Romantic gospel, almost infinitely variable in mood and purpose. He should be "wrapped up in his reflections," weak and melancholy, with a "pensive air of sadness" sitting upon his brow. He must be a person of "natural grace and refined susceptibility." He should be, above all, a man of philosophical thought. How can the theatre hope to capture the mystery of one who only "*thinks aloud*"? Kemble is too limited, in Hazlitt's view; he lacks "ease and variety," and seems unable to pursue any line of interpretation other than that of "determined inveteracy." Kean, conversely, is too "splenetic and rash," too nearly virulent, too lost in "sullen gloom" and given to *talking at* his hearers instead of being pensive and reflective. Hazlitt cannot conceive of an actor able to discharge the role of Hamlet in anything like its full register.

Hazlitt's dismay is all the more striking in that he appears to have had a high regard for Kean on other occasions. Kean was indeed much feted as the leading tragedian of his day. He made a lot of money, which he then squandered in drunkenness, ostentation, and generosity to his friends. He was praised by Kemble and Byron as well as by Hazlitt. Garrick's widow invited Kean to her house. A portrait of Kean as Sir Giles Overreach in Philip Massinger's *A New Way to Pay Old Debts* hangs in the Garrick Club in London. Yet to Hazlitt, Kean is simply not up to the part of Hamlet. But then, who could be? Better to read the play, discuss it with friends, ponder its enigmas, thrill to the subtle cadences of its wonderfully familiar language. As William Maginn put it (*Shakespeare Papers*, London, 1860): "*Hamlet* is, even more peculiarly than *Lear*, or *Macbeth*, or *Othello*, a play for the study." William Wordsworth wrote, in a letter to Sir George Beaumont,

1 May 1805, "I never saw *Hamlet* acted myself, nor do I know what kind of play they make of it."

London's theatres, beset by difficulties, responded by enlarging their audience capacities and by designing more visually spectacular productions, both aimed at drawing in new spectators. John Philip Kemble was Garrick's successor as lead actor at Drury Lane from 1783 (when he made his Drury Lane debut as Hamlet) to 1802 and as manager beginning in 1788. When he had difficulty in working with Richard Brinsley Sheridan as co-manager (Sheridan was also, of course, a famous playwright), Kemble moved to Covent Garden, where he remained active and successful in *Hamlet* and other plays from 1803 to 1808 and then from 1809 until his retirement in 1817. He died abroad in 1823. Under his leadership, Covent Garden became London's leading theatre. Both Covent Garden and Drury Lane were handsomely renovated in 1782 and 1792; both then burned, Covent Garden in 1808 and Drury Lane in 1809. Kemble rebuilt Covent Garden, more grandly than ever, and reopened in 1809, with increased admission charges that led to some sixty-nine days of riots and demonstrations for the restoration of old prices. Costs of production rapidly escalated. Audience capacity in both new theatres was huge, as can be seen from contemporary illustrations showing galleries along both sides rising to five tiers, with box seats over the stage (see Illustration 6). The new Covent Garden theatre featured an enlarged stage with proscenium arch and with wing-and-groove flats, enabling Kemble to indulge in his passion for resplendent pageantry. He freely adapted a number of Shakespeare's plays, in which, of course, he took the lead role.

Kemble's sister, the famous Sarah Siddons, was often his leading lady, in such Shakespearean roles as Queen Katharine, Isabella, Rosalind, Constance, Hermione, and Lady Macbeth. She played the Queen in *Hamlet* in 1796; she was also the first actress to undertake the role of Hamlet, in the Midlands in the 1780s and in a Dublin revival of 1802, thus anticipating later "breeches" performances of Hamlet by Charlotte Cushman, Sarah Bernhardt, and others, as we shall see. She was much admired by Hazlitt, Byron, Leigh Hunt, and Horace Walpole, among others, for her Shakespearean roles and for many others. She was painted in 1785 by Thomas Gainsborough (see Illustration 7), and, as the "Tragic Muse," by Sir Joshua Reynolds in 1784.

Illustration 6. The Drury Lane Theatre as rebuilt in 1812 after the fire of 1809, with a capacity of over 2,000 seats. The scene onstage is of *Hamlet*, act 1 scene 5, as Hamlet follows his father's armored ghost to a removed location on the battlements of the castle. Some gentlemen, in the boxes foreground, seem more interested in addressing the ladies and in being seen than in watching the play.

In his new theatre, Kemble performed before audiences of three thousand or more. Galleries stood along both sides of the house in four tiers; box seats flanking the stage could accommodate the Royal Family and other distinguished guests. Kemble's sets for *Henry VIII* and *Richard III* were noted for their colorful processions; his *Coriolanus* made use of Roman costumes; his *The Tempest* was handsomely masque-like. In *Hamlet*, and in other Shakespeare plays with kings and queens of former times, Kemble employed the court dress of Kemble's own era rather than that of historical period costuming. In his own role of Hamlet, Kemble set aside the traditional Van Dyck

Illustration 7. Sarah Siddons, sister of John Philip Kemble and Charles Kemble, 1785, by Thomas Gainsborough. Courtesy of ArenaPAL, London.

costuming of previous years for a contemporary court outfit of rich black velvet, with ruffles, powdered hair, and the Orders of the Garter and of the Elephant. (He was painted thus, at the gravesite of Ophelia, by Sir Thomas Lawrence in 1801.) Here, as elsewhere, Kemble was partial to unconventional effects. *Hamlet* was his second Shakespeare play at Covent Garden in 1803–4, following *Romeo and Juliet*. In this production, Kemble continued the tradition of cutting the Fortinbras material, Polonius's advice to Laertes, and the like, but with some restoration of the materials that Garrick had unwisely excised in 1772. Kemble's *Hamlet* was reportedly twenty minutes longer than anyone else's, in good part because he indulged in pregnant pauses, prompting Sheridan to quip that music should perhaps be employed to fill up the intervals. He was also noted for eccentric pronunciations, such as "hijus" for "hideous," "varchue" for "virtue," and "aitches" for "aches." We have Hazlitt's judgment that Kemble's Hamlet was too undeviating, too lacking in emotional range. His chief competition in 1804 seems to have been a child actor, William Henry West Betty, aged thirteen, who was known as "the young Roscius" after the famous actor of ancient Rome to whom Hamlet refers at 2.2.390–1. When Edmund Kean first appeared at Drury Lane in 1814, Leigh Hunt and William Hazlitt were among those who heralded the ascendancy of a bright new star, though, as we have seen, Hazlitt was convinced that Kean was not up to the extraordinary demands of acting Hamlet. At any rate, Kemble and Covent Garden soon lost ground to Kean and Drury Lane. Expensive sets and costumes aiming at historical correctness soon enabled Drury Lane to challenge its rival in the opulent style that Kemble had brought into prominence. Unfortunately, no visual synopses for his *Hamlet* have survived, but those for his *Richard III* and *Macbeth* in 1814, for example, are elaborate. For *Macbeth*, Kean brought on a "Romantic Landscape" with "Rocky Pass and Bridge," a "Gothic screen," a "Gallery in Macbeth's castle," and much more. William Capon, credited with having designed and executed some of the scenery, had been the exciting new scene designer for Kemble in 1794. *Bell's Weekly Messenger*, on 6 November 1814, applauded the "profusion of magnificence," proclaiming proudly that "our stage seems, indeed, to have reached its highest point of refinement, and we much question whether Rome, in all her luxury, and Greece, in all her elegance, could rival a British theatre" (2.110).

Kean's performance of Hamlet could be galvanizing. At the end of his painful interview with Ophelia in act 3, scene 1, he stopped as he was about to exit, returned to gaze intently on Ophelia's face for a few seconds, "and with a marked expression of tenderness on his own countenance, appeared to be choked in his efforts to say something, smothered her hand with passionate kisses, and rushed wildly and finally from her presence" (J. H. Hackett, *Notes, Criticisms, and Correspondence upon Shakespeare's Plays and Actors of Shakespeare*, 1863). Hazlitt, despite his serious reservations about Kean's interpretation of Hamlet overall, was stuck by this moment. "It had an electrical effect on the house," he wrote. "It was the finest commentary that ever was made on Shakespeare. It explained the character at once" (*Morning*

Chronicle, 14 March 1814). Then, during the acting of "The Murder of Gonzago" in act 3, scene 2, Kean as Hamlet crawled menacingly across the stage from his place at Ophelia's lap toward the enthroned Claudius and Gertrude as they watched the play within the play. This piece of stage business was to be copied by W. C. Macready in 1842 and was still in use in a 1920 German film starring Asta Neilsen as Hamlet (see the next chapter). Kean was intent above all on exploring Hamlet's introspective state of mind. To that end he abandoned the royal finery in which the character had been customarily dressed, choosing instead to present the prince in black velvet free of ornament.

Yet Kean proved a great disappointment as a manager or visionary; the times were not right for great Shakespearean theatre. Dissipated in his own personal life, he allowed the management of Covent Garden to fall into disrepair. Drury Lane too fell on hard times, partly in the hands of Kemble's brother Charles. The years 1816–37 were ones in which Shakespeare was repeatedly operatized, as in Frederick Reynolds's and Henry R. Bishop's *A Midsummer Night's Dream* in 1816. At a minor playhouse known as the Coburg (now the Old Vic), in 1828, Henry Milner adapted *Hamlet* to Gothic tastes: Hamlet, put on trial for the murder of his father and attempted murder of his mother, was saved only at the last minute by his mother's confession, whereupon he was proclaimed king. Not until the late 1830s, with the emergence of Charles's talented and beautiful daughter Fanny Kemble, and the appointment of William Charles Macready as manager at Covent Garden in 1837, did Shakespearean production find itself back on course.

In Canada and the United States during these years, Shakespeare was often performed, by the visiting Edmund Kean and others, in Montreal, Halifax, Quebec City, Philadelphia, and New York, among other cities. *Hamlet* was prominent among the favorites in the repertory, along with *Catherine and Petruchio, Richard III, Othello, The Merchant of Venice, Romeo and Juliet,* and *King Lear.* While touring in 1820–1 and then in 1825, Kean was accorded the title of honorary chieftain of the Huron Indians. The American tragedian Frederick Brown was a favorite as *Hamlet* in Montreal. Charles Kemble and his daughter Fanny crossed the Atlantic in 1832, again with *Hamlet* and a few other plays. The native-born Edwin Forrest began his sensational career in 1820 in Philadelphia and New York, and soon took on

Hamlet as a favorite role; see below for an account of his bitter rivalry with William Charles Macready.

During the years of the late eighteenth and early nineteenth centuries when theatrical interpretation languished, Romantic literary criticism of *Hamlet* seems to occupy another world. Goethe (*Wilhelm Meister*, 1778, 1795, later translated by Thomas Carlyle) led the way toward a new psychological insight into Hamlet as one who hesitates to act. "The time is out of joint. Oh, cursèd spite, / That ever I was born to set it right!" (1.5.197–8), cries Hamlet, when he has seen his father's ghost and has received the commission to revenge his father's murder. At other moments, to be sure, Hamlet expresses his urgent desire to act quickly and forcefully, but to Goethe the hesitation and delay are "the key to Hamlet's whole procedure." Earlier critics, though noting the delay, had not regarded it as a particular problem. For Goethe it is everything. "Amazement and sorrow overwhelm the solitary young man," writes Goethe. Hamlet is stunned by the realization that he is "unequal to the performance" of the Ghost's dread command. Goethe dwells on parallels between *Hamlet*'s Ghost and Wilhelm Meister's dead father. The book features at its core a production of Shakespeare's play.

Like William Richardson in 1784, Goethe conceives of Hamlet as "A beautiful, pure, noble, and most moral nature," but goes further to attribute to Hamlet a failure of nerve which makes him sink beneath a burden which "he can neither bear nor throw off." Not surprisingly, this influential piece of criticism comes from the pen of the man who wrote *The Sorrows of Young Werther* (1774), a prolonged, partly auto-biographical meditation on the exquisite melancholy of its young protagonist. Modern critics have wondered if Goethe, in attributing to Hamlet a paralysis of the will, is at least partly talking about himself.

Samuel Taylor Coleridge (*Notes and Lectures upon Shakespeare*, 1808), a great admirer of German Romanticism, developed this line of reasoning still further. For Coleridge, a major aspect of Shakespeare's genius is his ability to fathom the "deep and accurate science" of "mental philosophy." In order to understand Hamlet, "it is essential that we should reflect on the constitution of our own minds." When we pursue this line of investigation, we can see in Hamlet "a great, an almost enormous, intellectual activity, and a proportionate aversion to real action consequent upon it, with all its symptoms and accompanying qualities." Hamlet is undoubtedly brave and unconcerned about death, "but he vacillates from sensibility, and procrastinates from thought, and loses the power of action in the energy of resolve." The effect of this "overbalance of the imaginative power" is "the everlasting broodings and superfluous activities of Hamlet's mind."

As with Goethe, this perception of a delicate Romantic sensibility in Hamlet suggests that Coleridge is also looking inward at himself. Coleridge was able to write brilliantly on his best days, but his laudanum and then opium addiction and attempts to withdraw from it, his marital difficulties, and his economic dependence on others greatly intensified his sense of guilt and of failing spirits. "I have a smack of Hamlet in myself," Coleridge wrote. Is his Hamlet another self-portrait of a complex and sensitive genius suffering in romantic agony? Why, having been interrupted in its composition, was Coleridge unable to complete the fragmentary and wonderful "Kubla Khan"?

For other Romantic critics as well, Hamlet is introspective, even introverted, philosophical, and brooding. Charles Lamb (*On the Tragedies of Shakespeare*, 1811) speaks of his desire "to know the internal workings and movements of a great mind, of an Othello or a Hamlet for instance, the *when* and the *why* and the *how far* they should be moved." William Hazlitt aptly characterizes the penchant of the age for seeing one's own intellectual self in Hamlet. He insists,

It is *we* who are Hamlet. This play has a prophetic truth, which is above that of history. Whoever has become thoughtful and melancholy through his own mishaps or those of others; whoever has borne about with him the clouded brow of reflection and thought himself "too much i' the sun"; whoever has seen the golden lamp of day dimmed by envious mists rising in his own breast, and could find in the world before him only a dull blank with nothing left remarkable in it; whoever has known "the pangs of despised love, the insolence of office, or the spurns which patient merit of the unworthy takes"; he who has felt his mind sink within him, and sadness cling to his heart like a malady; who has had his hopes blighted and his youth staggered by the apparition of strange things; who cannot be well at ease while he sees evil hovering near him like a spectre; whose powers of action have been eaten up by thought . . . this is the true Hamlet. (1817)

To see Hamlet as like oneself in being a person whose powers of action are consumed by thought is to see the tender-hearted, blameless, and spiritually beautiful Hamlet of Goethe and Coleridge.

August W. von Schlegel (*Lectures on Art and Dramatic Literature*, 1809) is another disciple of Goethe. The burden that Hamlet faces "cripples the power of acting," writes Schlegel. "The weakness of his volition is evident: he does himself only justice when he says there is no greater dissimilarity than between himself and Hercules." "His far-fetched scruples are often more pretexts to cover his want of resolution." For Georg Wilhelm Friedrich Hegel, author of *Aesthetics* (based on lectures given in Berlin in the 1820s) and *The Philosophy of History* (lectures in 1830–1, published 1837), *Hamlet* is a useful and cautionary instance of Western civilization's uneven progression toward an ennobling spirit of consciousness: his hesitations and doubts are indicative of an inward struggle to know himself, but fail of their purpose when Hamlet achieves revenge only through chance and not through a full self-realization. Eugène Delacroix's 1839 painting of Hamlet and Horatio in the graveyard, with its dramatic lighting and storm-swept sky, captures the romantic mood of that famous scene. In America, Ralph Waldo Emerson comments in his essay on "Shakespeare, or The Poet" (*Essays*, 1841, 1847) that the very speculative genius of the nineteenth century is itself "a sort of living Hamlet."

Romantic contemplation of Hamlet as admirable in his thoughtfulness about human life inevitably raises a chorus of concerns about his treatment of Ophelia. "Poor Ophelia!" writes Anna Jameson. "Oh, far too soft, too good, too fair to be cast among the briers of this working-day world, and fall and bleed upon the thorns of life!" Ophelia's helplessness and innocence, says Jameson, can only melt us with profound pity. Her madness presents us with "an astonishing picture of a mind utterly, hopelessly wrecked! Past hope, past cure!" (*Characteristics of Women*, 1832). For Goethe too, Ophelia's "whole being floats in sweet, ripe passion," inviting us to discover "the movement of her heart" as she finds herself "forsaken, cast off, and despised" by Hamlet. Ludwig Tieck (*Dramaturgische Blätter*, 1824) admires Goethe's "fine observation" about Ophelia, adding his sympathy for the scene in which she must allow herself to be used as a decoy in addressing the young man she has loved so dearly, without "daring to breathe a word of vindication of herself."

What then of Hamlet's feelings for Ophelia? Thomas Campbell is persuaded that Hamlet's emotional commitment cannot have been profound. "It is anger with Laertes, not love for Ophelia, that makes Hamlet leap into the grave," Campbell insists. To make matters worse, "after the burial-scene, he seems utterly to have forgotten that Ophelia ever existed" (*Letters on Shakespeare*, *Blackwoods Magazine*, February,

1818, p. 505). Even Horatio is more solicitous of Ophelia than is Hamlet. In Schlegel's view, Hamlet "is too much overwhelmed with his own sorrow to have any compassion to spare for others." The deep concern about Ophelia will persist throughout the nineteenth century.

The Victorian age in Great Britain began, chronologically, at any rate, in 1837 with the coronation of the eighteen-year-old Queen Victoria. This is also the year in which William Charles Macready became theatre manager at Covent Garden. He moved to Drury Lane as manager from 1841 to 1843. Continuing what Kemble and Kean had set in motion, Macready emphasized two aspects of Shakespearean production: he restored texts to something more approximating textual integrity, and he mounted lavish productions with a serious attempt at historical reconstruction. He abandoned Nahum Tate's 1681 happy ending to *King Lear*, in which Lear was restored to Cordelia and to his throne. Tate's version had long held the stage for audiences who, in the so-called Age of Enlightenment, had found the original ending unendurably offensive to prevailing notions of poetic justice. A semblance of Shakespeare's original ending had been staged by Edmund Kean in 1823, but Macready's at Drury Lane in 1838 was the more thorough-going restoration. The play had been freed, in the words of *John Bull*, "from the interpolations which have disgraced it for nearly two centuries." (To be sure, the blinding of Gloucester was still left out as something more brutishly violent than contemporary audiences could be expected to endure.) Other important restorations by Macready included *The Tempest* and *A Midsummer Night's Dream*.

Probably Macready shortened his *Hamlet* (1837) as a matter of practical necessity, as he did also with *King Lear*, but Garrick's wholesale rearrangements were now generally a thing of the past. Macready acted the part of Hamlet from 1823 to 1851, thus continuing the tradition of longevity in the role as seen in Betterton (1661–1709), Garrick (1742–76), Kemble (1783–1817), and Edmund Kean (1814–32). Macready played Hamlet in an exaggeratedly manic way during the performance of "The Murder of Gonzago," as some actors have done since, notably Kenneth Branagh in his 1996 film version.

In the devising of scenic splendor, *Hamlet* seems to have occupied a prominent and early place in Macready's campaign to provide a heretofore unrivalled magnificence of costume and scenery in the staging of Shakespeare. *The Examiner* marveled, on 2 October 1837, that "the scenes of *Hamlet* were a series of glorious pictures," and Macready's own *Diary* was quick to agree: "The play was put beautifully on the stage. The audience noticed with applause several of the improvements." What some of these "improvements" may have been like can be seen in a contemporary depiction of the gravedigging scene (5.1) in the *Illustrated London News*. Hamlet, holding a skull, is attired in a knee-length tunic, over which he wears a long, flowing black cloak. The poniard of his sword is visible. His headpiece is extraordinarily tall, extending to perhaps fifteen inches above the crown of his head. Horatio is outfitted in tunic and short cape, a sword at his side, and a feathered hat under one arm. The Gravedigger is behind, sitting on the brink of his pit. The painted set backstage is picturesque. Trees on either side flank a Gothic-windowed building connected to a masonry archway, with perhaps a garden behind.

A retrospective painting by Daniel Maclise (1842; see Illustration 8) indicates how richly the set was decorated for Macready's staging of "The Murder of Gonzago." The play-within-the-play is centered

Illustration 8. William Charles Macready as Hamlet watching the play-within-the-play (3.2). Laertes and Ophelia are on the left as we view the painting; Polonius, Gertrude, and Claudius are on the right. A painting by Daniel Maclise, 1842. Courtesy of the Victoria and Albert Museum, London.

backstage, carefully framed within a little theatre structure. To stage right are Laertes, Ophelia, ladies and gentlemen of the court, and spear-carrying armored guards, while to stage left are the King and Queen, Polonius, and more courtiers. All are handsomely dressed in an approximation of period costuming. The entire stage space is festooned with banners, drapes, curtains, statuary, and simulations of carved paneling. Claudius, backstage, looks frowningly away from the action.

Further insights can be gained about the splendor of Macready's productions from accounts of his staging of the history plays. His aim in staging *King John* in 1842 was to bring to the theatre an "animated picture of those Gothic times" in which the play was set. Costuming was scrupulously attentive to verisimilar detail. The actors, including hundreds of supernumeraries, assembled in front of an impressive medieval backdrop painted by William Telbin, so that the stage was "thronged with the stalwart forms of the middle ages" (*The Times*, 25 October). Macready seems to have been eager to outdo Kemble's earlier grand spectacles of *King John*, with Sarah Siddons in 1783 and in revivals down to 1823. All this, of course, was very expensive.

Drury Lane and Covent Garden fell on hard times when, in 1843, the royal patents that had given them absolute control for so long of the London theatrical scene were abolished. (Provincial touring by other companies had been allowed for some time.) Drury Lane later made a comeback, but the fact that these two acting companies declined so rapidly in 1843 and afterward suggests that the opening up of performance rights to other groups was much overdue. Quick to seize the opportunity were Samuel Phelps at the new Sadler's Wells Theatre in Islington from 1843 until 1862, and Charles Kean (the second son of Edmund Kean) at the Princess's Theatre in Oxford Street. Phelps had acted for Macready in the late 1830s, with such success that Macready enviously tried to hold him back. As one of the founders of Sadler's Wells in 1843, Phelps managed the company so astutely for nearly twenty years that he succeeded in "making Shakespeare pay." He produced no fewer that thirty-four of Shakespeare's plays, arguably doing more to popularize that dramatist than any other theatre manager in the history of the London stage. He gave up managerial responsibility in 1862. Thereafter he chiefly acted at a re-energized Drury Lane. He died in 1878.

Charles Kean had acted Hamlet at Drury Lane in 1838 and at the Haymarket in 1843. He managed the Princess's Theatre from 1850 to

1859, where his overly elaborate scenic designs were the object of some criticism. The years immediately following 1853 were especially splendiferous at the Princess's under Kean's management. Many actors who had performed at Drury Lane and Covent Garden, finding themselves without permanent employment in 1843 and afterwards, did star turns occasionally at the new theatres or toured the provinces. The need for new theatre buildings and for new actors fed each other in a wave of frenetic activity. An acting company at the Haymarket, which had opened in 1821 and then had been permitted, in the years immediately before 1843, to extend their season to ten months in direct competition with the patent right theatres at Drury Lane and Covent Garden, naturally flourished once those patent rights were ended. Under the management (since 1837) of Benjamin Webster and extensively renovated by him, the Haymarket quickly moved to a top position in 1843 and afterwards. It was both fashionable and charming. So was Sadler's Wells. Some smaller theatres took advantage of the new freedom from patent restriction, especially the Theatre Royal in Marylebone, where in 1850 Gustavus Vaughan Brooke took the lead role in a production of *Hamlet*, and the Olympic in Wych Street, rebuilt after a fire in 1849.

The decades following 1843, then, were prosperous ones of spectacle and music in the staging of Shakespeare. Phelps and Charles Kean, obviously in competition with each other, developed their distinctive styles of production. Phelps at Sadler's Wells paid special attention to poetic touches, faithfulness to the Shakespearean text, and tasteful scenic arrangements managed within a modest budget; Kean played for big effects with a sizable budget and large casts. Part of this was simply pragmatic; Phelps had limited resources and a smaller house. To be sure, Phelps's *Henry V* in 1852 did its best: some forty supernumeraries outfitted as English soldiers marched at Agincourt, each carrying two wickerwork armor-clad dummy warriors with wax heads modeled by Madame Tussaud, to create the illusion of three marching abreast. Still, Kean at the Princess's Theatre could boast of employing as many as 550 actors in his most sumptuous spectacles. Judging from a contemporary picture in the *Illustrated London News*, Kean used all the men at his disposal (even if not quite 550) in staging the battle of Shrewsbury in *1 Henry IV*, on the occasion of the Shakespeare Tercentenary in April 1864. Kean's *Henry V*, performed in 1859, was his last production before he stepped aside from the management of the Princess's. Here the big scenes were the siege of Harfleur and an interpolated staging of Henry's triumphal entry into London on his return from Agincourt. For the triumphal entry, Kean brought on the Mayor and Aldermen of the City, citizens in profusion, boys outfitted with angels' wings, and a singing company of Prophets. Brass instruments resounded as the procession approached London Bridge and the Tower.

Charles Kean did *Hamlet* some fourteen times in 1850–1, with more to follow. Phelps performed Hamlet with Isabel Glyn as Gertrude before she left Sadler's Wells in 1851; an engraving after a daguerreotype by Paine of Islington shows Phelps in a declamatory attitude, dressed in a black, belted knee-length tunic and tights, bareheaded, with a medallion around his neck presumably containing a likeness of his dead father, while Glyn sits in a white robe and regal cape and a crown on her head as she listens disconsolately to Hamlet's lecture on her moral failings (3.4). The set is not elaborate. Another engraving based on Paine of Islington shows Charles Kean as Hamlet, also in a knee-length black tunic and bareheaded, this time with a sword at his side and a cape hung about his shoulders. The curtained Gothic set behind him and the chair on which he leans are visibly more handsome than in the Phelps illustration. Indeed, Kean's staging was, as in his treatment of other plays, elaborate in the style of Macready. Kean's sets for *Hamlet* included the guard platform of the castle in act 1, scenes 1 and 4, another part of the battlements for scene 5, the royal presence chamber inside the castle and its own framed theatre, where "The Murder of Gonzago" could be put on, the Queen's private chamber for Hamlet's interview with his mother in act 3, scene 4, and an ancient burial ground near to the palace to which Ophelia was borne with impressive if maimed rites.

The German-born French actor Charles Fechter, having left the French stage for London in 1860 and performing thereafter in English, scored a great success at the Princess's in 1861 and then at the Lyceum in 1864 with a novel and controversial *Hamlet*. Fechter did away with traditional courtly dress in favor of rustic Viking costumes. The set and furnishings were similarly primitive. The architecture was more medieval Norman than Scandinavian, but Fechter himself as Hamlet sported flaxen hair. Rosencrantz and Guildenstern were thick-bearded Viking warriors in rugged cross-gartered leggings. The Ghost, addressing Hamlet at length in act 1 scene 5, stood first in what appeared to be full moonlight; then, as dawn neared, the lighting on the Ghost seemed gradually to diminish until he vanished altogether. This remarkably innovative effect was produced by having the Ghost stand behind a large concealed wheel, which, as it slowly rotated, caught up increasing amounts of tinted transparent material and thus progressively obscured what the audience could see. The Ghost appeared to do what Macbeth says of the three Weird Sisters: "what seemed corporal melted / As breath into the wind" (Macbeth, 1.3.81–2). Later, for the burial of Ophelia, Fechter created the illusion of a brilliant sunset, as though to contrast the insensate beauty of nature with the grief and cruelty of humankind. Fechter avoided what he regarded as the unseemly grappling of Hamlet and Laertes in Ophelia's grave, as had been staged by Macready and Kemble and others before them.[1] Fechter brought his Hamlet to America in 1870 and performed it often until his retirement in 1877.

Henry Irving raised the art of Shakespearean production to new heights of costly splendor during his years at the Lyceum from 1878 until his retirement from the theatre in 1902. He had played Osric at the Princess's Theatre in 1860, and then produced Hamlet in 1874 with an unprecedentedly successful run of two hundred nights. The costs of producing Shakespeare were already dangerously high, owing to the emphasis on elaborate spectacle; Charles Kean ran into financial difficulties. F. B. Chatterton, manager at Drury Lane from 1864 until 1878–9 during which time the financial situation of that company grew worse, famously declared that "Shakespeare spells ruin." Yet while it lasted, Irving's tenure was as successful as it was costly. The Lyceum gained a position of clear dominance in Shakespearean production, and retained that title until Irving stepped aside. Irving also toured North America eight times between 1883 and 1903, with Ellen Terry as his leading lady in all but the last of these.

Though he took major roles in his productions, including that of Hamlet, Irving excelled more as a manager than as an actor. (A satirical cartoon printed in an extra-illustrated copy of William Winter's Henry Irving, 1885, suggests that Irving might have done well to heed Hamlet's advice to the players not to "saw the air too much with your hand, thus," etc., 3.2.4–5; see Illustration 9.) He gathered around him a luminous group of players, including Ellen Terry as his leading lady, Forbes Robertson, William Terriss, George Alexander, Jessie Millward, Winifred Emery, and Genevieve Ward. His production of

HAMLET (*To Mr. Irving*) : " Nor do not saw the air too much with your hand thus ; but use all gently ; for in the very torrent, tempest, and (as I may say,) whirlwind of your passion, you must acquire and beget a temperance, that may give it smoothness."

Illustration 9. Hamlet advises Henry Irving not to saw the air too much with his hand. A cartoon from an extra-illustrated copy of William Winter's *Henry Irving*, 1885.

Hamlet, with Terry as Ophelia, ran for 108 performances in 1878–9. Henry James described her in this production as "a somewhat angular maiden of the Gothic ages, with her hair cropped short, like a boy's, and a straight and clinging robe" (quoted in Donald Mullin, *Victorian Actors and Actresses in Review*, Westport, CT: Greenwood Press, 1983, p. 441). Terry also starred in the years that followed as Portia in *The Merchant of Venice* (1879), Desdemona in *Othello* (1881), Beatrice in *Much Ado About Nothing* (1882), Juliet in *Romeo and Juliet* (1882), Viola in *Twelfth Night* (1884), Lady Macbeth in *Macbeth* (1888), Queen Katharine in *Henry VIII* (1892), Cordelia in *King Lear* (1892), and Imogen in *Cymbeline* (1896). Irving himself went on to be honored with a knighthood.

Irving's interpretation of Hamlet was of a man stricken with love for Ophelia—a not surprising emphasis, given the sympathy expressed by many nineteenth-century critics for the suffering of such a tender, innocent, and beautiful young woman. Even as Hamlet mocked her in their painful overheard conversation (3.1), Irving's Hamlet could not hide the depths of his feeling for her; in the words of a contemporary reviewer, "his whole frame seemed to tremble with heartfelt longing." To put this failed love relationship in a fuller perspective, and to bestow on Hamlet the emotional sensitivity worthy of such a lovelorn young man, Irving followed some of his predecessors in deleting Hamlet's soliloquy of implacable determination to send the kneeling Claudius's soul to hell (3.3.73–96). Gone too were Hamlet's wry comments on his disposing of the dead body of Polonius, most of the business in act 4 about Hamlet's being sent to England and Laertes's plotting with Claudius to poison Hamlet, and still more. As a result, act 4 focused chiefly on Ophelia's touching bouts with madness, played by Ellen Terry at the top of her form. Except for Hamlet's grim resolve not to slay Claudius at prayer in act 3 scene 3, his soliloquies were preserved intact throughout. The production ended with Hamlet's "the rest is silence" (5.2.360), thus literally giving him, rather than Fortinbras, the last word. Irving was, in this as in all things, the quintessential nineteenth-century actor-manager, playing up his favorite scenes, putting himself and his leading lady always in the spotlight, and cutting where necessary to accommodate the massive sets that were needed for the changes from scene to scene.

Even though Irving's staging of *Hamlet* in 1878–9 was not as extravagant as his *Henry VIII* in 1892, with its rich pageantry and elaborate processions, *Hamlet* was still produced in high style. Irving chose an Elizabethan decor, blended tastefully with some suggestions of antique Denmark, so that his actors could be as handsomely costumed as possible. Several scenes were notable for their pictorial splendor. The battlements of Elsinore stood in front of the palace and its illuminated windows in the background, while the star to which Bernardo alludes (1.1.40) glistened in the sky above. The Ghost made his appearance in a remote area of the battlements, among massive rocks, in the soft light of the moon, until the pale dawn, shimmering over a vast expanse of water, warned of the coming of day. Later, Ophelia was buried in a sloping hillside graveyard near the palace, through which the funeral cortège slowly ascended in the carrying out of its "maimèd rites" (5.1.219). (Franco Zeffirelli's handsome filming of a hillside graveyard in his 1990 film may have been inspired by this innovative staging.)

As Irving himself wrote, in a prefatory note to his acting version of *Hamlet*: "It is but natural that, in attempting to place one of Shakespeare's works on the stage worthy of the great master, the utmost care should now be exercised with regard to the scenic decorations and other accessories of the play.... The first object of a manager, no doubt, should be to obtain capable representatives of the various characters; but . . . their efforts will be aided and not hampered by a due attention to the effectiveness and beauty of their scenic surroundings. Shakespeare, if well acted on a bare stage, would certainly afford great intellectual pleasure; but that pleasure will be all the greater if the eye be charmed, at the same time, by scenic illustrations in harmony with the poet's ideas." One could hardly ask for a more insightful statement of the credo of most late-nineteenth-century London Shakespearean stage-managers.

These were also years of rapid growth internationally in the production of Shakespeare. Macready and Irving both made several trips to America, where Lewis Hallam Jr had introduced *Hamlet* to the American colonies in 1759 and 1761 (see chapter 4). The celebrated American actor Edwin Booth (son of the English actor Junius Brutus Booth and brother of the John Wilkes Booth who assassinated President Lincoln in 1865 and of Junius Brutus Booth Jr), having succeeded greatly with *Hamlet* in San Francisco in 1853 and then with a consecutive run of 100 nights at the Winter Garden Theatre, New York, in 1854–5, took the play to London's Princess's Theatre in 1880–1. Although many Americans were disappointed at its reception in a London theatre world dominated by Irving at the Lyceum, the show ran for 119 nights. His Hamlet was described as "dark, mad, dreamy, mysterious," "as far removed as possible from the plane of actual life." Booth had played Hamlet to Irving's Laertes in Manchester in 1861. Booth's success in the role of Hamlet eclipsed that of the American actor Edwin Forrest, who also became involved in a bitter rivalry with Macready that led to the Astor Street riot in New York in 1849 in which 31 people were killed and over 100 injured. American audiences idolized Forrest with his youthful, untrained, and freewheeling interpretation of Hamlet as differentiated from the traditional and cultivated style of the British-educated Macready, thus epitomizing and polarizing a conflict between American populism and English elitism; but when the New York authorities fired on the rioting American crowds, the populist Shakespeare that had rapidly become an integral part of American's new-world experience was dealt a severe blow of official repression.[2]

Literary interpreters of *Hamlet* in Victorian England continue to be fascinated by the question of Hamlet's delay, with widely varying hypotheses. To Jones Very (*Essays and Poems*, 1839), Hamlet is a thoughtful and tormented man, "more than commonly liable to the fear of death," forever questioning whether "To be or not to be" and indecisive for that reason. A number of German critics similarly follow Goethe and Coleridge in attributing Hamlet's delay "to an excess in him of a reflective, meditative habit of mind" (F. T. Vischer, *Kritische Gänge*, 1861). Ferdinand Freiligrath, in 1844, compares Hamlet's hesitancy to act to that of Germany in its seeming inability to move toward liberty and political reunification: as he puts it, "Deutschland ist Hamlet" (see John Clavin, *Critical Responses to "Hamlet," 1600–1900*, vol. 3, New York: AMS Press, 1995-2006).

Yet disagreements with this recognizably Romantic interpretation are increasingly to be heard. William Minto (*Characteristics of English Poets from Chaucer to Shirley*, 1874) finds the explanation of the delay not in fear or in psychological paralysis, but in Hamlet's final reliance on "a blind, inexplicable, vague trust that some supremely favorable moment will occur." Destiny "is ripening the harvest for him." Hamlet is "resolved not to strike till the most favorable moment," and that moment is handed to him by a turn of events he could not have predicted. The German Hermann Ulrici (*Shakespeare's Dramatische Kunst*, 1839, translated 1846) sees the purported delay as prompted not by psychological paralysis but by Hamlet's perception that the code of revenge cannot be reconciled with Hamlet's own Christian faith. He is beset with doubts and scruples that are highly moral and in accord with his Christian teaching, so that in him "we behold the Christian struggling with the natural man." Ulrici implicitly ignores Hamlet's bloodthirsty speech of wishing to send the kneeling Claudius's soul to hell, as did a number of theatre directors, including David Garrick and Henry Irving.

Edward Dowden (*Shakspere: A Critical Study of His Mind and Art*, 1875) essentially agrees with Minto that Hamlet resolves his own questionings by submitting to the will of heaven. Dowden argues,

however, that this comforting reliance on divine purpose is not Shakespeare's own view. "The providence in which Shakespeare believed,"
writes Dowden, "is a moral order which includes man's highest
exercise of foresight, energy, and resolution." Alongside Hamlet's
providential interpretation of his own story, we hear in the play's last
scene the voice of Horatio, who "delivers us from the transcendental
optimism of Hamlet, and restores the purely human way of viewing
things." The play for Dowden is thus a profound study in incertitude,
but it is not the paralysis of will championed by Goethe and Coleridge.
Other critics, too, such as (in Germany) L. Schipper (1862), J. L. F.
Flathe (1863), and Karl Werder (1875), firmly assert that Hamlet shows
no signs of indecision or hesitation or morbid, self-tormenting consci-
entiousness; if anyone delays, it is Claudius. Algernon Charles Swin-
burne (*A Study of Shakespeare*, 1880) is sure that "the signal
characteristic of Hamlet's inmost nature is by no means irresolution
or hesitation or any form of weakness, but rather the strong conflux of
contending forces." Friedrich Nietzsche, in *The Birth of Tragedy, or:
Hellenism and Pessimism* (1872), contends that Hamlet is held back not
by excessive thought but by tragic knowledge of the utter futility of
action in the corrupted world in which he has found himself. These
arguments may indeed be closer to ways in which Elizabethans viewed
Hamlet in 1599–1601 (see chapter 3) than are the Romantic and post-
Romantic interpretations of Hamlet as immobilized by psychological
paralysis of the will.

In pursuit of moral idealism in the play, Victorian critics turn to
Horatio with no less admiration than for Hamlet. Henry N. Hudson,
for one, proclaims Horatio to be "one of the very noblest and most
beautiful of Shakespeare's male characters," a perfect model of friendship in his unselfish gracefulness and his scholarly, calm skepticism
(*Shakespeare: His Life, Art, and Character*, 1872, 2.268). Hermann Ulrici
(*Shakespeare's Dramatische Kunst*) similarly sees in Horatio a man who
"alone is without any ends of his own; he does not aim at making any
profit for himself, but devotes himself entirely and unreservedly to his
friend." Ulrici is confident that Horatio will reap a suitable reward for
this disinterested conduct: Fortinbras is sure to assign him "to the high
but responsible office of restoring peace and order to the racked and
disjointed kingdom."

This last remark is symptomatic of another tendency of late eigh-
teenth- and nineteenth-century literary criticism: to imagine what a

Shakespeare character would have been like before and after the action of the play, or in some other imagined situation. Maurice Morgann had done much to establish this fashion of critical thinking in his *Essay on the Dramatic Character of Sir John Falstaff*, 1777. To bolster his appreciation for Falstaff as a lovable human being of honor, dignity, and courage (!), Morgann downplayed Falstaff's incorrigible carryings-on, asking his readers instead to imagine what it would have been like to know Falstaff as a real person on occasions other than those dramatized by Shakespeare. *Hamlet* invited similar speculations. Critics permitted themselves to imagine a Hamlet who did not wish to send Claudius's soul to hell or arrange the deaths of Rosencrantz and Guildenstern, but was instead a gentle soul with whom one could debate philosophical issues of life and death. Horatio, as his dear companion and upholder of the highest moral ideals, deserved a little story of his own, in which Denmark could flourish under him as joint ruler with Fortinbras.

Many writers in the nineteenth century take up the question of whether Hamlet's madness is real or feigned, generally opting (as do Victor Hugo in 1864 and Hippolyte-Adolphe Taine in 1866) for the latter, though sometimes conceding that Hamlet may well be afflicted by a melancholy that amounts to a mental disease. Another topic of perennial interest is that of asking whether Gertrude was an accessory before the fact of murder. The general consensus is to give her the benefit of the doubt as to her prior knowledge of the killing of her husband, though an anonymous essay devoted to the subject, *Hamlet. An Attempt to Ascertain whether the Queen were an Accessory, before the Fact, in the Murder of her First Husband*, 1856, does suspect her of adultery before the murder (as was true of Gertrude's counterpart in Belleforest's *Histoires Tragiques*; see chapter 1).

Along with its critical absorption in the philosophical and moral implications of *Hamlet*, nineteenth-century literary criticism turns also to dramaturgical matters, admiring the play's stagecraft and dramatic construction. Joseph Hunter (*New Illustrations of the Life, Studies, and Writings of Shakespeare*, 1845, 2. 205) declares that "Nothing in the dramatic art ever exceeded the skill with which the First Act is throughout constructed." An unsigned article in *The Quarterly Review* of 1847 documents such a claim by noting how adroitly Shakespeare motivates Bernardo's nervousness as the first scene begins. Having seen the Ghost twice before, and fearing now, as he is about to start his midnight watch, that the Ghost is likely to reappear at any moment, Bernardo is understandably "distilled / Almost to jelly with the act of fear" (1.2.205–6). This anxiety can explain why Bernardo asks the opening question, "Who's there?" when it is Francisco, the guard currently on watch, who should issue that challenge. Francisco's "you come most carefully upon your hour" is no less skilfully calibrated by the dramatist to underscore the guards' terrified realization that the hour of rendezvous has just struck. And so the article proceeds, with a close analytical reading that is new to critical investigation of *Hamlet* and at the same time is also dedicated to the purpose of demonstrating both "The universality of Shakespeare's genius" and the splendid "compression of the scene."

The German critic G. G. Gervinus (*Shakespeare Commentaries*, 1849, translated 1863) explores the dramatic purpose in the play of having Hamlet so well acquainted with the art of acting, as seen in his instructions to the players, his appreciation of skillful delivery of speeches, his scorn of Polonius as an actor, and therefore his logical choice of a play-within-the-play as a device to "catch the conscience of the King" (2.2.606).

A study of Shakespeare's chronological development, and of the place of *Hamlet* in that process, becomes an important focus of literary study during this period. Advances in philological method, sometimes in the work of German scholars and supported by the first professional Shakespeare organization in history, the *Shakespeare Gesellschaft*, improved knowledge of the dating of Shakespeare's plays and thus led to a better understanding of their chronological order. A major contribution in this vein was Edward Dowden's study of Shakespeare's mind and art (1875) cited above. Dowden sees *Hamlet* as standing midway between Shakespeare's early years of apprenticeship and his latest work, written when Shakespeare had become a master dramatist. This mastery can be seen in the development of his thought, imagery, and style. It bespeaks a personal self-mastery as well: *Hamlet* is the work of an author who "had entered upon the full maturity of his manhood."

Part of what is so universal about Shakespeare's insights into human character can be found, according to some Victorian male critics, in Hamlet's misogyny directed particularly against his mother: "Frailty, thy name is woman!" (1.2.146). Edward Strachey, in what must be the first book-length study of *Shakespeare's Hamlet* (1848), applies this principle to Hamlet's observations on Gertrude. "Nothing is more universal (though often nothing more puzzling)," writes Strachey, "than that characteristic of the female mind which, even in grave and thoughtful women, and much more in the light and trifling, enables them to receive impressions, and make observations, without bringing them before their minds in distinct consciousness. Women feel and act with an intuitive wisdom far superior to that of men, but they have not the same power of reflecting on their feelings and acts, and translating them into the shape of *thoughts*." Therefore, Gertrude's lack of any clear perception of her own situation "is in perfect keeping with her whole character." Such a generalization reveals something not uncommon in Victorian literary criticism of the play: writers praise Shakespeare's universality in such a way as to enlist Shakespeare on the side of the general truths that the writers themselves wish to endorse. Shakespeare, our contemporary, must also feel as we do about women (or politics, or what have you). In the present instance, Shakespeare is seen as though he were a typical Victorian male in his readiness to judge women as inherently gifted in intuitive and emotional wisdom but deficient in rationality and the resolve to act decisively. Another Victorian characteristic of this line of thought is the easy assumption that we can read Shakespeare's mind in the words of Hamlet.

One consequence of the Victorian appreciation of moral character, as we have seen, is the desire to get to know Shakespeare's characters better, as though they were real people with whom we might like to visit. George Eliot (*Mill on the Floss*, 1860, book 6, chapter 6) longs to know more of the story than Shakespeare has set down for us, especially of the love affair of Hamlet and Ophelia. "If his [Hamlet's] father had lived to a good old age, and his uncle had died an early death," Eliot writes, "we can conceive Hamlet's having married Ophelia, and got through life with a reputation of sanity, notwithstanding many soliloquies, and some moody sarcasms toward the fair daughter of Polonius, to say nothing of the frankest incivility to his father-in-law." Edward Strachey (1848) similarly wonders what sort of wife Ophelia would have made for her gloomy wooer. Mary Cowden Clarke, in "Ophelia, the Fair Rose of Elsinore" (*The Girlhood of Shakespeare's Heroines*, 1851–2), sets about to envisage the "girlhood," and Helen Faucit (*On Some of Shakespeare's Female Characters*, 1885) the "afterlife," of Shakespeare's heroines. About Hamlet, Henry N. Hudson writes that, notwithstanding the diversity of opinions one encounters in various writers, yet "all agree in thinking of Hamlet as an actual person" (*Introduction to* "*Hamlet,*" 1870).

Ophelia remains throughout the Victorian period a favorite subject for writers, critics, and actor-managers. The hero of William Makepeace Thackeray's *Pendennis* (1848–50) falls in love with an actress, Miss Fotheringay, in her role as Ophelia on stage. Ophelia is also vividly portrayed in paintings and illustrations, suggesting the extent to which lovers of Shakespeare during this period were taught to think of his plays in visual terms. Beginning in the 1780s and 90s, John Boydell, one-time Mayor of London, commissioned an array of well-known artists to devise pictures based on scenes from Shakespeare to be put on display in Boydell's Shakespeare Gallery in Pall Mall. Engravings of these illustrations appeared in an edition of Shakespeare in 1802. They have become collectors' items today. Scenes from all the plays are included. A considerable number depict subjects that Shakespeare invokes through his poetry but does not attempt to put on stage, like Mercutio's "Queen Mab" fantasy in *Romeo and Juliet* and the wedding of Petruchio and Kate in *The Taming of the Shrew.* All the stages of Jaques's "Seven Ages of Man," from act two, scene 7 of *As You Like It,* are pictorialized, along with Jaques's mordant disquisition on the weeping deer that he report-edly has beheld in the forest (2.1.31–3). Such piquant details seem positively to invite artists to give the image a material substance. Bottom's love affair with Queen Titania similarly offers a subject that the artist Henry Fuseli explores with unbounded visual creativity. (Fuseli also painted a scene, for the Boydell Shakespeare Gallery, of Hamlet on the battlements of Elsinore Castle being restrained by his friends as the Ghost beckons him to "a more removèd ground," 1.4.61.)

The irresistible subject of this sort in *Hamlet* is the drowning of Ophelia, as reported by Gertrude. John Everett Millais's painting of this moment (1852; see Illustration 10) is justly celebrated, as is its realization on film in Laurence Olivier's *Hamlet* (1948), with Jean Simmons floating downstream past a bank of flowers, singing and dressed in a white gown that will soon pull her "from her melodious lay / To muddy death" (4.7.183–4). Less well known is Henry Tre-sham's earlier painting, as reproduced in an etching of 1794 by Francesco Bartolezzi, of Ophelia as she clambers out onto the "pendent boughs" in order to hang her garland there (173–4) before falling in the water. Three female figures are visible on the farther

Illustration 10. John Everett Millais's painting, *Ophelia*, 1852, depicting Ophelia as she is borne up, "mermaid-like," awhile by her garments until they become heavy with water and pull her "from her melodious lay / To muddy death" (4.7.183–4). Courtesy of the Tate Gallery of British Art.

shore in attitudes of alarm, presumably by way of explaining how it is that Gertrude knows of Ophelia's drowning but without having been able to rescue her (see Illustration 11). The Boydell Shakespeare Gallery includes still another representation, in an engraving by J. Parker of Richard Westall's painting (1803) of Ophelia clinging to a branch as she is about to fall into the stream. Ophelia's mad scenes also fascinated artists, including the English painter Henrietta Rae in 1890. The American soprano Mignon Nevada was painted as the mad Ophelia in 1910. Artistic representations of great actors in their stage roles are to be found in the eighteenth century, to be sure, as in Benjamin Wilson's 1761 painting of David Garrick as the King in the storm scenes of *King Lear*, but in such depictions the subject is the actor as theatre performer. Romantic and Victorian artists seek inspiration in the dramatic story itself, beautifully told in words by Shakespeare but still in need of the artist's visualization of the imaginary.

Hamlet inspired a number of musical scores in the classical repertory in the course of the eighteenth and nineteenth centuries. An operatic

Illustration 11. A painting by Henry Tresham as reproduced in an etching by Francesco Bartolezzi, 1794. The mad Ophelia, reaching out to hang the "fantastic garments" she has woven on the "pendent boughs," is seen at a distance by Queen Gertrude and some other women, unable to save Ophelia from imminent drowning (4.7.169–73).

Hamlet at the Haymarket in London, 1712, mentioned in chapter 4, was based chiefly on Saxo Grammaticus's *Historia Danica*. Charles-Louis-Ambroise Thomas's French opera in 1868, written with alternative endings, devoted its fourth act for the most part to the mad Ophélie. Hector Berlioz's *Tristia* consists of three short pieces for orchestra and chorus, of which the third and best known is a "*Marche funèbre pour la dernière scène d'Hamlet*" (1844), composed for a stage performance that never took place. Franz Liszt wrote a symphonic poem called *Hamlet* in 1858. Another *Hamlet* (1888) is the last of Pyotr Ilich Tchaikovsky's symphonic poems based on Shakespeare and other literary sources.

Editing of Shakespeare in the nineteenth century grew to the proportions of an industry. Among the many editions, some of the most noteworthy are those of Charles Knight (1838–43), John Payne Collier (1842–4, 1853, 1858), Henry N. Hudson (1851–6, 1880–1), Nicolaus Delius (in Germany, 1854–61), Alexander Dyce (1857, 1864–7, 1875–6),

S. W. Singer (1856, 1875), Richard Grant White (1857–65), Howard Staunton (1858), Thomas Keightley (1864), and Charles and Mary Cowden Clarke (1864, 1868). Prior to these were the so-called Variorum editions in 1773, 1778, 1785, and 1793, briefly described in the previous chapter. Perhaps the most influential edition of the century was the so-called Cambridge Shakespeare, edited in nine volumes by William George Clark and William Aldis Wright in 1863–6 and issued also in a more compact edition known as the Globe Shakespeare in 1864. The act-scene-line numbering of that edition soon became standard for works of reference and critical study.

These editions offered a variety of materials for a reading public eager to embrace Shakespeare as a central figure of cultural heritage for the English-speaking world and beyond. Many of these editions were elaborately illustrated, in a tradition inaugurated by Nicholas Rowe in 1709 but now greatly expanded. The cultural values of Victorian England were put on display. Commentary notes were substantially augmented. An improved understanding of the early Shakespeare quartos resulted in more reliable texts. Editors endeavored to give potential book-buyers what they seemingly wanted in endless profusion: a complete set of Shakespeare's works, handsomely bound and well designed to adorn many a middle-class home as a kind of biblical text and as a visible token of the buyers' comfortable means and cultural sophistication. Family values naturally became an important criterion in the business of acquiring such a possession. An expurgated *Family Shakespeare*, edited first by Henrietta Bowdler and then in collaboration with her brother Thomas (1807, 1818), provided a "safe" text for family reading by removing passages that were deemed indelicate, especially for women and children. Sexual double entendre, part of the incessant wordplay that Samuel Johnson had deplored, was assiduously rooted out (though the Bowdlers inevitably let stand some bawdy passages they seem not to have comprehended).

Charles and Mary Lamb's *Tales from Shakespeare* (1807), not an edition but a redaction of Shakespeare's plots, similarly provided a Shakespeare that would not bring a blush to the most modest of maidenly cheeks. Charles wrote graceful prose versions of six tragedies; his sister, Mary (who had killed their mother in a fit of bipolar rage and had to be looked after by her bachelor brother for the rest of his life), said in a letter that she did fourteen comedies. The history plays and Roman plays were omitted, perhaps as too sensational and bloody. Though intended for young readers, the book also won the hearts of adult audiences caught up in a Romantic swirl of Shakespeare bardolatry.

Scholarly reference volumes began to appear in the late nineteenth century, thereby greatly assisting the work of essayists and critics. Perhaps the most important was *A Complete Concordance or Verbal Index to Words, Phrases, and Passages in the Dramatic Works of Shakespeare*, with a supplementary concordance to the poems, compiled by John Bartlett in 1896 and often reprinted. His work had been anticipated by Mary Cowden Clarke for the plays in 1845 and by Helen Kate Furness for the poems in 1875. E. A. Abbott published *A Shakespearian Grammar* in 1870, systematically categorizing and describing Shakespeare's usages of nouns and noun-formations, verbs, adjectives, adverbs, conjunctions, exclamations, and the like. New editions of this *Grammar* appeared in 1886 and in subsequent years. C. T. Onions's *A Shakespeare Glossary* (1911), by now an old standby, has been revised and updated in 1986 by Robert D. Eagleson (Oxford: Clarendon Press). Marvin Spevack's *The Harvard Concordance to Shakespeare* (Cambridge, MA: Harvard University Press, 1973), is more accurate than Bartlett's, which had been done without the advantage of computers.

The growth of learned societies devoted to Shakespeare is another testimonial to his increasing centrality as a cultural icon. Perhaps surprisingly, the first such society came into being in nineteenth-century Germany. The *Shakespeare Gesellschaft,* or Shakespeare Society, is today (though having split into two societies, East and West, during the Cold War years) the oldest such organization still in existence; it was founded in Weimar in 1865. Other societies around the world would establish themselves and expand their learned activities in the twentieth and twenty-first centuries.

Several eighteenth- and nineteenth-century novelists have found occasion to make fun of *Hamlet*, aimed not at the play itself but at the ways in which the play has increasingly been served up to credulous audiences by self-serving actor-managers, rank amateurs, and charlatans. Henry Fielding is perhaps the first, with his jocose description, in *Tom Jones*, 1749, of Partridge's naive response to David Garrick's stage presentation of *Hamlet* (see chapter 4 above). Charles Dickens similarly makes comic capital of a *Hamlet* performance in *Great Expectations* (1861, chapter 31). There, Pip and his friend Herbert Pocket go together to see Mr Wopsle, the church clerk from Pip's home town, in his role as the hapless star of a provincial company now performing *Hamlet* in London. Wopsle's stage name is Waldengarver. The production is hilariously inept. The Ghost, uncertain of his lines, prompts himself from a script wrapped around his truncheon. The Queen is so be-hooped with decorative metal bands that she is christened "the kettledrum" by some members of the noisy audience. When Wopsle as Hamlet raises the point rhetorically as to "Whether 'tis nobler in the mind / To suffer," and so forth, a lively debate ensues among those in the audience who say yes, those who say no, and still others who opt for "toss up for it." After the performance of the play-within-the-play in act three, scene 2, Hamlet is handed a little black recorder (the musical instrument, not a recording device) bearing a suspicious resemblance to a musical instrument that has just been passed out from the orchestra. Hamlet is called upon by the audience to play "Rule Britannia." And so it goes. After the performance, Pip and Herbert are reluctantly escorted to Wopsle's dressing room by the dresser, whose only criticism of the performance just ended is that "Waldengarver" has not always shown off his stockinged legs to best advantage.

Mark Twain's *Huckleberry Finn* (1884, chapters 21–2) offers an equally brilliant spoof in its depiction of two con men who work their way up and down the Mississippi River as Shakespearean actors, gulling naive frontier audiences into thinking they are being given a taste of culture only to learn too late that the con artists have slipped out of town with their ill-gotten gains. Mark Twain knew whereof he spoke, having grown up in Hannibal, Missouri, along the great river. An "Immortal Soliloquy" from *Hamlet* naturally figures as part of the bill of fare offered by the Duke, posing as David Garrick the younger, of Drury Lane Theatre, London, and the Dauphin, posing as Edmund Kean the elder, of the Royal Haymarket Theatre, Whitechapel, Pudding Lane, Piccadilly, London. The two rogues also offer the "Balcony Scene" from *Romeo and Juliet* and a "Broad-sword conflict" from *Richard III*. Hamlet's soliloquy turns out to be an uproarious mix of Shakespearean passages in total disarray, with snatches of *Macbeth, Richard III,* and whatever else might lie at hand. "To be, or not to be; that is the bare bodkin / That makes calamity of so long life," the speech begins, going on to this climax: "But soft you, the fair Ophelia: / Ope not thy ponderous and marble jaws, / But get thee to a nunnery—go!" The "bare bodkin" (an erroneous substitute for "respect") is from a few lines later on in the soliloquy; the "ponderous

and marble jaws" are from Hamlet's first addressing his father's ghost at
1.4.50; "get thee to a nunnery" is from Hamlet's upbraiding of Ophelia
at 3.1.122–31. Twain clearly suggests that too much of Shakespeare in
America is just a lot of the flapdoodle that Huck so wisely mistrusts.
Twain's wry combativeness here is of a piece with the scorn he
directed at New England blueblood authors like Henry Wadsworth
Longfellow and William Cullen Bryant and James Russell Lowell, all
of them scions of British literary culture.

    The nineteenth century was also a golden time for parodies of
Shakespeare on stage. Richard W. Schoch's *Not Shakespeare: Bardolatry
and Burlesque in the Nineteenth Century* (2002) and Stanley Wells's
Nineteenth-Century Shakespeare Burlesques (1977–8) offer many illustrations, including John Poole's *Hamlet Travestie* (1810), the anonymous
A Thin Slice of Ham Let! (1850), Barton's *Hamlet According to an Act of
Parliament* (1853, in which Hamlet meets his father drunk), the anonymous *Hamlet! The Ravin' Prince of Denmark* (1866), Robert Craig's
Hamlet, or, Wearing of the Black (1866, in which Queen Gertrude drinks
to her son from a mug of beer into which her husband has dropped an
onion), W. R. Snow's *Hamlet the Hysterical, a Delirium in Five Spasms!!!*
(1874, in which the likenesses of Hamlet's father and uncle that he
shows to Gertrude in act 3, scene 4 are empty picture frames),
J. Comyns Carr's *A Fireside Hamlet* (1884, with a young H. Beerbohm
Tree), and William Yardley's *Very Little Hamlet* (1884).

    In several of these parodies, Hamlet and Laertes fight each other
with boxing gloves instead of rapiers, while the courtiers cheer them
on. In *Hamlet! The Ravin' Prince of Denmark*, the hero boasts of his
pugilistic expertise:

> Here I stand, the Danish Chicken
> Ever fit to face the foe.
> Won't he get a fearful lickin'?
> Does I tremble at him? Oh, dear, no!

In the same parodic work, Hamlet laments the decline of tragedy on
the contemporary stage by intoning, "Oh, for some bard to consecrate
the scene / And bid the drama be what she hath been!" Ophelia's
distraught account to her father of Hamlet's strange behavior toward
her in her "closet" or private chamber (2.1.77–102) goes as follows:

> No shoes at all, and only half a stocking,
> Burst into the nursery without ever knocking,

Then seized the infant by its little throttle,
And drank the dead king's health in its milk-bottle!

The play's most famous soliloquy (3.1.57–89) begins "To be or not to be, that is the question. / Oh, dear, I'm suffering from the indigestion!," only to end abortively with "I really can't go on, for people say / This is the noblest passage of the play." To be sure, all these spoofs are implicitly admiring of what Shakespeare wrote; the skylarking is an acknowledgment of a genius too great to be degraded by sendups.

Better than all these is *Rosencrantz and Guildenstern*, by W. S. Gilbert of Gilbert and Sullivan fame, first published in the periodical *Fun* in 1874, though evidently not performed in public until 1891. The cast for a 1904 performance included Gilbert himself, George Bernard Shaw, and some others. In it, Claudius confesses to Gertrude the appalling sin of his youth: he wrote a five-act tragedy. Rosencrantz (in love with Ophelia) and Guildenstern contrive, with Ophelia's help, to steal the script of Claudius's play from Ophelia's father so that Hamlet may be tricked into performing in it in the presence of the King. As a consequence, Hamlet is banished to "Engle-land," where his distressing tendency to lengthy soliloquizing will go unnoticed by the natives, since they are as mad as he. (The joke about wanting to be left alone on stage to soliloquize is one that Gilbert returned to in *The Mikado*, 1885, in which Ko-ko twice objects testily to being interrupted, first by Pish-Tush—"Now then, what is it? Can't you see I'm soliloquizing? You have interrupted an apostrophe, sir!"—and later by Nanki-Poo: "Go away, sir! How dare you? Am I never to be permitted to soliloquize?")

Literary allusions to Hamlet in the late eighteenth and in the nineteenth centuries are, to be sure, generally admiring. Goethe's *Wilhelm Meister's Apprenticeship* (1778, 1795) tells how the autobiographical hero joins a troupe in order to play an "entire and unabbreviated" *Hamlet* (book 5). Mary Wollstonecraft, in her *Vindication of the Rights of Women* (1793), uses *Hamlet* to illustrate the vital importance of her cause by citing Hamlet's attack on Ophelia (3.1.122ff.) as an instance of an all-too-prevalent misogyny in Western culture. The mat-weaving episode in Herman Melville's *Moby Dick* (1851, chapter 47), without actually mentioning the play, inspires a searching meditation on the resemblance between the warp and weft of a nautical net and Hamlet's reflections on the intertwined roles of free will and necessity in human life in act 5, scene 2 ("There's a divinity that shapes our ends, / Rough-hew them how we will," etc.). Melville's *Pierre* (1852) draws a series of parallels between its central figure and Hamlet, especially in the close relation of son and mother and the son's struggles to be a writer. In George Eliot's *Felix Holt, the Radical* (1866), the eponymous hero borrows the language of Hamlet's inquisition of Ophelia (3.1.122ff.) in his tirade against Esther. In *The Mill on the Floss* (1860), Eliot draws comparisons between Maggie Tulliver and Hamlet. Karl Marx, in *Das Kapital* (1867), deliberately misquotes Hamlet's "Well said, old mole!" (1.5.171) with a modern substitution, "Well grubbed, old mole!" to express Marx's expectant cry of jubilation at the imminent and inevitable collapse of the capitalist system.

In summary, the appreciation of Shakespeare in the nineteenth century in the theatre, in the library, and in publishing houses signaled an ever-increasing celebration of Great Britain's greatest poet-dramatist as the fountainhead of culture at home and around the world. Throughout the Romantic and Victorian eras, *Hamlet* stood at the very heart of this cultural enterprise. Its hero was seen as the quintessential Romantic protagonist, sensitive, melancholic, ill-suited to act in a bad world but inspirational as a thinker. Ophelia and Horatio were similarly lauded as innocent and morally upright. Shakespeare's texts were often pruned to emphasize these qualities. Theatres and productions grew in cost, size, and splendor. Not coincidentally, this awesome rise to prominence of Shakespeare as national poet-dramatist came at a time of the Industrial Revolution, of growing prosperity for the middle class, of flourishing parliamentary democracy, and of commercial and political success around the globe for British colonialism. Many British people saw their own Victorian age as the natural and appropriate fulfillment of progressive cultural, political, and economic development set in motion in the Renaissance and enhanced by Enlightenment thinking in the eighteenth century. Even the many spoofs of *Hamlet* attest to the limitless fondness of the English-speaking world for Shakespeare as an observer and champion of English culture. Shakespeare, with *Hamlet* as his quintessential play, epitomized the amazing rise to prominence of Great Britain as a nation. Shakespeare's freedom of spirit, his seemingly limitless imagination, and his deep insights into the human condition were seen as splendidly representative of what had made Great Britain great.

6

Reform It Altogether: *Hamlet*, 1900–1980

Perhaps no actor-manager at the turn of the twentieth century captures more perfectly the prevailing style of lavishly expensive productions of Shakespeare than does Herbert Beerbohm Tree, presiding genius at Her Majesty's Theatre from its inception in 1897 until his death in 1917. (That theatre became His Majesty's Theatre in 1901 when Queen Victoria died at the age of eighty-two, having reigned for some sixty-four of those years and having been succeeded by her nearly-sixty-year-old playboy son, Edward VII.) Tree had produced *Hamlet* in 1892 at the Haymarket Theatre, taking the lead role himself and casting his wife as Ophelia. The show ran for 116 performances.

As manager at Her Majesty's in 1897 and afterwards, Tree did all he could to outdo his great predecessor, Henry Irving. Tree's production of *King John* (1899) made an elaborate tableau of the King's yielding to his barons at Runnymede in 1215, even though Shakespeare never breathes a word about Magna Carta. In Tree's *Antony and Cleopatra* (1907), the famous meeting of the lovers on the river of Cydnus took place in the theatre with as much pomp and circumstance as Tree could muster, thus actualizing the verbal account spoken by Enobarbus in Shakespeare's play to Maecenas and Agrippa (2.2). The number of scenes in the play had to be greatly reduced to make room for the spectacle. In a similar vein, live rabbits scampered through a carpet of thyme, wild flowers, and blossoming thickets in Tree's *A Midsummer Night's Dream* (1904). Olivia's Italian-style garden in *Twelfth Night* (1901) featured statues, fountains, terraces, a handsome staircase, real grass, and a scenic backdrop of hills and trees. Effects like these were not only costly to build; they were not easily moved, so that Tree found it expedient to rearrange the scenes with the action at Olivia's house presented in a continuous sequence rather than interspersed, as in Shakespeare's text, with scenes at the palace of Duke Orsino or on the seacoast of Illyria. Tree returned to *Hamlet* in 1909 and 1910 at His Majesty's, as part of a London Shakespeare Festival.

Yet a seismic shift was at hand. Johnston Forbes-Robertson chose a simpler style of staging for his *Hamlet* in 1897, albeit with an orchard full of apple-blossoms for Ophelia's mad scenes. Encouraged by George Bernard Shaw, Forbes-Robertson restored the long-absent Fortinbras to the final act, thus ending the production with an impressively dignified funeral cortège in honor of the fallen hero. F. R. Benson's *Hamlet* at the Shakespeare Memorial Theatre in Stratford-upon-Avon in 1899–1900 went still further in restoring Shakespeare's text: this uncut second-quarto/Folio version ran to no less than six hours, from 3:30 to 11:00 p.m. with a sizable interval for dinner. A performance of this sort had to rely on simple scenic effects and rapid movement. Benson needed to be able to take his productions on tour. A full-length production of *Hamlet* had seemingly never been attempted before, probably not even in Shakespeare's day. The undertaking struck some reviewers as academic and the performances by Benson's provincial repertory company inclining to be spotty, but the challenge to nineteenth-century staging orthodoxy was plain for all to see.

More significantly still, on 16 April 1881 William Poel had directed a single amateur reading of *Hamlet* at St George's Hall on Regent Street, London, based on the 1603 quarto, on an unadorned stage surrounded on four sides by red curtains through which the entrances and exits were effected. Along with Poel's other work, this experimental venture signaled a new direction that the theatre was to take. William Poel, visionary and eccentric, established the Elizabethan Stage Society in 1894 with a view to putting on plays by Shakespeare and his contemporaries in something like their original theatrical settings. He wished to learn more about Elizabethan stage practice, partly as a matter of scholarly interest but more largely as a means of challenging the costly and spectacular production methods of Irving and Tree. The discovery in 1881 of Johannes de Witt's 1596 sketch of the Elizabethan Swan Theatre (see Illustration 2) provided Poel with the rationale he needed for mounting productions on an open stage with continuously swift-paced action by a troupe of ensemble players in close proximity with their audience. His revivals paid close attention to Elizabethan period costuming. He made use of an inner stage as well as the open platform. He eschewed cuts as much as possible, and did away for the most part with intermissions. He and his collaborator, Philip Ben Greet, hired vacant halls or theatres on low budgets to see what could be learned about the texts of the plays when they were put on in something approaching the conditions of the original Globe Theatre. *Henry V* appeared thus at the Lecture Theatre in Burlington Gardens in 1901, and *Twelfth Night* in 1903 at the Court Theatre. Poel produced *The Comedy of Errors* in 1895 at Gray's Inn, where it had been staged by Elizabethan actors in 1594. He cast a girl of fourteen as Juliet and a youngster of seventeen as Romeo in his *Romeo and Juliet*, 1905. George Bernard Shaw was impressed, and indeed was an enthusiastic supporter of the reforms to which he and Poel were both committed. Poel revived his production of *Hamlet* at the Little Theatre in London in 1914.

Harley Granville-Barker, at the Savoy Theatre in 1912–14, was inspired by Poel's example to recapture the fluidity and presentational openness of Elizabethan staging, though in modified ways that were sensitive to the demands of a commercial theatre, thereby avoiding what must have seemed cultish and even pedantic in some of Poel's experiments. Granville-Barker opened with a rapid-paced *The Winter's Tale* in 1912, with no footlights or scenic backdrops and with the action limited to three acting areas. He also did away with the broadly burlesque style of acting in which the below-stairs characters had often been presented.

In his *Preface to Hamlet* (1936), Granville-Barker maintained stoutly that Shakespeare did not conceive the play (or any other, for that matter) in five-act form, and that imposing such a structure on stage production is hypothetical at best: "It cannot but to some extent thwart his technique." Indeed, at what is conventionally marked as the end of act 3 and the beginning of act 4, after Hamlet's killing of Polonius, the indication of an act division may be, as Granville-Barker says, seriously misleading. It was not introduced in editorial practice until the sixth quarto of 1676, long after the Folio of 1623. In the earlier texts, Hamlet exits from his mother's chamber, dragging in the dead body of Polonius, whereupon in the Folio text Claudius enters ("*Exit Hamlet tugging in Polonius. Enter King*") seemingly to Gertrude, who is not named in the exit stage direction. A plausible inference is that she remains on stage throughout, thus contradicting the conventional marking of act 4. The first quarto of 1603 can be similarly interpreted: the stage direction reads "*Exit Hamlet with the dead body. Enter the King and Lordes*," not naming the Queen, who nevertheless speaks both before and after this stage direction and thus may (or may not) have been on stage throughout. No exit is indicated for her in the second quarto text either, though the stage direction does then specify that she is to come on stage with her husband after Hamlet's exit ("*Enter King, and Queene, with Rosencraus and Guyldensterne*"), so that the Q2 text might seem to indicate that a scene break has occurred. The absence of an exit for Gertrude in Q2 does not necessarily mean that she remains on stage; original stage directions often fail to specify exits, presumably because actors could be counted on to know when they should get off stage. On the other hand, only rarely on the Elizabethan stage do we find an exit and bare stage followed immediately by the re-entrance of one or more of the exiting characters.

The point here is that Granville-Barker's attempts to understand Elizabethan staging alerted him to the hazards of giving too much credence to neoclassical conventions of act-scene division. These observations were prompted by Granville-Barker's own production of *Hamlet* in London in 1936, in which, despite Granville-Barker's misgivings, a scene break was provided, whereupon a new scene took place in "*the King's dressing-room.*" (Recently it has been argued, by Gary Taylor, in Taylor and John Jowett, *Shakespeare Reshaped, 1606–1623*, Oxford: Clarendon Press, 1993, pp. 3–50, that after about 1608 Shakespeare *did* conceive his plays in five acts, probably as a result of indoor performances in the Blackfriars theatre, but *Hamlet* was, of course, written and performed several years before that proposed date.)

In 1912, Edward Gordon Craig, illegitimate son of Ellen Terry, co-directed (with Konstantin Stanislavsky) and designed a renowned *Hamlet* at the Moscow Art Theatre. Craig had played Hamlet earlier, in 1897, at the Olympic Theatre, wearing Henry Irving's costume from a decade before. His set in 1912 made use of elaborately symbolic non-representational screens that were hinged in such a way as to facilitate a quick shift from interior to exterior. He championed a new method in stage lighting by doing away with traditional footlights in favor of lights placed above. Color and light were central to his concepts of stage picture. Fervently dedicated to the proposition that theatre is the craft of the director, he strove to highlight relationships between movement and sound and between line and color. Throughout he aimed at integration of a concept uniting the acting company with its theatrical milieu. Experiments such as these inevitably opened up *Hamlet* to new interpretations and new staging methods. Through his use of screens, subtle lighting, and minimal amounts of painting, Craig offered suggestion and subtlety in place of theatrical overstatement. Such at any rate became the battle cry among adventurous younger directors in the early years of the twentieth century.

Japanese audiences witnessed some performances of *Hamlet* in a non-traditional mode during these years, notably that of Otojiro Kawakami in 1903 and Shoyo Tsubouchi in 1906 (abridged) and 1911 (with a male actor playing Gertrude), followed later by Tsuneari Fukuda in 1955. In China, Gu Wuwei's 1916 amalgam of *Hamlet* and *Macbeth*, entitled *The Usurper of State Power*, aimed its political message at Yuan Shikai's attempted overthrow of the republic. Jiao Juyin, in 1942, staged the play in a Confucian temple in Sichuan Province to which the Chinese government had retreated in the face of Japanese attack, in order to make the political point that nicety and delay could be fatal.

The acting company at the Old Vic Theatre, which had been built in 1818 and renamed the Royal Victoria in 1833, adopted the new style of production under the leadership of Philip Ben Greet and his theatre manager, Lilian Baylis. Greet staged a production of *Hamlet* in this theatre in 1916 based on a full text of the 1604 quarto. In 1930, still under the management of Lilian Baylis, Harcourt Williams directed John Gielgud, aged 26, in *Hamlet* at the Old Vic (and then at the New Theatre in 1934, where it ran for 155 performances) in a memorable and largely uncut production (see Illustration 12).[1]

To be sure, some well-known Shakespearean actors of the early twentieth century continued to please audiences with what we would probably recognize today as traditional interpretations of Hamlet. In America, Walter Hampden, as a kind of successor to E. H. Sothern, was a favorite in the role of Hamlet, in New York and on tour, right after World War I. John Barrymore, making his debut in the role of Hamlet at New York's Sam Harris Theatre in 1922, with Arthur Hopkins as director, performed in the role for 101 nights, breaking Edwin Booth's record of 100 performances in 1854–5. Barrymore succeeded in London as well, with Fay Compton as his Ophelia. Although Robert Edmond Jones's set design for the 1922 production

Illustration 12. John Gielgud as Hamlet, at London's New Theatre, 1934.
Photograph by Yvonne Gregory. Courtesy of ArenaPAL, London.

was innovative, with its single playing area and a flight of steps leading
upward toward a distant sky instead of the multiple sets typical of
Irving's or Tree's staging plans, Barrymore as Hamlet was a matinée
idol. Contemporary reviewers credited him with grace of movement,
a compelling presence, and lofty skills of elocution, even if to today's
listeners of old recordings his deep-voiced emotional tremor is apt
to sound overwrought. George Bernard Shaw complained that the
Hamlet–Ophelia scene (3.1) reminded him too much of Romeo and
Juliet. Barrymore wore the familiar tunic and black tights. Barrymore's
influence was visibly felt in the Hamlet of Raymond Massey on
Broadway in 1931, with its arrangement of stairs, levels, and platforms.

Maurice Evans, after playing at the Old Vic in 1935, scored his greatest triumph as Hamlet in New York in association with Katharine Cornell in 1938 and afterwards, whereupon he toured the production in its "entirety." As a member of the U. S. armed forces in 1941, Evans took his "G. I. Hamlet" on tour in the South Pacific and then, in 1945, in New York. He was trumpeted by one critic in 1938 as "the finest Hamlet that we have seen in our town since John Barrymore's classic portrayal of the role" (13 October, *New York Herald-Tribune*). "Classic portrayal" is a telling phrase. These popular successes were, not surprisingly, transatlantic. Leslie Howard played *Hamlet* on Broadway in 1936 in a production that fared poorly in New York, owing to its being in competition with that of Gielgud, but did better on tour.

John Gielgud was also in some ways a "classic" heir to Barrymore in the 1930s and 1940s. Gielgud did indeed dress traditionally in his early performances, but he also aligned himself with cutting-edge directors and acting companies, and became an innovative director himself. During the 1930s and 1940s he played Hamlet hundreds of times and in several productions: at the Old Vic in 1930 as mentioned above, at Stratford-upon-Avon in the 1930s, at London's New Theatre in 1934 with himself as director (see Illustration 12), at New York's Empire Theatre in 1936 (directed by Guthrie McClintic, with Lillian Gish as Ophelia and Judith Anderson as Gertrude), at the Lyceum in London in 1939 and at Elsinore Castle in Denmark (with production design by Motley) in the same year, at London's Haymarket in 1944–5 (directed by George Rylands), and then on tour in the Middle and Far East. By then he was in his early 40s, ready to move on to other things. In 1964 he would direct Richard Burton as Hamlet (see below). Princely and elegant, gifted with a superbly resonant voice, Gielgud was identified for decades more than any other actor with Hamlet, in good measure because he thought through the part with such extraordinary intelligence. He was not afraid to acknowledge his inheritance of a rich stage tradition, yet he also knew how to make the part uniquely his own.

The role of Hamlet has been coveted not only by male actors but by many actresses, long accustomed to being on stage in male attire in such plays as *As You Like It* and *Twelfth Night*. Charlotte Cushman took on the "breeches" part of Hamlet in 1851. (Previously, she had played Romeo to her sister Susan's Juliet in a very successful run of *Romeo and Juliet* at the Princess's Theatre in 1845; she also played Cardinal Wolsey in *Henry VIII*.) Sarah Bernhardt, after playing a manly and resolute Hamlet in male attire (in French prose translation) at the Adelphi Theatre in 1899 (see Illustration 13), pioneered in a five-minute silent filming of the dueling scene in *Hamlet* shot at the Paris Exposition of 1900. She also brought her Hamlet to North America.

Perhaps the most unusual "breeches" performance of Hamlet was that of Asta Nielsen in a German seventy-eight-minute silent film of 1920, directed by Svend Gade and Heinz Schall. In this version, Hamlet (Nielsen) appears at first (to most of the other characters, though not to us) to be a man, but is discovered in the final scene to be a woman, having been sheltered thus by her protective mother from the perils of a cut-throat, male-dominated world of courtly

Illustration 13. Sarah Bernhardt in her "breeches" role as Hamlet, at the Adelphi Theatre, *c.* 1899. Courtesy of ArenaPAL, London.

politics. This idea of a female Hamlet who is disguised as a male to preserve his/her lineage came to the film directors from Edward P. Vining's *The Mystery of Hamlet* (Philadelphia, 1881), in which the hero's female identity helps explain the purported inability to carry out revenge. In the film version, similarly, the last-minute identification of Hamlet as a woman offers, in retrospect, a possible explanation as to why he/she has been so reluctant to act and why he/she feels such deep fondness for Horatio.

Other "breeches" Hamlets have included Judith Anderson, on a tour of the United States and in Carnegie Hall, 1970–2, at the age of 73; Angela Winkler, in a production directed at Hamburg and Edinburgh in 1999 by Peter Zadek (who had previously staged the play at Bochum in 1977); Teresa Budzisz-Krzyzanowska in Andrzej Wajda's production at Krakow, Poland, in 1989; Frances de la Tour at a London fringe theatre, the Half Moon, in the 1980s; Diane Venora, under Joseph Papp's direction at the Public Theater, New York, in 1982–3; and Black Eyed Susan, in Ethyl Eichelberger's female version called *Hamlette* for Charles Ludlam's Ridiculous Theatrical Company in 1990.

The year 1925 saw the first modern-dress *Hamlet*, under the direction of Barry Jackson and H. K. Ayliff, first at the Birmingham Repertory Theatre and then at London's Kingsway Theatre. Colin Keith-Johnston, as Hamlet, belonged entirely to the modern world: he smoked, dressed casually, and confronted those he despised with studied rudeness. He could be violent. A balanced cast gave depth to the other characters as well; this was an ensemble *Hamlet*. The set was suitably spare; for the scene at the gravesite of Ophelia (Muriel Hewitt), a large flower-decorated grave stood mid-stage in front of a tall, simple cross and a non-scenic back wall, while the mourners gaped at the spectacle of Hamlet (in plus fours) fighting with Laertes (Robert Holmes). Modern dress also freed the cast to break with traditional interpretations of character. Polonius (A. Bromley-Davenport), no longer doddering, was instead dapper and shrewd. Ophelia was a child of the flapper generation in the 1920s, fascinated with the prospect of an enlarged sexual freedom while at the same time repressed and anxious (see Illustration 14).

Other modern-dress productions soon followed on the Continent, in Prague (Karel Hilar, director) and Berlin (Leopold Jessner). In a sense, modern-dress production was not new: Shakespeare and his

Illustration 14. A. Bromley-Davenport as Polonius and Muriel Hewitt as Ophelia (1.3) in the first modern-dress production of *Hamlet*, directed by Barry Jackson and H. K. Ayliff at the Birmingham Repertory Theatre in 1925. Photograph by Lenare. Courtesy of ArenaPAL, London.

fellow actors dressed generally as Elizabethans or Jacobeans, and Restoration actors looked on stage as if they had just wandered in from the Stuart royal court. Yet modern dress in the twentieth century took on a polemical edge, if only because it was sharply defying the convention of historically "realistic" set designs and costumes that had reigned for so long. Modern dress lent itself to political interpretation: Jessner, for one, viewed *Hamlet* as a political play, far more compelling as such for contemporary audiences than the "worn-out" psychologizing of a man presumably incapable of action.

The post-World War I disillusionment on display in Jackson and Ayliff's 1925 production set the standard for other modernist interpretations intent on finding social and political relevance in Shakespeare's great tragedy. Leopold Jessner's 1926 production in Germany was not just in modern dress; it also presented itself as a highly politicized critique of Kaiser Wilhelm and the German ruling class, with Hamlet (Fritz Kortner) as the rebel hero defying the autocratic regime of Claudius. This left-leaning view of the play did not suit the purposes of the Nazis when they came to power in the 1930s. In their opinion, Shakespeare really should be thought of as a German author; Germans generally were immensely proud of the Schlegel-Tieck translations and regarded these texts as more authentically Shakespearean and more contemporary (because in modern German) than the English text. Accordingly, the Third Reich encouraged interpretations that cast the playwright more in the role of German national poet, with Hamlet as the fair-haired Saxon son of a brave Nordic prince who had "smote the sledded Polacks on the ice" (1.1.67), as the Germans were to do again in the late 1930s. Gustaf Gründgens was a national-socialist hero in this mold in a 1936 production that ran for some 130 performances. In Russia, a production at the Moscow Art Theatre in 1924–5 under Michael Chekhov's direction ran into trouble with the Soviet authorities for its anti-authoritarian (and hence "reactionary") political slant. Theatrical performances of *Hamlet* were subsequently banned until after Stalin's death in 1953. Boris Pasternak had to proceed cautiously in order for his 1930 translation of Shakespeare to be published.

Tyrone Guthrie's 1937–8 Freudian interpretation of *Hamlet* responded to the growing crisis of a Europe between two world wars by exploring the psychological dimensions of existential uncertainty and dilemma. Laurence Olivier, in the role of Hamlet, was a tragic protagonist for an era fascinated with psychoanalysis as a key to understanding of the human psyche. Ernest Jones's *Hamlet and Oedipus* (1910 in essay form, revised for book publication in 1949) had given wide currency to Sigmund Freud's hypothesis that Hamlet is driven by a subconscious incestuous desire for his mother and hence a psychological inability to punish his uncle for having done what Hamlet fears most in himself—an explanation, in psychoanalytic terms, for the presumed delay in Hamlet's quest for revenge that had so fascinated Goethe and Coleridge. (I shall say more about Freud shortly.) Guthrie and Olivier adopted the Freudian interpretation as their governing concept in 1937–8, although in practice Olivier was so athletic, forceful, and muscular that some critics wondered how such a Hamlet could have succumbed to self-scrutiny and doubt. The set, with its platforms and ramps, gave Olivier ample room for a display of frenetic vigor. His duel with Laertes (Michael Redgrave) was protracted and spellbinding. The production was taken to Kronborg Castle near Helsingör (i.e. Elsinore) in Denmark for a short run in late spring, ignoring the inconvenient fact that the castle we can visit today was extensively restored and remodeled after a fire in the 1630s and Swedish bombardment in 1658–60. The first performance had to be moved indoors, owing to inclement weather, with unexpectedly beneficent results: the improvised event, staged as theatre-in-the-round, proved to be a revolutionary experience for the participants. Alec Guinness called this opening night "the most exciting theatrical experience most of us ever had" (Barry Gaines, in *Inside Shakespeare: Essays on the Blackfriars Stage*, ed. Paul Menzer, Selinsgrove, PA: Susquehanna University Press, 2006). Olivier later directed a production of *Hamlet*, starring Peter O'Toole, at London's National Theatre in 1963, Olivier having just been appointed as the company's first artistic director.

Olivier carried the idea of psychological paralysis forward into his film version of *Hamlet* in 1948, shortly after Alfred Hitchcock's *Spellbound* (1945) bore witness to a trendy belief in psychoanalysis as a potential cure-all for mental illness. In the film *Hamlet*, Olivier is alternately despondent and alive with energy. At one moment we see him meditating on suicide in a voice-over of "To be or not to be" while Hamlet gazes down "from the dreadful summit of the cliff / That beetles o'er its base into the sea." At other moments the castle becomes a living presence as the camera follows Hamlet through the winding passageways and staircases of Elsinore. In his conversations with Horatio (Norman Wooland) and the gravedigger (Stanley Holloway), Olivier's Hamlet is wisely compassionate and insightful about death and destiny. He interrupts the "maimèd rites" of Ophelia's burial in act 5 with a brave proclamation of his royal title: "This is I, / Hamlet the Dane" (5.1.219, 257-8; see Illustration 15). The finale is visually emblematic in a way that film can do so well: Claudius (Basil Sydney), unable to prevent Gertrude (Eileen Herlie) from drinking the poisoned cup intended for Hamlet, since he cannot publicly confess that it is poisoned, is stabbed by Hamlet and falls to the floor, reaching out desperately toward the throne, the crown, and his queen—the

Illustration 15. Laurence Olivier as Hamlet at Ophelia's grave (5.1) in Olivier's 1948 film.

guilty possessions for which he has committed his terrible crime and that will now elude him forever. Hamlet dies reconciled to his mother. A grieving Horatio brings the film to a close with the hope that "flights of angels" will sing Hamlet to his rest (5.2.362). The deletion of the Fortinbras story and all its political ramifications focuses the film instead on the death of a noble prince who, had he been invested in the throne, would have "proved most royal" (400). Soldiers carry the dead Hamlet to the ramparts.[2]

Innovative period setting and costuming offered yet another way to steer interpretation of *Hamlet* towards a commentary on the contemporary world of the mid-twentieth century. Period setting became very popular with Shakespearean theatre companies at about this time, in good part because it offered the director a rich opportunity to put the mark of his concept on his work. Modern-dress productions, as in 1925 and 1926, had made the point of topical relevance. Michael Benthall carried the idea a significant step further by proposing that the abandonment of Elizabethan mise en scène need not mean limiting

the choice to modern dress. Benthall established an important prece-
dent at Stratford-upon-Avon in 1948 by setting *Hamlet* in Victorian
times. Presumably his intent was to ask audiences to ponder the
Victorian-like complacencies of their own bourgeois existences. No
less original was Benthall's decision to cast two actors, Paul Scofield
and Robert Helpmann, in the title role on alternate nights, thereby
exploring multiple approaches to Hamlet's psyche and dilemma.
Benthall's experiment was soon followed by period-setting productions of other Shakespeare plays: *All's Well That Ends Well* set in
Edwardian England of the 1900s (Tyrone Guthrie, Stratford, Canada,
1953), *Much Ado About Nothing* set in the American frontier southwest
(American Shakespeare Festival, 1957), the same play in midwest
America at the end of the Spanish–American War of 1898 (New
York Shakespeare Festival, A. J. Antoon, 1972), and many more.

In the years following World War II, the political temperature
heated up more and more rapidly in performance, as it did in the
society being mirrored on stage and in film. Grigori Kozintsev's
Hamlet, produced in Leningrad in 1954 immediately following the
death of Joseph Stalin in 1953, was the work of a director who had
spent much of the war in a prison camp. His mission was to analyze
what, in his words, was "happening in the prison state around him."
The Hamlet of this production was an existential hero in his resistance
to oppression, as in Leopold Jessner's anti-authoritarian German production of 1926, in Russian versions by Sergei Kirov in 1932 and by
Yuri Lyubimov at Moscow's Taganka Theatre in 1971–80 starring
the protest poet Vladimir Vysotsky, in Poland (Crakow) in 1956,
in Czechoslovakia (Prague) in 1941 at the Vinohrady Theatre, and as
an absurdist farce in 1978 at the Balustrade Theatre in Rumania
(Bucharest) in 1989, among others; see Anthony B. Dawson, "International Shakespeare" and Wilhelm Hormann, "Shakespeare on the
Political Stage," in *The Cambridge Companion to Shakespeare on Stage*
(2002).

For his black-and-white film version of 1964, Kozintsev teamed up
with Boris Pasternak as textual translator and with Dmitri Shostako-
vich as musical composer, both of whom were as passionately committed as was Kozintsev to the cause of artistic freedom in a police
state. Kozintsev's intent, to be sure, was not solely political: as a film
artist, he saw his work in metaphorical and visual terms as a study in the
elemental natural forces of earth, sea, stone, and fire. The film images

are thus both topical and universal. Hamlet's thinking is dangerous to the state because it is political. The many monumental statues of Claudius (Mikhail Nazvanov) are suggestive of the Stalinist cult of personality. The instructions of Polonius (Yuri Tolubeyev) to Reynaldo to keep a close watch over Hamlet in Paris are in perfect keeping with the eavesdropping mentality of the Danish court. The constrictive metallic corset and petticoats of Ophelia (Anastasia Vertinskaya) are emblematic of a lost personal freedom. Elsinore, with its stone walls, drawbridge, and huge spiked portcullis, becomes a state prison. A runic monumental cross in Ophelia's graveyard, timeworn and neglected, testifies to the forgetfulness of human history. The gravedigger's hammer resounds with harsh impersonality as he nails down the lid of her coffin. Sand and dirt pour out of Yorick's skull as it is held up by Hamlet (Innokenti Smoktunovsky) in his ironic inquiry into the senseless triviality of a human existence drained of spiritual meaning (see Illustration 16). Against this hollowness stands Hamlet as existentialist rebel and sacrificial victim.

John Gielgud's successful Broadway 1964 modern-dress *Hamlet*, at the Lunt-Fontanne Theatre with Richard Burton in the title role, was reformulated by Bill Colleran for Electronovision in that same year. Several hand-held cameras, variously positioned in the course of three live performances, provided a multiple perspective shot from various angles. Collated into a single show, this *Hamlet* was then broadcast four times to some 976 movie theatre audiences throughout the United

Illustration 16. Innokenti Smoktunovsky as Hamlet at Ophelia's grave (5.1) in Grigori Kozintsev's black-and-white film, 1964.

States. Partly because Electronovision was as yet a relatively untried technology, the broadcast was of poor quality in picture and in sound. The cameramen with their hand-held cameras had to manage as well as they could with the production's stage lighting; no compromises were allowed here. Still, by means of cutting and selecting among the alternative shots, the producers did at least capture a truly memorable performance by Burton. Rejecting entirely the melancholy and pensive Hamlet of Goethe-Coleridgean tradition, Burton, the son of a Welsh coal-miner who had found his theatrical metier in the Oxford University Dramatic Society, is virile, witty, sardonic, tempestuous, and rough-edged; he swaggers, pouts, threatens, and brawls. His soliloquies are internalized rather than directed to the audience. The informal costuming consists of open-necked shirts and wool sweaters and the like, as if at a rehearsal (see Illustration 17). The setting, as in the original staging, is utilitarian and unadorned. A nearly uncut text enables us to see Hume Cronyn in the role of Polonius, Eileen Herlie as Gertrude (her role also in Olivier's 1948 film), John Gielgud as the

Illustration 17. George Rose as the First Gravedigger, Richard Burton as Hamlet, and Robert Milli as Horatio, in act 5, scene 1 of *Hamlet* at the Lunt-Fontanne Theatre, New York, 1964.

off-camera voice of a shadowy Ghost, Alfred Drake (not successfully) as Claudius, and Linda Marsh as Ophelia. Flawed it undoubtedly is, but we can still be grateful that it is available today in voice recordings and on videocasette. Burton insisted in his contract that all copies be destroyed, and his wishes were carried out almost to completion, but one surviving copy has been discovered.

Discouragement about contemporary social and political life in the era following the outbreak of the nuclear arms race, Civil Rights activism and its backlash, the assassinations of Martin Luther King and of Jack and Bobby Kennedy, controversy over the Welfare State, and the increasing social unrest over military actions in Vietnam and elsewhere (including the Falkland Islands crisis of 1982) all prompted a search for challenging questions in Shakespearean productions, as though asking what that mighty playwright would have thought of the 1960s, 1970s, and early 1980s if he were to come back to life. A prevailing mood of cynicism led some directors to see Hamlet as no longer a hero against despotism, but instead a sufferer of universal ennui. Peter Hall, directing *Hamlet* for the Royal Shakespeare Company at Stratford-upon-Avon in 1965, wrote in his program notes that the production "was about the disillusionment which produces an apathy of the will so deep that commitment to politics, to religion or to life is impossible." The impasse that divided Denmark from Norway in this production reminded audiences of Europe's Iron Curtain. David Warner as Hamlet responded unheroically to the utter helplessness of his situation. His declaring to Rosencrantz and Guildenstern that "Denmark's a prison" (2.2.244) took on an ominous topical resonance. Glenda Jackson played Ophelia as a neurotic shrew. Hall's production came only a short time after Peter Brook, also at Stratford-upon-Avon, had staged his enormously influential *King Lear* (1962), with Paul Scofield in the title role, based on the apocalyptically dark reading of that play in Jan Kott's *Shakespeare Our Contemporary* (translated into English in 1964). (Less famously, Scofield played Hamlet under Brook's direction at Birmingham and then at London's Phoenix Theatre in 1955.) During these same years, at the Heile Selassie I Theatre in Ethiopia, Tsegaye Gebre-Medhin had great success with a *Hamlet* attuned to audiences for whom magic, ghosts, fate, and warrior kings were familiar icons.

The noble and sensitive prince of *Hamlet* tradition, though thoughtfully embodied in Michael Pennington's graceful performance for the

Royal Shakespeare Company at Stratford-upon-Avon in 1980, with John Barton as director, was becoming more and more a thing of the past. Stratford, as the home of the Shakespeare industry, might still be hospitable to intelligently traditional readings, but elsewhere the mood of the Vietnam and post-Vietnam era was one of disillusionment.

Nicol Williamson, as Hamlet in a production directed by Tony Richardson at London's Roundhouse Theatre in 1969, was anything but the delicate aristocrat of nineteenth-century tradition: he was tough and serious, snarling, ill-tempered, facing the harsh realities of his situation with splenetic determination. Williamson's non-standard British speech, his mumblings, pithy rhythms, and other vocal mannerisms caused quite a stir. The show was taken to New York and then (1969) was filmed, with Tony Richardson as director, Anthony Hopkins as Claudius, Judy Parfitt as Gertrude, Mark Dignam as Polonius, and Marianne Faithfull as Ophelia. No attempt was made, in the filming as in the stage production, to hide the industrial origins of the Roundhouse as a circular building with a turntable in the center that had once enabled railroad locomotives to be housed, repaired, and rotated onto new sets of tracks. In his rebellious attitude toward the Establishment, Williamson as Hamlet seems a plausible stand-in for the Angry Young Men of postwar Great Britain: dissatisfied, underemployed, and despairing of a world given over to ethnic and racial tensions and calamitous post-imperialist wars. A claustrophobic sense of No Exit is enhanced by close-up shots. Williamson is brilliant, willful, unpredictable, not very likeable, stuffy, and self-important. Alienation is at the heart of this portrayal.

Buzz Goodbody (the first woman to direct a major British *Hamlet*), in a Royal Shakespeare Company studio production at The Other Place at Stratford-upon-Avon and then at the Roundhouse in London in 1975–6, pursued Peter Hall's prison image by converting the whole auditorium into the playing space, so that when Hamlet (Ben Kingsley) commanded, at 5.2.314, "Oh, villainy! Ho, let the door be locked!," the audience realized with a start that the theatre doors were indeed being shut upon them. The set designed by William Dudley for Richard Eyre's 1980 production at London's Royal Court was in effect another prison: the armed guards stationed at the many doors were a manifestation of a state control so oppressive that Hamlet (Jonathan Pryce) was under constant surveillance. When, in act 4, he attempted to evade his pursuers, he opened one *trompe l'oeil* door after another only to find an armed spy behind each. Polonius (Geoffrey Chater) was a self-satisfied, miserly bully, the creature of a police state.

Even more revisionary and experimental stage interpretations of *Hamlet* appeared in the decades leading up to the 1980s, on the Continent as well as in the United Kingdom and the United States. In New York, at the Public Theater in 1968, Joseph Papp went well beyond Peter Hall in jarring his audiences with a psychological nightmare of Oedipal and incestuous conflict. The opening image on stage was of Hamlet (Martin Sheen) in a coffin-like cradle at the feet of a huge bed occupied by Hamlet's hated uncle and Hamlet's mother, thus literalizing in the theatre Hamlet's obsessive imaginings of the two of them living "In the rank sweat of an enseamèd bed, / Stewed in corruption, honeying and making love / Over the nasty sty" (3.4.94–6). Heiner Müller's *Die Hamletmachine*, written in 1977 and produced in Paris in 1979, explored from an East German point of view the angst of the artist/intellectual in an era of Soviet domination in Eastern Europe. Müller later directed a seven-and-a-half-hour version (in which *Die Hamletmaschine* served as the play-within-the-play) in Berlin, 1989–90, as a dirge for a regime that was about to collapse and leave in its wake an uncertain world of globalized conflict. This play was not an adaptation so much as a strenuously avant-garde disquisition between two speakers, one of them schizophrenic and impotent (Hamlet) and the other implacably revolutionary (Ophelia). The *Hamlet* of the Polish director, Andrzej Wajda, in 1982, dressed Fortinbras in the uniform of the hated Polish Security Forces. Liviu Ciulei, directing the play at the Arena Theater in Washington, D.C., in 1978, chose as his mise en scène the world of Bismarckian Germany.[3]

Literary criticism of *Hamlet* in the twentieth century down to the 1980s begins with A. C. Bradley's *Shakespearean Tragedy*, 1904, and its affinities to the soon-to-vanish Victorian world of Henry Irving and Beerbohm Tree. *Hamlet* is one of the four "great" Shakespearean tragedies studied by Bradley in this influential book, along with *Othello, King Lear*, and *Macbeth*. What these four plays have in common, in Bradley's view, is that they deal with universal issues of good and evil, temptation and sin, self-knowledge and self-betrayal. The Roman and classical plays, including *Julius Caesar, Antony and Cleopatra*, and *Coriolanus*, focus on political conflict; the great plays of

Shakespeare's "Tragic Period" are more profoundly spiritual and moral in their concerns. In these terms, Bradley refuses to see Hamlet as "one-sidedly reflective and indisposed to action," as Goethe and Coleridge had maintained. Instead, Bradley views Hamlet as an idealist of deep moral sensibility, who is for that very reason unusually vulnerable to the violent shock presented to him by the murder of his father and his mother's over-hasty remarriage. His passion for generalization prompts him to reflect, perhaps "too curiously" (5.1.205), on the larger meaning of everything he observes. The violent shock and his generalizing imagination conspire to drive him into a deep melancholy. "His whole mind is poisoned." He can never think of Ophelia as he did before, since she is a woman, like Hamlet's own mother. "He can do nothing." Hence "his vain efforts to fulfil this duty [of revenge], his unconscious self-excuses and unavailing self-reproaches, and the tragic results of his delay."

In all this, Bradley seems to sum up the best of nineteenth-century criticism, with its close attention to the study of character as a model for human behavior. Shakespeare's tragic world is, to Bradley, ultimately explicable and moral in the most enlightened sense of that term. Great dramatic literature should be "improving" and inspirational. As Bradley writes (of *King Lear*): "Good, in the widest sense, seems thus to be the principle of life and health in the world; evil, at least in these worst forms, to be a poison. The world reacts against it violently, and, in the struggle to expel it, is driven to devastate itself." Bradley is, like Henry Irving, one of the last of the Victorians.

Just as theatrical performances in the early twentieth century increasingly sought a return to a simpler and more "Shakespearean" open stage, scholarly criticism too mounted a crusade for better historical understanding of theatrical methods and conditions in early modern England. Sir Walter Raleigh (Professor of English Literature at Oxford, not to be confused with the Raleigh or Ralegh of the Elizabethan and Jacobean court) emphatically rejects the premises of nineteenth-century character criticism, insisting that "A play is not a collection of the biographies of those who appear in it." Character is not "a chief cause of the dramatic situation," nor is *Hamlet* "a Moral Play, like one of Miss Edgeworth's stories" (*Shakespeare*, London: Macmillan, 1907). Raleigh turns his attention instead to the artistic methods by which this play affects spectators in the theatre. The poet Robert Bridges takes a similar approach, as can be judged from the title of one of his *Collected Essays* (London: Oxford University Press, 1927–36), "The Influence of the Audience on Shakespeare's Drama." E. K. Chambers, an invaluable researcher into Elizabethan archives, insists that the tired old question of the nineteenth century, "Was Hamlet mad?" is "not merely insoluble; it cannot even be propounded in an intelligible guise" (E. K. Chambers, ed., *The Tragedy of Hamlet*, London: Blackie, 1894). The German scholar Levin L. Schücking studies ways in which Shakespeare strives more for vivid dramatic effects than for coherence, partly because the brutally Gothic nature of his primitive source story has not been fully assimilated into *Hamlet*'s Christian European world (*Character Problems in Shakespeare's Plays*, 1917, translated, London: G.G. Harrap, 1922).

The title of Edgar Elmer Stoll's *Art and Artifice in Shakespeare* (1933, London: Methuen, 1963) suggests a rigorously historical commitment to the idea that reliable factual scholarship should not allow itself to be seduced by moral, biographical, or psychological interpretation. A play, he argues, is an artifice arising out of a particular historical milieu. Its structure and method are governed by a set of conventions to which the playwright, the actors, and the spectators implicitly agree. To be ignorant in our modern age of these conventions is to invite anachronism and romantic flimflam. Following this principle, Stoll deduces that *Hamlet* is not a play about moral scruples or psychological paralysis; it is instead a revenge story constructed out of certain conventional revenge motifs and reshaped by the resourceful dramatist. Hamlet's delay serves the purpose of testing Claudius's guilt; it is a device needed to carry the story forward to its exciting conclusion. Postponing the catastrophe is a stratagem often found in blood tragedies, as in Sophocles's *Oedipus the King* (see Stoll's *Hamlet: An Historical and Comparative Study*, Minneapolis: University of Minnesota Press,1919).

Lily Bess Campbell, in *Shakespeare's Tragic Heroes: Slaves of Passion* (New York: Barnes & Noble, 1952), pursues a similarly historical line of argument: a play like *Hamlet* cannot be adequately understood without a knowledge of Elizabethan ideas on melancholy and the moral function of tragedy in offering consolation for grief. *Hamlet*, she argues, is a study in the passion of grief, in Fortinbras and in Laertes no less than in Hamlet himself. Claudius and Gertrude represent the mortal sin of allowing passion to overwhelm reason.

Historical scholarship of the twentieth century has added greatly to our knowledge of dramaturgy on Shakespeare's stage and has introduced many lively debates. John Dover Wilson (*What Happens in Hamlet*, 1935) takes exception to the work of some historical scholars like Schücking who insist that Shakespeare, in refashioning an old story and an old play, has not succeeded in fusing the old with the new. Wilson's intent is to show that Shakespeare knew what he was doing. Wilson asks a number of probing questions. "What is the dramatic purpose of the long conversation between Hamlet and the First Player immediately before the play ["The Murder of Gonzago"] begins? Why is the play preceded by a dumb show? Why does not Claudius show any signs of discomfiture at this dumb show, which is a more complete representation of the circumstances of the murder than the play which follows it? What is Hamlet's object in making the murderer the nephew and not the brother of the king?" These are essentially dramaturgical questions of the sort not often asked before Wilson posed them, and they are ones that demand an extensive knowledge of early modern culture as well as of theatrical conditions.

No less intriguing is the question for which Wilson's book is perhaps best known: does Hamlet suddenly perceive, through some noise or movement backstage, that he is being eavesdropped upon by the King and Polonius as he converses with Ophelia, and is this discovery the explanation as to why he turns on her suddenly with "Get thee to a nunnery" and "Where's your father?"? (3.1.122–31). Wilson insists that some such stage action is implied and necessary. This present book, in chapter 2, has argued that an Elizabethan audience probably would not need such stage business because the audience would be able to see everything, including the hidden eavesdroppers; but that is not the point here. Wilson's position on the matter is not as important as the kinds of questions he is now posing.[4]

Historical criticism can provide a useful way of thinking about ghosts and other spirits. We need to get over the anachronistic notion, in Wilson's view, that Shakespeare and his audience were generally skeptical of ghosts. Eleanor Prosser, in *Hamlet and Revenge* (Stanford: Stanford University Press, 1967), also urges that we must attempt to understand such metaphysical matters in Elizabethan terms, although she arrives at a very different and more problematic conclusion. When we accept that the world of *Hamlet* is a Christian world, says Prosser, then we must acknowledge that the ghost of Hamlet's father is "demonic" and that his commandment of revenge should not be obeyed. Most critics (including myself) find this too simplified a view of revenge in *Hamlet*, but Prosser is at least asking an important question.

Historical information on Shakespeare's intellectual and cultural background is especially relevant to *Hamlet*, with its searching inquiries into so many philosophical matters. Theodore Spencer's *Shakespeare and the Nature of Man* (New York: Macmillan, 1942) discusses Shakespeare's indebtedness to challenging new thinkers in the Renaissance like Machiavelli, Montaigne, and Copernicus. Hamlet's generalizing mind is much preoccupied with the question of humankind's place in the cosmos. What books has Shakespeare been reading when he has Hamlet discourse on "this goodly frame, the earth," "this most excellent canopy, the air," "this brave o'erhanging firmament, this majestical roof fretted with golden fire," all of which now seem to him only "a foul and pestilent congregation of vapors" (2.2.299–304)? Spencer suggests Thomas Digges's free translation of Copernicus in his *Perfect Description of the Celestial Orbs* (1576) as one possible answer, along with the writings of neoplatonists like Pico della Mirandola (1463–94), in his *Oration on the Dignity of Man*. In view of the importance of melancholy in *Hamlet*, should we read carefully a treatise on the subject by Dr André Du Laurens called *Of the Diseases of Melancholy*, published in 1599, shortly before Shakespeare wrote *Hamlet*? Where do Shakespeare's ideas on Reason and Nature come from? What did he need to know about classical stoicism to enable him to write so insightfully about Hamlet's admiration for Horatio as "one, in suffering all, that suffers nothing, / A man that Fortune's buffets and rewards / Hast ta'en with equal thanks" (3.2.65–7)? A. O. Lovejoy's *The Great Chain of Being* (1936) is another rich source of background information on *Hamlet*'s intellectual universe.[5]

The so-called "New" Criticism, championed in the 1930s and afterwards by G. Wilson Knight, D. A. Traversi, L. C. Knights, and others, mounted a frontal assault on historical criticism, thereby ushering in what was often to become a century of confrontational debate centered on seemingly irreconcilable ideological oppositions. The New Criticism was a revisionary movement, championed by those for whom traditional historical research was the purview of the academic Establishment and a hidebound educational curriculum that unduly valorized research skills in historical archives and the acquisition of many dead languages. As such it was too often dry, philological, lifeless, out of touch with ways in which Shakespeare should affect us by his poetic power. The New Critics insisted that criticism pay close attention to poetry and language without the encumbrance of lengthy historical or biographical research.

G. Wilson Knight accordingly reads *Hamlet* as centered thematically around images of "an unweeded garden," a "prison," a "pestilent congregation of vapors," a "quintessence of dust," all of this silhouetted against a superficial courtly world of gaiety and color (*The Wheel of Fire*, London: Oxford University Press, 1930). Lesser but still powerful image patterns call our attention to "clouds," "windy," "fruitful river," a "sea of troubles," oceans, tempests, all "Mad as the sea and wind" (*The Shakespearian Tempest*, London: Oxford University Press, 1932). Derek Traversi sees Shakespeare, after having written *Troilus and Cressida*, as struggling in *Hamlet* "to reduce to order a whole group of disturbing impressions, to give them ordered significance in a balanced work." By uniting in one character the metaphysical and the human in a common experience, Shakespeare provides us with greater "poetic mastery" and "dramatic power" than ever before in his writings (*An Approach to Shakespeare*, 3rd ed., London: Hollis & Carter, 1968–9).

T. S. Eliot, though he also praises the historical critic E. E. Stoll for confuting the "character" interpretations of Goethe and Coleridge, insightfully anticipates some of the preoccupations of New Criticism in his analysis of *Hamlet*'s failure to achieve an "objective correlative": Hamlet is dominated by "an emotion which is inexpressible, because it is in *excess* of the facts as they appear" ("Hamlet and His Problems," *Selected Essays, 1917–1932*, 1932). L. C. Knights reads Hamlet as self-indulgent and neurotic; the play itself is a compromise between an "objective study of a peculiar kind of immaturity" and "a spontaneous and uncritical expression of Shakespeare's own unconscious feelings." One can be clear-sighted about Hamlet's weaknesses and yet experience a "lively dramatic sympathy" (*Explorations*, London: Chatto & Windus, 1946). Histrionic and even melodramatic postures impress upon us "the static quality of Hamlet's consciousness" (*An Approach to Hamlet*, London: Chatto & Windus, 1960). Harry Levin examines in *Hamlet* a dialectic structure of "thesis, antithesis, synthesis" achieved through "interrogation, doubt, irony." Hamlet's ironic viewpoint becomes the synthesis through which we can attempt to comprehend the play's pervasive questionings (*The Question of Hamlet*, 1959).

Common to these critical investigations are an interest in tone, imagery, verbal texture, and dramatic construction. They are roughly contemporary with the developments we have seen in the theatre toward experimental rejection of traditional Victorian interpretations based on lofty appraisals of moral character. Caroline F. E. Spurgeon's *Shakespeare's Imagery and What It Tells Us* (Cambridge: Cambridge University Press, 1935) provided New Critics with a storehouse of image patterns in *Hamlet*, as noted also by G. Wilson Knight above: diseases, blisters, ulcers, mildewed ears, apoplexies, and self-deceptions that "will but skin and film the ulcerous place, / Whiles rank corruption, mining all within, / Infects unseen" (3.4.154–6). Wolfgang Clemen's *The Development of Shakespeare's Imagery* (London: Methuen, 1951) adds to imagery study the perspective of how imagery changes in the course of Shakespeare's writing career and how *Hamlet* occupies a pivotal position in that pattern of development. Nigel Alexander, in *Poison, Play, and Duel: A Study in "Hamlet"* (London: Routledge & Kegan Paul, 1971), focuses on the three images of his title as controlling the play's structure and language. Maurice Charney's *Style in "Hamlet"* (1969) enlarges the scope of imagery analysis to include the visual: that is to say, stage picture, actors' gesture, and all that happens in the theatre. These matters are further explored in Charles Forker's "Shakespeare's Theatrical Symbolism and Its Function in *Hamlet*" (*Shakespeare Quarterly* 14, 1963, 215–29). For Inga-Stina Ewbank, language is a major thematic concern through which we can explore the possibilities and limitations of speech in *Hamlet* ("Shakespeare and the Power of Words," *Shakespeare Survey* 30 (1977), 85–102). C. S. Lewis, though hardly a New Critic as defined here, gives a thematic reading of the play as about fear and doubt generated by the unanswerable questions that death poses concerning human life and the nature of the cosmos (*Hamlet, the Prince or the Poem*, British Academy Lecture, 1942).

Psychological interpretation of *Hamlet* becomes a staple of Shakespeare criticism in the twentieth century, for the obvious reason that to many readers Hamlet seems to have a problem of delay. Freud bases his analysis of that problem, in *The Interpretation of Dreams* (1899, 3rd ed., translated by A.A. Brill, New York: Macmillan, 1911), on his newly formulated theory of the unconscious, according to which Hamlet is driven by an unacknowledged incestuous desire for his mother and is accordingly unable to punish his uncle for having done the very thing that Hamlet himself subconsciously wishes to commit, that is, sleep with Gertrude. Freud gives to this unresolved psychological dilemma the name of "Oedipus complex," in recollection of the ancient classical myth, as dramatized by Sophocles in his *Oedipus the King*, of the tragic hero whose fate it is to discover that he has killed his own father and married his mother. Ernest Jones elaborates this theory in his *Hamlet and Oedipus*, as we saw above. Freud sees his interpretation as a great advancement in psychoanalytic theory, not only as a new reading of *Hamlet* but more fundamentally as a way of understanding a shift in human civilization from an early, archaic culture in which parricidal and incestuous desires were acted upon to a more modern culture in which those feelings are repressed.

In a sense the psychological analysis of Freud and Jones is a continuation of the "character" criticism of the nineteenth century, asking essentially the same question as did Goethe and Coleridge: why does Hamlet delay? Freud rightly insists that he has formulated a bold new way of understanding human motivation, but his presupposition that Hamlet's delay is the result of an emotional imbalance unduly limits the field of critical examination. The classical dictum that a great tragedy must have, in Aristotle's terms, a *hamartia* or "tragic flaw" also encourages too easily the explanation that Hamlet's delay is his tragic flaw. But what if Shakespeare was not thinking in Aristotelean terms and did not necessarily regard such a "flaw" as the key to understanding Hamlet's tragedy? Or what if we translate Aristotle's *hamartia* as "tragic error" or "mistake," rather than as "tragic flaw"?

Given their presupposition, psychologically oriented critics do provide a range of possible interpretations to the celebrated question of delay. K. R. Eissler's *Discourse on Hamlet and "Hamlet,"* 1971, learnedly reviews the extensive critical literature on Hamlet's supposed madness, pointing out that the first intimations of emotional imbalance come from what Horatio says about Hamlet's "wild and whirling words" (1.5.139), not from Hamlet himself. Similarly, Hamlet's feigned madness is a motif of the plot derived from Saxo Grammaticus, a story in which the hero is anything but hesitant to enact his bloody revenge. Eissler allows some plausibility in Freud's and Jones's Oedipal interpretation but sets it off against a simpler reading of "the manifest content of the play" in which Hamlet bungles his opportunities; the result overall is that Shakespeare makes "at least two readings possible, and at that, two quite opposite ones." Avi Erlich proposes quite a different reading from that of Freud and Jones, as implied in Erlich's title, *Hamlet's Absent Father* (1977), namely, that Hamlet's greatest emotional longing is for a strong authority figure who can replace the lost father and thus recover for Hamlet his sense of personal identity. Polonius, Old Fortinbras, Priam, Achilles, Osric, Yorick, and even Horatio are all insufficient fathers in their various ways.

Theodore Lidz gives a lucid account, in his *Hamlet's Enemy: Madness and Myth in "Hamlet"* (1975), of the psychiatrist's attraction to *Hamlet* and the various modifications that have been offered to Freud's Oedipus Complex theory as related to the role of the family in intra-psychic conflicts, adding his own emphasis on what we can learn psychologically from the myth of Hamlet as found in Saxo Grammaticus, in the story of Lucius Junius Brutus as founder of Rome's republic, in Euripides's *Orestes*, in Suetonius's account of *The Lives of the Twelve Emperors*, in Nero's incestuous attachment to his mother, in Kyd's *The Spanish Tragedy*, and in the Fool of folk drama, all of this germane to a study of Ophelia and the female "Oedipal" transition. Norman N. Holland, in *Shakespeare's Personality* (Berkeley: University of California Press, 1989), asks what we can perhaps learn about the author himself from the way he depicts Oedipal conflict.[6]

A correlative line of investigation has been that of mythological criticism. This method offers a way of exploring, anthropologically and psychologically, the "collective unconscious" of the human race. In part, the movement traces its intellectual origins to the Swiss psychologist Carl Jung (1875-1961). Gilbert Murray's *Hamlet and Orestes: A Study in Traditional Types* (British Academy Annual Shakespeare Lecture for 1914) studies the archetype of revenging the murder of a father as an ancient and tribal custom. Such an investigation can give to *Hamlet* an anthropological universality, seeing his struggle in terms of the primitive and the civilized on both an inner and societal level. Francis Fergusson similarly looks at *Hamlet* in the context of Greek tragedy and ancient ritual, arguing that the Elizabethan theatre fostered a myth-ritual pattern; *Hamlet* in these terms can be understood as a species of ritual drama drawing much of its psychic force from "a great deal of the religious culture of the Middle Ages" that "was still alive in Shakespeare's time" (*The Idea of a Theater*, 1949). Northrop Frye pursues an archetypal line of investigation in his *Anatomy of Criticism* (Princeton: Princeton University Press, 1957), *A Natural Perspective: The Development of Shakespearean Comedy and Romance*

(New York: Columbia University Press, 1965), and *Fools of Time: Studies in Shakespearean Tragedy* (Toronto: University of Toronto Press, 1967), showing how we respond unconsciously to mythic patterns in our culture by communal participation in drama. All drama celebrates in one form or another the primal myths of seasonal change and rebirth, expressing culturally a constant cyclical movement. In these terms, *Hamlet* is appropriately autumnal, wintry, melancholic. Robert Ornstein picks up nicely on this idea in his "The Mystery of Hamlet: Notes Toward an Archetypal Solution" (*College English*, 1959), in which he proposes that Hamlet "is a ritual scapegoat" with a particularly modern twist: "he is Dying God *as* Juvenile Delinquent." John Holloway examines *Hamlet* from an anthropological point of view in *The Story of the Night: Studies in Shakespeare's Major Tragedies* (London: Routledge & Kegan Paul, 1961).

Two particularly impressive studies of *Hamlet* can perhaps suggest ways in which the critical approaches surveyed thus far need not, and indeed should not, maintain themselves on separate courses. Maynard Mack, in "The World of *Hamlet*" (*Yale Review*, 41 (1952), 502–23), looks at that world not in the narrow geographical sense of Denmark but in the artistic and theatrical sense of "the imaginative environment that the play asks us to enter." This is a world dominated by the interrogative mood, reverberating with questions, doubts, enigmas, riddles, and mysteries, all forcing upon us a painful awareness of the problematic nature of reality. Shakespeare's choice of key words, such as "apparition," "seems," "assume," "put on," "shape," "show," "act," and "play" underscores uncertainty and puzzlement, on Hamlet's part and on ours. Hamlet's greatest task, and ours as well, is to come to terms with such a world and learn thereby to understand what it is to be human. Mack's interpretation of *Hamlet* is thus vividly attuned to image patterns and verbal details, as in the New Criticism that Mack knew well enough from teaching at Yale, but it is also informed by a larger moral vision hearkening back to the best of what A. C. Bradley had to say about the play.

Fredson Bowers's "Hamlet as Minister and Scourge" (*PMLA*, 70 (1955), 740–9) is also closely attentive to language, especially in the scene of Hamlet's confronting his mother about her marriage. "Heaven hath pleased it so / To punish me with this, and this with me, / That I must be their scourge and minister" (3.4.182) points to Hamlet's realization that he must (as scourge) pay a just retribution to heaven for having killed a man, even while he has unwittingly been heaven's agent or minister in meting out to Polonius a fate that the old man has brought on himself. Bowers shows how the rest of *Hamlet* plays out just as Hamlet has here predicted: Ophelia goes mad, Laertes returns to Denmark, a duel is fought, and at last all accounts are settled, in a way that Hamlet could not have planned. Both essays combine careful close reading with a well-informed historical perspective and with a complex awareness of the play's overall architectonic shape.

The work of Mack and Bowers, then, along with that of Stoll, Campbell, Wilson, Spencer, Knight, Traversi, Knights, Eliot, Spurgeon, Erlich, Murray, Fergusson, and others can provide some indication cumulatively of what twentieth-century criticism down to about 1980 has to offer in the way of historical, new critical, psychological, and mythological perspectives on *Hamlet*, much as A. C. Bradley can stand as a summary and capstone of nineteenth-century character criticism. In a similar way, the stage and film productions of Poel, Granville-Barker, Ben Greet, Jackson, Ayliff, Benthall, Guthrie, Olivier, Burton, Hall, Williamson, and others, rebelling against but also partly absorbing the work of traditionalists like Barrymore, Evans, and Gielgud, embody innovative and rapidly changing commentary on the cultures in which they were fashioned. Still to come was the brave new world of the 1980s, 1990s, and 2000s, carrying even further the processes of experimentalism and social critique in Shakespeare production and interpretation. It is to these three most recent decades that we turn for the current story of postmodern *Hamlet*.

7

There Is Nothing Either Good or Bad But Thinking Makes It So: Postmodern *Hamlet*

The year 1980 is, of course, an approximation in marking the advent of postmodern *Hamlet* as well as postmodern everything else, but it will perhaps do as well as any other. In that year, Stephen Greenblatt published his epochal *Renaissance Self-Fashioning: From More to Shakespeare*, quickly hailed as model and archetype of the so-called New Historicism. Taking its inspiration in part from revisionist historians like Lawrence Stone (*The Crisis of the Aristocracy, 1558–1641*, 1965) and cultural anthropologists like Clifford Geertz (*Negara: The Theatre State in Nineteenth-Century Bali*, 1980), this critical school fixed its gaze on government as an organism devoted to the manipulating of illusions, using the public ceremonials of statecraft as the means of engendering self-fulfilling myths of control and power. The approach was inherently skeptical of political authority. In California, at least, where many of the early New Historicists studied and taught, the movement was a response to the new Great Communicator on the scene, Governor (later President) Ronald Reagan. It was closely parallel to and allied with the critical movement known as Cultural Materialism, then making its presence known in the United Kingdom in the work of Jonathan Dollimore (*Radical Tragedy*, 1984), Dollimore and Alan Sinfield (*Political Shakespeare*, 1985), John Drakakis (*Alternative Shakespeares*, 1985), Terry Eagleton (*Shakespeare and Society*, 1967; *William Shakespeare*, 1986), and others. These critics, who generally regarded Raymond Williams as their spiritual father, taught mostly in the new universities of the United Kingdom, not at Oxford or

Cambridge, and were thus avowedly anti-Establishment and class-conscious in their ideology. More than the New Historicists in the United States, they tended to promote radical political interpretation of literary texts in the cause of rapid political and cultural change.

More or less concurrently, feminism as a critical movement loomed into new prominence. The year 1980 saw the publication of a landmark collection of essays edited by Carolyn Ruth Swift Lenz, Gayle Greene, and Carol Thomas Neely called *The Woman's Part: Feminist Criticism of Shakespeare*. The feminist movement itself was not new, of course, but in the world of teaching and scholarship it caught the revolutionary spirit that was in the air in the early 1980s. Appointments of women to college and university faculties, long in abeyance since the days of the Suffragette movement in the early twentieth century, when a few women had become professional scholars, now began to achieve some momentum. Juliet Dusinberre's *Shakespeare and the Nature of Women*, first published in 1975, became a beacon of inspiration for other feminist scholars, including Lisa Jardine, whose *Still Harping on Daughters* (1983) adopted a defiant stance towards the repression and oppression of women in Shakespeare's plays, including Gertrude and Ophelia in *Hamlet*. Marianne Novy's *Love's Argument: Gender Relations in Shakespeare* (1984) and Carol Thomas Neely's *Broken Nuptials in Shakespeare* (1985) followed soon after.

Meantime, the school of criticism known as post-structuralism or deconstruction burst upon the scene, first at Yale University, where the linguistic and semiotic concepts of Ferdinand de Saussure, Michel Foucault, and Jacques Derrida were imported from Europe to insist that language is a system of difference in which the signifiers (i.e., words and gestures) are essentially arbitrary. "Meaning" and "authorial intent" are ultimately impossible to determine. Instead of the once-familiar author of literary tradition, we now had multiple points of view, indeterminacy of meaning, and a multiplicity of texts. The method of linguistic analysis known as "speech–act theory," developed by the philosopher J. L. Austin, offered ways of exploring language as a series of linguistic acts. At its best, as in Patricia Parker and Geoffrey Hartman's *Shakespeare and the Question of Theory* (1985), the new deconstructive method facilitated a flexibility of linguistic meaning able to uncover new resonances of verbal play in what Shakespeare wrote. Chapter 5 of Parker's *Shakespeare from the Margins: Language, Culture, Context* (Chicago: University of Chicago

Press, 1996) explores in *Hamlet* the resonant language of conveyance, translation, and representation in deconstructing meaning and interpretation.

Textual scholarship soon picked up on the excitement of the post-modern revolution with Gary Taylor and Michael Warren's edited collection of essays called *The Division of the Kingdoms* (Oxford: Clarendon Press, 1983), insisting that *King Lear* exists in not one but two early texts, each with its own integrity. The implications for *Hamlet*, with its three early texts, were soon being explored by Bernice Kliman, Paul Bertram, Ann Thompson, and Neil Taylor, among others; see chapter 3 and the suggestions of further reading for that chapter. The battle cry of postmodern editing, that we need to acknowledge the existence of multiple texts rather than a single text, thus marched in tandem with the insistence on indeterminacy of meaning that is the premise of deconstructive analysis, just as the critical move to set aside canonical definitions of literary greatness and to interpret a work of art as caught up in the social practices of its time bears a close resemblance to recent performance history. These developments are thus all part of a large movement of reassessment.[1]

The new critical movements of the 1980s were quickly at odds with more established forms of critical discourse and with one another. At a meeting of the Modern Language Association in New York in December, 1976, an overflow audience listened raptly to a debate between Hillis Miller, championing the new deconstructive method, and Meyer Abrams, insisting that deconstruction opens the floodgates to total indeterminacy of language by allowing any utterance to mean what the speaker or listener or reader wishes it to mean. Wayne Booth took part as well. (The papers were published subsequently in *Critical Inquiry*.) At a meeting of the Shakespeare Association of America in Boston in 1988, in a session on "Feminism vs. New Historicism," the feminist critics (Lynda Boose and Kathleen McLuskie) declared war on the New Historicists (represented on the panel by Louis Montrose) for paying little or no attention to issues of concern to women. Some New Historicists were taken aback and even hurt by this antagonism: could not feminists and New Historicists unite in a common cause against the older and more traditional modes of literary analysis? Yet the feminists had a point, in that few New Historicists at that time were women (Leah Marcus's *Puzzling Shakespeare* would not appear until 1988, Annabel Patterson's *Shakespeare and the Popular Voice* in 1989), and the concerns of the New Historicists were predominantly political in ways that men found particularly fascinating. Easier for the New Historicists was to declare war on the critical formalism of the by-now-no-longer-new "New" Critics. Literary study needed to focus on historical context and social practice. When Greenblatt inaugurated the journal *Representations* at Berkeley in 1983, the Shakespeare world understood that formalist critics need not apply.

Hamlet was certain to be a crucial text for the new schools of literary theory and analysis. A case in point is Stephen Greenblatt's *Hamlet in Purgatory* (2001), discussed earlier in chapter 3. Greenblatt picks up on the Ghost's account of his sojourn in Purgatory in act 1, scene 5, as he and Hamlet encounter each other on the battlements of Elsinore Castle. Purgatory is not named as such, but the Ghost's meaning is unmistakable in his reference to his being "Doomed for a certain term to walk the night / And for the day confined to fast in fires, / Till the foul crimes done in my days of nature / Are burnt and purged away" (1.5.11–14). Greenblatt's new historical method is to surround this interview with a rich store of information about late medievalism and the sixteenth-century English Renaissance, when the newly estab-lished Anglican Church did away with the doctrine of Purgatory as part of a Protestant effort to redeem Christianity from the "false" accretions of what were regarded as centuries-old instances of Roman Catholic abuse. One major result, Greenblatt notes, is that ordinary Christians, long taught to seek salvation through the church and through the intercession of the saints and the Virgin Mary, now found themselves deprived of this consoling large and family-like structure of support. Individual Christians were now more on their own, not only for themselves but for their dearly departed loved ones. Chantries erected in churches to endow prayers for the dead in perpetuity were no longer allowed in England, along with monas-teries, abbeys, and other institutions once able to assist in commemor-ation of the dead. Favorite legends about ghosts, saints' lives, pilgrimages, and the like were under attack as superstition by the reformers, as in Reginald Scot's *Discovery of Witchcraft* (1584) and Samuel Harsnett's soon-to-be-published *Declaration of Egregious Popish Impostures* (1603).

Greenblatt details the rise and fall of Purgatory as an institution, both as a doctrine and as a source of income for the Roman church. With its demise, as Greenblatt shows, an enormously comforting means of negotiating with the dead was suddenly taken away, leaving in its wake a longing for remembrance of, and contact with, the dead that had to be met by other means. The book is thus "New Historicist" in its analysis of how English culture, and implicitly other cultures as well, go about dealing with change and loss, and how literature—here, drama in particular—serves a particularly vital function. Purgatory was for the late medieval world a piece of poetry, as Greenblatt sees it. Its presence in *Hamlet* bespeaks a kind of "magical necessity" for which tragedy provides the ideal genre. The play becomes a showpiece for what Clifford Geertz calls "cultural poetics."[2]

An early landmark in gender studies in the postmodern era is Coppélia Kahn's *Man's Estate: Masculine Identity in Shakespeare* (1981, pp. 132–40), taking a careful and enlightening look at the hazards faced by young males as they consider how to fulfill their quest for adult male sexuality and thus eventually take the place of their fathers. Hamlet is a prominent example. His struggle to achieve self-understanding is immensely complicated by his father's death, his mother's sexual disloyalty, Hamlet's consequent sense of shame in being the son of a cuckolded husband, and his conflicted feelings for a young woman whose behavior seems to confirm all his misogynist revulsions toward the entire sex: "Frailty, thy name is woman!" (1.2.146). Marjorie Garber, whose *Coming of Age in Shakespeare* was published in the same year, asks similar questions about sexual maturation and about Hamlet's obsessive comparing and contrasting of himself with others, including Hercules and Phaethon (pp. 198–215).

Important to these and later feminist critics were such anthropological studies as Claude Lévi-Strauss's *The Elementary Structures of Kinship* (1949, translated into English in 1969), with its analysis of the cultural practice of patriarchal males who marry their daughters to men outside the tribe in order to promote "exogamous" business ties beneficial to the patriarchal structure; and Victor Turner's *The Ritual Process*, 1969, itself indebted to the work of Arnold van Gennep (*The Rites of Passage*, translated, 1960), describing the hazardous transitions of birth, puberty, marriage, and death, especially when young women find themselves facing the challenge of transferring their allegiances and whole way of life from one male-dominated family to another. As applied to Ophelia in *Hamlet*, this approach offers sympathy for a young woman caught between dominant males in conflict with one another (Polonius, Hamlet, Laertes), to all of whom her feelings of attachment are strong.

Gertrude faces a similar dilemma in her uncomfortable position as a dowager queen, dependent now on the support of her new husband and yet unable to appease the son whom she bore in her marriage with her now-dead spouse. Lawrence Stone's *The Family, Sex, and Marriage in England, 1500–1800* (1977) also provided a wealth of information on social history for new feminist studies of Shakespeare.

In "Man and Wife Is One Flesh: *Hamlet* and the Confrontation with the Maternal Body," 1992, Janet Adelman builds on the earlier work of Coppélia Kahn. Despite the differences between old Hamlet and his murderous brother Claudius, argues Adelman, the fathers in this play "keep threatening to collapse into one another, annihilating in their collapse the son's easy assumption of his father's identity." In its dual portrayal of Gertrude and Ophelia, moreover, "the play conflates the beloved with the betraying mother, undoing the strategies that had enabled marriage in the comedies." The structure of *Hamlet* "is marked by the struggle to escape from this condition, to free the masculine identity of both father and son from its origin in the contaminated maternal body." The image of the mother is thus bifurcated into the familiar Freudian opposites of "virgin and whore, closed or open, wholly pure or wholly corrupt." This essay demonstrates, as does the work of Kahn and some others, the fruitful crossover between psychological and feminist criticism.[3]

Postmodern psychoanalytic criticism of *Hamlet* tends to follow and extend the theories of Freud, Ernest Jones, K. R. Eissler, Avi Erlich, Theodore Lidz, and others detailed in the previous chapter. John Russell's *Hamlet and Narcissus* (1995) is a post-Freudian reading of "the failure of the mother" and its impact on Hamlet as a consequence of the crucial relationship "between the infant and its maternal environment." Jacques Lacan, noting the insistent theme of loss and mourning in *Hamlet*, and the manifest inadequacy of the rituals employed to mourn the deaths of old King Hamlet, Polonius, and Ophelia, posits a gap or hole resulting from the primary Oedipal loss that the mourners attempt in vain to remedy (*Écrits*, Paris: Éditions du Seuil, 1966). What Lacan thus describes in psychoanalytic terms bears a striking resemblance to the psychic loss that Greenblatt accounts for historically in the Reformation's abandonment of the comforting doctrine of Purgatory.

For postmodern practitioners of deconstruction, *Hamlet* is a feast of indeterminacy. Jacques Derrida (*Specters of Marx*, translated by Peggy

Kamuf, New York: Routledge, 1994), in a contemporary political analogy addressed to the question of "Whither Marxism?" sees Hamlet's delay as a "waiting without horizon of expectations" for a future so bedeviled by uncertainties that hesitation is the only rational stance for him (or for any modern thoughtful person, faced by a world of underemployment, contradictions in the free market, and economic war) to adopt. Only the language of deconstruction can find a way to deal with the complex binaries of life and death, matter and spirit. Aaron Landau's "'Let Me Not Burst in Ignorance': Skepticism and Anxiety in Hamlet" (*English Studies* 82, 2001, 218–29) argues for a "comprehensiveness and instability of ideological systems in the play" that encourages critics "to come to many different conclusions about *Hamlet*'s religious content." The very indeterminacy of ideological meaning is a distinct asset to the play: it encourages audiences and readers to find questions rather than answers. Hamlet's anxiety about ascertaining the guilt of Claudius is an essential part of his relationship with the stoical and skeptical Horatio. The marked difference between Hamlet's own Christian-providential interpretation of his own story and Horatio's secular reading of that same story in act 5 leaves the play where it should reside, in the realm of mystery and uncertainty.

Howard Felperin provides a foundational deconstructive analysis of *Hamlet* in his *The Uses of the Canon: Elizabethan Literature and Contemporary Theory* (Oxford, 1990, pp. 1–15), according to which the play may be imagined to reflect eighteenth-century London or twentieth-century Berkeley just as plausibly as medieval Denmark; its notions of mimesis, nature, and history "are no more secure or self-evident" in Hamlet's speech on these topics "than they are in the diverse discourses of drama—classical, medieval, Renaissance—on which he somewhat indiscriminately draws."[4]

A major critique of modern literary theory is to be found in Margreta de Grazia's *"Hamlet" without Hamlet* (2007). De Grazia refreshingly asks if the quest for a modern Hamlet has left us with a protagonist who is "distinguished by an inner being so transcendent that it barely comes into contact with the play from which it emerges." De Grazia spots this critical trend as beginning in the ages of Enlightenment and Romanticism in the late eighteenth and early nineteenth centuries, when Hamlet first becomes a deep and introspective thinker, rather than the action hero of a tale of dispossession and revenge. Modern deconstructive or psychological criticism simply continues the one-sided emphasis on Hamlet's personal angst. The basic premise of the play, de Grazia insists, needs to be foregrounded instead: namely, that the son of a murdered father, entitled by the patrilineal system to inherit his father's throne, has had that inheritance stolen away from him by his villainous uncle. Though obliged at first to keep silent about his wrongs, Hamlet never forgets that Claudius has "Popped in between th'election and my hopes" (5.2.65). The regicide and usurpation have broken his needed attachment to his land of Denmark. The play is filled with contests over land, involving Norway, Poland, and, of course, Denmark. Modern criticism, argues de Grazia, has largely forgotten Hamlet's investment in these things.

De Grazia's title, then, *"Hamlet" without Hamlet*, with its wordplay on the common expression, "Hamlet without the Prince," is not a call for criticism to detach the protagonist from his play, but quite the opposite. Her project is to search not for the play's original meaning (whatever that might be), but for what it can mean today when we strip away the critical errors imposed on the play by Romantic sensibilities of two hundred years and more. To do this will be to take away the "monadic exclusivity" that alienates Hamlet from the rest of the play and thereby restore to him the complexity and centrality that he should enjoy in the context of the whole work. De Grazia's study is thus not a throwback; it is fully modern in the process of redefining what "modern" should mean in an interpretation of Shakespeare's great play. It requires sensitivity to meanings of words often concealed from modern readers, like "hide" denoting a measurement of land as well as a skin, or "Doomsday" in its conjoining of "domain" and "doom," land and judgment, or "groundlings" as a name for those who pay ground rent for a place to stand in the theatre. Some normally rejected readings from the 1603 first quarto, like "guyana" for "Vienna" in the second quarto and the Folio at 3.2.236, and "Nor Turke" for "nor man" or "or Norman" at 3.2.32, take on new and plausible value for de Grazia in light of the play's incessant wordplay and fascination with periods of decline in human history. De Grazia's insight is invaluable: *Hamlet* began to look "modern" in the nineteenth century because his presumed psychological makeup was perceived then as modern, but the time has come today to reinvent Shakespeare's *Hamlet* in the light of a modernism that can see the whole play and its protagonist in as multiple a cultural context as the play deserves.

Many stage productions of *Hamlet* in the early 1980s manifested the intellectual and political preoccupations of the postmodern generation of critics coming into prominence at about the same time. Jan Kott's *Shakespeare Our Contemporary* (translated from the Polish punningly titled *Szkice o Szekspirze* in 1964), responding to the profound disillusionment especially in Eastern Europe in the aftermath of World War II, had already galvanized the world of theatre with its apocalyptic vision of a civilization on the brink of disaster. His concept of *Hamlet*, as indeed of other Shakespeare plays as well, was of a bleak comedy of the absurd through which "we ought to get at our modern experience, anxiety and sensibility." *Hamlet* for Kott is "only a drama of political crime," centered on a young protagonist who is "deeply involved in politics, sarcastic, passionate and brutal," a "young rebel who has about him something of the charm of James Dean" and for whom "action, not reflection, is his forte" (pp. 51–65). In his absurdist reading of cultural nihilism, Kott was attuned to the powerfully influential existentialist philosophy of Jean Paul Sartre and Albert Camus, the revisionary theatrical concepts of Antonin Artaud (*The Theater and Its Double*, 1958) and Jerzy Grotowski (*Towards a Poor Theatre*, 1968), and such absurdist plays as Eugène Ionesco's *The Chairs* (translated by Martin Crimp, London: Faber & Faber, 1997) and *The Bald Soprano* (New York: Grove Press, 1958). These challenging ideas had been around since the end of World War II, and had shown themselves, as we have seen in the previous chapter, in stage and film productions by Grigori Kozintsev, Peter Hall, Tony Richardson, Buzz Goodbody, and others. Now, in the early 1980s, the tempo of protest accelerated in the climate of postmodern revolution.

Jonathan Miller envisaged his austere production of *Hamlet* at London's Warehouse Theatre in 1982 as portraying a world in which "politics are a game and a lie." Miller unheroically conceived of his protagonist, played by Anton Lesser, as "a rather unattractive character, a tiresome, clever, destructive boy who is very intelligent but volatile, dirty-minded and immature." Claudius for Miller was "a sort of Prussian *Junker*" (*Subsequent Performances*, New York: Viking, 1986, pp. 110–11). Adrian Noble's production of a full-length *Hamlet* for the Royal Shakespeare Company at London's Barbican Theatre and then at Stratford-upon-Avon in 1992–3, with Hamlet played by Kenneth Branagh, employed a Victorian mise en scène only to expose the hollowness of that cultural tradition and the fragmentation of the postmodern world. Glimpses "backstage" of the actors getting ready for their performances in the play-within-the-play called attention to the theatre itself as the centerpiece of Noble's design: everything was staged. In a modern-dress production at Chicago's Wisdom Bridge Theatre in 1985, Robert Falls staged the first court appearance of Claudius (1.2) as a modern media event: Claudius, visible only on two television monitors flanking the stage to left and right, blandly offered political assurances about his new administration in the unmistakable style of President Ronald Reagan, while on stage his political operatives and handsome young women in cocktail dresses were busy preparing a public relations reception for the press.

The Romanian director Alexander Tocilescu, at Bucharest's Bulandra Theatre in 1985, similarly conceived of a Hamlet (played by Ion Caramitru) who coped as heroically as he could with the corrupt regime of Claudius—in other words, of the Stalinist Romanian dictator Nicolai Ceauçescu, who would be executed in 1989. (Caramitru was one of the leaders of the revolution against the government.) Peter Zadek, in a Brechtian German production of 1977 restaged in 1999 (mentioned briefly in the previous chapter), assigned the part of Hamlet to a fifty-year-old actress, Angela Winkler, who portrayed the protagonist as too abused and psychologically crippled to plot a revenge. The stage in Otomar Krejca's version of the play in Düsseldorf (1977) was dominated by a huge mirror; that of Jürgen Flimm in Hamburg (1986) centered visually on a huge wall. In Lin Zhaohua's staging of *Hamlet* in Beijing in 1989–90, the actors playing Hamlet, Claudius, and Polonius exchanged roles at various points in order to underscore the production's emphasis on existential angst unrelieved by a tragic vision; the only permanent prop was a barber's chair, symbolizing at various times a throne, a bed, or a rock beside Ophelia's grave.

Productions of the twenty-first century have continued to innovate. John Caird's concept for his *Hamlet* at London's National Theatre in 2000 and transported to the United States in 2001–2, starring Simon Russell Beale, took the visible form of a huge cross dominating the set. Elimination of the Fortinbras plot focused this version on spiritual and psychological issues. Beale's Hamlet was intelligent, caustic, emotionally wounded, yearning to return to a student's life, awash in grief, disheveled, able at last to confront his enemy in the play's final scene with calm and resolution. The set was both a prison and a cathedral, low-lit and dark, with church-like hanging lanterns and ecclesiastical background music. Sound effects, blocking, and set design were all focused on Caird's central idea of an existential and familial drama.

Mark Rylance, the artistic director of the new Globe Theatre on the Bankside from its completion in 1997 until 2007, played *Hamlet* under the direction of Giles Block in 2000 (see Illustration 18). Rylance portrayed a delicate mind on the brink of clinical depression and even madness, lightened by flashes of wit and whimsical dottiness. In the Globe space that invites chumminess and overstatement, Rylance was resourceful in developing a rapport with audiences. He pointedly hurled at them Hamlet's line about how "groundlings" are "capable of nothing but inexplicable dumb shows," then adding, after they had objected vociferously at this, "*and noise*" (3.2.11–12). Despite swift-paced action on a Jacobean non-scenic stage, the show at three and a half hours was too long for inexperienced playgoers, some of whom were indeed noisy. Reviewers generally felt that Rylance achieved the not inconsiderable feat of creating a subtle and fascinating character in the face of considerable odds.

Illustration 18. Mark Rylance as Hamlet as he considers whether or not to stab Claudius (Tim Woodward) at prayer (3.3), in the Globe Theatre production of 2000 directed by Giles Block. Photograph by Francesca Dalla Pozza. Courtesy of the new Globe Theatre.

Steven Pimlott wrote of the protagonist (played by Samuel West) in his four-hour modern-dress *Hamlet* at Stratford-upon-Avon in 2001 that Hamlet is "a killer. He wants truth at all costs, and the costs, when you think about it, are Ophelia, Claudius, Polonius, Gertrude, etc., etc." The "etc." would of course include Laertes, Rosencrantz, and Guildenstern. This Hamlet belonged to a youth culture rebelling against an unfeeling world. To provide a backdrop for a tale of carnage, the modern setting was drab and grey. The stage was essentially an empty space swept by searchlight-like lighting effects and watched over by surveillance cameras. The "spin doctoring" presided over by a suave Claudius (Larry Lamb) in scene 2 reminded audiences of George W. Bush and Tony Blair. Rosencrantz and Guildenstern offered a marijuana joint to Hamlet. He and the gravediggers in act 5, scene 1 shared beer and sandwiches, then tossed Yorick's skull back and forth as though it were a rugby ball. In the final scene, Hamlet nicked Claudius with his poisoned sword, forced him to drink the poisoned cup, and then shot him with a revolver. When Fortinbras took the seat of royal authority, the courtiers pressed forward, hesitantly at first, then enthusiastically, to show their devotion to the new political order.

At the Birmingham Repertory Theatre and Edinburgh International Festival in 2003, Calixto Bieito's cynical and flippant *Hamlet*, with George Anton in the lead role, emphasized seediness, corruption, surveillance, drug culture, and kinky abuse. Michael Bogdanov, who had previously directed *Hamlet* in 1977–8 for the Young Vic, staged the play again in 2005 at the Grand Theatre, Swansea, in a production that took aim at aggressive war in Iraq and around the globe. Philip Bowen, as Hamlet, found himself in a world of insane competition for wealth and power.

The Wooster Group's production of the play at New York's Public Theater, 2007, and in other locations, took as its inspiration the Gielgud–Burton *Hamlet* of 1964 (see previous chapter). Under the direction of Elizabeth LeCompte, fleeting film images of Burton on screen were juxtaposed with Scott Shepherd as Hamlet and other actors on stage—Ari Fliakos as Claudius, Marcellus, and Ghost, and Kate Valk as both Gertrude and Ophelia—giving solid form to the evanescent phantoms behind them. The effect, as Ben Brantley wrote for the *New York Times* on November 1, was that of "an aching tribute to the ephemerality of greatness in theater."

Jude Law's Hamlet, as directed by Michael Grandage first at the Donmar Warehouse in London and Elsinore Castle and then at New York's Broadhurst Theatre opening on September 12 in 2009, was bound to be a media sensation; after all, Law had been named among the Top Ten most bankable Hollywood movie stars in 2006, as well as being one of the most handsome males in show business. With many successes on stage and in film, Law has gone on more recently still (2009–10) to the role of Doctor Watson in Guy Ritchie's film adaptation of *Sherlock Holmes*. For John Lahr, reviewing the Broadway production in the 19 October 2009 issue of *The New Yorker*, this "slick, streamlined three-hour production" did not reach the level of "inspired nuance" of David Warner or Jonathan Pryce (see previous chapter), but was nonetheless admirable for Law's sharp critical intelligence and clear, crisp delivery of the lines. Lahr's chief reservation was that Law could not hide his dashing, charismatic sense of being so at ease with himself; emotional paralysis and self-doubt were beyond his register. Ben Brantley wrote in the *New York Times* that "Law approaches his role with the focus, determination and adrenaline level of an Olympic track competitor staring down an endless line of hurdles." (For some reflections on a similar media blitz in David Tennant's Hamlet of 2009, see below in a discussion of film and television productions.)[5]

Shakespeare on film and on television in the 1980s and afterwards has enjoyed a considerable and sustained success, both artistically and financially, even more so than in the spate of Shakespeare films right after World War II, chiefly by Laurence Olivier and Orson Welles. That earlier generation of Shakespeare on film yielded only one *Hamlet*, by Olivier, in 1948; the more recent era has seen at least four notable productions, in addition to a very capable and straightforward BBC *Hamlet* of 1980 with Derek Jacobi as Hamlet. The four major films are, as one would expect, considerably less avant-garde than the stage productions of the same era. Commercial films, even those with intellectual aspirations, need to reach out to large audiences. Indeed, the story of filming *Hamlet* in the three decades or so since 1980 is one of attempting to bring *Hamlet* back into the prominence it once enjoyed on stage while at the same time interpreting the play in the light of contemporary mores. The result is that *Hamlet* is well-known today by large numbers of people, who have thereby been invited to think of *Hamlet* as a fable for our time. It is, of course, widely taught in schools and universities. *Hamlet* is our contemporary, in the English-speaking world and more broadly still. The play's success as visual entertainment has been bolstered by, and has contributed to, the successful filming of other Shakespeare plays, including *Henry V*, *Much Ado About Nothing*, *Othello*, *Twelfth Night*, *A Midsummer Night's Dream*, *Love's Labour's Lost*, and still others.

Franco Zeffirelli's 1990 film *Hamlet* is a blend of updating and tradition. On the one hand, the film goes Hollywood in its casting, thereby suggesting analogies to contemporary popular entertainment; on the other hand, it is fairly conventional in visual design and in concept. The director's decision to cast Mel Gibson as Hamlet, along with Alan Bates as Claudius, Glenn Close as Gertrude, Helena Bonham Carter as Ophelia, Ian Holm as Polonius, and Paul Scofield as the Ghost was transparently a move to woo audiences with box office pizzazz. The film's commercial success was in fact respectable, even if its twenty-million-dollar gross profit in the United States (at a cost of fifteen million dollars) could not match that of Gibson's other action films. Zeffirelli's *Hamlet* is an action film in its way; with Gibson as the star, audiences would, of course, expect things to happen. Gibson as Hamlet is ceaselessly in motion as he chases after his father's ghost on the guard platform, outmaneuvers Rosencrantz

Illustration 19. Mel Gibson as Hamlet and Helena Bonham Carter as Ophelia (3.1) in Franco Zeffirelli's 1990 film.

and Guildenstern, urges Ophelia to get herself to a nunnery (see Illustration 19), stabs Polonius behind the arras in the Queen's chamber, browbeats his mother, and overpowers his enemies in the play's scene of final reckoning. Manliness displaces the introspection of traditional interpretation. A pruning to less than forty percent of the play's original length makes room for the action sequences. Film reputations are exploited to similar effect in the other major characters as well. Glenn Close, the passionately seductive "other woman" of *Fatal Attraction*, becomes in Zeffirelli's film a widowed queen who is infatuated with her new lover, with no hint of hesitancy or bewilderment. Given this interpretation, Alan Bates is well cast as the object of Gertrude's sexual longing: he is, as he is often seen in other films or plays, an attractive male for whom a woman like Gertrude might forget nearly everything else in her desire for him. Bates's Claudius is so winsome and jovial in his pleasure-taking that one tends to forget that he has murdered his brother. Helena Bonham Carter, familiar to modern audiences as the attractive, jittery, feisty sufferer of unhappy love relationships in films like *Twelfth Night* and *Howards End*, is, as Ophelia, another sympathetic loser. Zeffirelli embraces celebrity type-casting at every turn.

Nor does Zeffirelli deny the viewer any of the lavish scenic effects for which he is justly famous in earlier films like his *The Taming of the Shrew* (1967) and *Romeo and Juliet* (1968). Especially gorgeous is his depiction of the hillside graveyard where Ophelia is buried. The costumes and architecture are richly appropriate to a film intent on providing visual splendor. Zeffirelli is a star of his own production. The film is vividly contemporary in these terms while lavishing its attention on what Hollywood has to offer. It is a conservatively "safe" film, apolitical, commercially appealing to audiences desirous of entertaining action and romantic intrigue. As such it appropriately brings to a close the decade of the 1980s dominated by Margaret Thatcher in Great Britain, Ronald Reagan in the United States, and the apathetic and acquisitive Baby Boomer generation.

Kevin Kline and Kirk Browning had the bad luck to choose that same season of 1990 as the year in which to do their PBS production of *Hamlet* for WNET/Thirteen's "Great Performances" series. Based on an earlier New York Public Theater production (1989) with Kline in the role of Hamlet, this version was shown only once on PBS public television. The timing was disastrous. Pitted hopelessly against the

Zeffirelli–Gibson juggernaut, Klein's *Hamlet* has been generally and undeservedly forgotten. This is a great pity. Never showy or blatantly commercial, focusing quietly on superb performances and insightful interpretation of the script, this production is the opposite of the Zeffirelli film in every way. Dana Ivey as Gertrude, Diane Venora as Ophelia, Brian Murray as Claudius, Michael Cumpsty as Laertes, Peter Francis James as Horatio, and Kline as Hamlet understand every word they say, and provide just the right gestures. No doubt this version has been penalized because it is a low-budget studio production without Hollywood glitz, but by the same token we are given the opportunity to observe nuanced acting at close range. The film is extraordinarily intelligent without being avant-garde. It seemingly offers no suggestive analogies to the contemporary 1980s scene. Costuming is traditional. This *Hamlet* attempts to be timeless, and perhaps that is another reason it did not capture public attention in competition with Zeffirelli's Hollywood blockbuster. The version is available on DVD.

Kenneth Branagh, having challenged Laurence Olivier with his film version of *Henry V* in 1989, turned to *Hamlet* in 1996–7. (*Much Ado About Nothing*, with which Branagh had great success in 1993, was not on Olivier's list of accomplishments as film actor-director.) Olivier's *Henry V* in 1944 and *Hamlet* in 1948 had set the standard for Shakespeare on film in mid-century Great Britain, and Branagh, brash and ambitious, was keen to fashion himself in the role of successor to his great father-figure. Perhaps Branagh's most striking decision in determining how to go beyond Olivier's black-and-white *Hamlet* was to film the play in its entirety and in color. Branagh had already starred as Hamlet in a full-length stage production in 1992–3 (mentioned earlier), directed by Adrian Noble for the Royal Shakespeare Company at the Barbican Theatre in London. At four hours in length, the film required an intermission for the screenings, and produced considerable anxiety among Branagh's financial backers. He persisted, and the result is that today we can savor the whole thing, including all of the fourth act that is so often severely abridged.

Derek Jacobi, the Hamlet of the BBC production in 1980 mentioned above, is quite remarkable as Claudius in 1996–7: he is presentable as a king, efficient as an administrator, savvy as a politician, and deeply tormented with guilt for the terrible thing he has done. Julie Christie as his queen is touchingly persuasive in her big scene with Hamlet (3.4), as she moves from defensiveness and denial to painful

Illustration 20. Derek Jacobi and Julie Christie as Claudius and Gertrude, in their first court appearance (1.2), in Kenneth Branagh's 1996–7 film.

acknowledgment of guilty sorrow. Kate Winslet expertly manages the emotional distance she must traverse from a hesitantly unsure young woman to one who is distraught, deranged, and confined to a strait-jacket. Richard Briers as Polonius rejects the usual comic role of doddering old fool for that of a counselor who is surprisingly sagacious. Exterior shots of Blenheim Palace, and studio interiors representing its great halls and waiting rooms, make for an impressive mise en scène. The choice of a late nineteenth-century time frame lends itself to elegantly handsome costuming (see Illustration 20).

Like Zeffirelli, Branagh exploits the celebrity status of some well-known film actors, mainly in cameo appearances. Robin Williams lends his zany, offbeat style of acting to the foppish Osric. Charlton Heston sonorously intones the part of the Player King. Some of the brief appearances are not very successful: Jack Lemmon as Marcellus in act 1 is generally regarded as something of a disaster, and Gérard Depardieu in the minor role of Polonius's servant Reynaldo seems oddly cast, with his distinctive French accent, as though he has wandered onto the wrong filming location. Billy Crystal as the Grave-digger, with his Brooklyn accent, seems no less out of place. Silent appearances by John Gielgud and Judi Dench add little, other than to the name-dropping roster. (Dench had played Ophelia to John Neville's Hamlet at the Old Vic in 1957.) Still, these brief star turns give celebrity gloss to the film without impinging on the major roles.

Branagh is, of course, counting on his own stardom to enhance the audience's interest in his performance of the lead role.

Branagh chooses other ways to update his *Hamlet* for a wide audience wishing to see the story as reassuringly modern and accessible. In a flashback he shows us Hamlet and Ophelia in bed together, thus erasing any doubt as to whether they have been lovers in the fully sexual sense. To modern sensibilities, if Hamlet and Ophelia have been attracted to each other, why shouldn't they consummate the relationship sexually? Yet the film's choice erases cultural distance between the present day and a centuries-old court in which Ophelia would lose everything if she were to take a chance like that. As both her father and brother emphatically insist, her value on the marriage market would be reduced to nothing at all if she were to give in to Hamlet's supposed "unmastered importunity" (1.3.32). In the play she seems to listen carefully to their advice, but a modern film for popular audiences has reason to choose otherwise.

Similarly, the quake-like moving of the earth in Hamlet's scene with the Ghost gives a visual demonstration of the Ghost's otherworldly ability to "work i'th'earth so fast" (1.5.171), thereby providing this modern popular film with nearly-mandatory special effects. Blenheim Palace is subjected in the film's last scene to a gratuitous invasion by Fortinbras's army, smashing windows and leaping over railings in a way that would presumably have delighted Zeffirelli and Mel Gibson. Still, this is an important and generally successful film. It resonates powerfully with remembrances of current events in the late 1990s, including the sensational death of Princess Diana in 1997, other garishly publicized scandals in Great Britain's royal family, the recent collapse of Soviet communism, and millennial apprehensiveness about an approaching apocalypse and the end of history.

Michael Almereyda's *Hamlet* (2000) demonstrates brilliantly how a low-budget, modern-setting adaptation can be made to illuminate Shakespeare's text at least as effectively as the more costly and showy enterprises of Zeffirelli and Branagh. Almereyda chooses as his mise en scène the steel-and-concrete canyons of Manhattan near Times Square, where Claudius (Kyle MacLachlan) is Chief Executive Officer of a multinational conglomerate enterprise named the Denmark Corporation. He has recently married his deceased brother's widow (Diane Venora), a well-groomed suburbanite for whom luxurious creature comforts mean everything. Together they savor the sybaritic

Illustration 21. Ethan Hawke as Hamlet, Diane Venora as Gertrude, and Kyle MacLachlan as Claudius in Michael Almereyda's 2000 film set in Manhattan.

pleasures of stretch limousines and a private swimming pool in their luxury high-rise Elsinore Hotel. Yet all is not well. The Ghost of Hamlet's father (the playwright Sam Shepard) ominously appears and vanishes on the building's closed-circuit video monitor security system and on the high concrete balconies that serve as this movie's battlements.

Hamlet (Ethan Hawke), in this fallen world of decadent privilege and secret crime, is a rebel with a cause. Outfitted in a Peruvian woolen hat and informal attire, he stands out as an alienated and misunderstood youth (see Illustration 21). Being a film geek, he naturally undertakes to test the intentions of his hated uncle with an experimental film of his own making—Almereya's ingenious substitution for Shakespeare's "The Murder of Gonzago." Gadgetry meaningfully pervades this reflexively multimedia and metatheatrical film about film. Hamlet is astute enough to detect the wiretap that Polonius (Bill Murray) and Claudius have planted on Ophelia (Julia Stiles) for her interview with Hamlet. Hamlet communicates with Ophelia on her answerphone. When Hamlet is being escorted on an overnight flight to England by Rosencrantz and Guildenstern, he has the bright idea of investigating their laptop computer in the overhead luggage rack while they are asleep. Finding there an incriminating message they are conveying to the King of England with orders for the execution of Hamlet, the Prince simply backspaces the computer message and substitutes their names for his. Media stunts such as these illustrate the cleverness with which Almereyda has updated *Hamlet* to the early twenty-first century. The performances (also with Liev Schreiber as Laertes) are first rate.

David Tennant's Hamlet, under the direction of Gregory Doran for the Royal Shakespeare Company at the Courtyard Theatre in Stratford-upon-Avon from July to November in 2008 followed by a West End run at the Novello Theatre, enjoyed such a phenomenal success that it was then filmed for BBC2 with Tennant (of Doctor Who fame) still in the title role and with Patrick Stewart as Claudius/Ghost, Penny Downe as Gertrude, and Mariah Gale as Ophelia, all from the original company, along with Edward Bennett, who had substituted for Tennant (sidelined with spinal surgery) as Hamlet during part of the stage run, now as Laertes. As a substitute for Elsinore Castle, the producers and director chose as their filming location the deconsecrated nineteenth-century missionary school chapel and surrounding cloisters of St Joseph's College in the north London suburb of Mill Hill. This three-hour modern-dress version, based substantially on the second quarto of 1604, includes Rosencrantz, Guildenstern, Fortinbras, and even the often-deleted Reynaldo. Yorick's skull, as in the stage version, is that of the concert pianist André Tchaikowsky, who bequeathed this object to the RSC for just this kind of theatrical use. The extensive familiarity of the cast with the play and with one another through repeated stage performances makes for a production that is intense and intelligent. The BBC2 film version was broadcast in the United States on 28 April 2010.

Rory Kinnear's Hamlet, in a modern-dress production by Nicholas Hytner at London's National Theatre and shown on film in the winter of 2010-2011, earned special praise for its ability to give new meaning to the play's remarkable and familiar language. As reviewed by (among others) Ben Brantley for the *New York Times* (1 January 2011), this version capitalized on close-ups in the eavesdropping scenes with insightful interpretations of the play's well-known lines. The effect was to give immediacy and poetic power to Hytner's concept of a

fascist Denmark constantly under the surveillance of grey-coated security men with cell phones and listening devices. Kinnear's Hamlet
was a thinking man and Renaissance prince whose feigned madness
eloquently underscored a genuine malaise and emotional distress.
Gertrude (Clare Higgins), in her searing encounter with her son in
her chambers, appeared to see the Ghost of her former husband,
despite her denials to Hamlet. She was an alcoholic, afraid of her
new husband Claudius (Patrick Malahide), who was, to be sure, a
cold-blooded tyrant. Polonius (David Calder) seemed aware of his
own pomposity as he bore down on his son with fulsome advice about
being true to oneself. The careful attention to language and meaning
throughout was materially enhanced by a new technological advance
(also put recently to use in broadcasting opera and symphonic music)
of filming the production to live audiences in selected movie theaters,
as part of the National Theatre Live series of performances.

As befits such a famous play that lends itself so well to screen
interpretation, *Hamlet* is available today in more film versions than is
any other play by Shakespeare or indeed any other dramatist who ever
wrote. All of the films described here deserve careful attention.
Together they provide an unequaled opportunity for comparing different interpretations. Still other famous Hamlets on film include
Maurice Evans (NBC, 26 April 1953), John Neville (Old Vic Production on CBS's Show of the Month, 24 February 1959), and Christopher Plummer (BBC/Danmarks Radio, 1964), taped at Elsinore Castle
in Denmark.[6]

The commercial filming of *Hamlet*, then, has found ingenious means
of interacting with contemporary culture. The potential for a broad-
ening of the appeal of Shakespeare, and of *Hamlet* in particular,
manifests itself in other cultural venues as well: in foreign-language
films; in adaptations, musicals, and rock operas; in musical scores
inspired by the play; in spin-offs, spoofs, and parodies; in numberless
allusions incorporated into modern plays, films, works of fiction,
poetry, political cartoons, television sit-coms, and just about every
imaginable facet of modern culture; and in *Hamlet*'s enormous if
often unacknowledged impact on the very language that we speak
today. These multiple and ever-expanding transformations of the
twentieth and twenty-first centuries will bring our history of *Hamlet*
to a close for the present.

Hamlet has been produced filmically in widely divergent cultures worldwide: India (1935 in Hindi and 1955 in Urdu, directed by Kishore Sahu), Austria and West Germany (1960–1, directed for television by Peter Wirth and Maximilian Schell, with Schell as Hamlet), France (1962–3), Hungary (1963), the Soviet Union (by Grigori Kozintsev, 1963–4), northern Ghana (1964, in Tongo, the home of the Frafra people), Canada (*The Trouble with Hamlet*, 1969, and a complete *Hamlet* in 1973), Brazil (Ozualda Ribiera Candeias's *A Herança*, 1970), Japan (1977, and Yukio Ninagawa's Noh theatre *Hamlet* in 1998), Turkey (Metan Erksan's film *Intikam Melegi–Kadin Hamlet*, 1977), Italy (*Amleto*, 1978), the Netherlands (1980), Poland (1981), Sweden (1984, with Stellan Skarsgård as Hamlet), Mauritania (Dev Virahsawmy, 1995 and 1997), China (Shanghai Peking Opera's *Revenge of the Prince*, 2005), Saudi Arabia (as in Sulayman al-Bassam's *The Al-Hamlet Summit*), and still others.

In an aggressively postmodernist Spanish film of 1976, directed by Celestino Coronado, twin Hamlets (Anthony and David Meyer) soliloquize jointly in a duologue before confronting Ophelia (Helen Mirren) from the contrasting points of view of a divided sensibility. "I did love you once," one of them insists, only to be refuted by his twin: "I loved you not" (3.1.116–20). (The idea of two actors in the role of Hamlet as a key to his divided sensibility had actually occurred earlier, in the 1930s, to the courageous Russian director Vsevolod Meyerhold, who was shot in 1940 on Stalin's orders for having dared to stand up to the Soviet regime; his sadly unfulfilled wish was to have carved on his tombstone, "Here lies a man who never played or produced Hamlet"). Heiner Müller staged a collage of his *Hamlet-machine* and his own translation of *Hamlet* in a seven-hour marathon at the Deutsches Theater in East Berlin in 1990, complete with a radio broadcast of Stalin's funeral, a stage littered with artifacts of European history, and clown routines. We have seen how *Hamlet* has been put to work as an ideological protest against dictatorship in Russia and eastern European countries. *Hamlet* has proved to be no less powerful as an ideological weapon in Egypt as well, particularly in opposition movements against Gamal Abdel Nasser as President from 1956 to 1970.

Adaptations of Shakespeare have often been motivated by a wish to update the plays and show how "relevant" they can be to burning contemporary issues today. *10 Things I Hate About You* (Gil Junger, 1999, currently being refashioned into a TV sitcom series) transfers the

story of *The Taming of the Shrew* to a high school in Seattle, where
Cameron James (Joseph Gordon-Levitt) falls for Bianca Stratford
(Larisa Oleynik) only to learn that her obstetrician father, Dr Walter
Stratford (Larry Miller), fearful of premarital pregnancy, will not let
her go out on a date until her stridently feminist older sister Kat (Julia
Stiles) can learn to relate to some member of the opposite sex. The
intrepid Joey Donner (Andrew Keegan) takes on the daunting assignment of getting Kat to go out with him. In Tim Blake Nelson's *O*, the
protagonist of Shakespeare's *Othello* is transformed into Odin James, or
"O. J." (Mekhi Phifer), a black high school South Carolina basketball
star with a white girlfriend named Desi Brable (Julia Stiles) and a
jealous buddy, Hugo Goulding (Josh Hartnett), who bitterly resents
having been displaced as the basketball team's first player. Paul
Mazursky's 1982 *Tempest* begins the story of that play in late-twentieth-
century New York, when a disillusioned architect (John Cassavetes)
decides to escape from civilization with his teenage daughter Miranda
(Molly Ringwald) to a Greek island, where he takes up with a twice-
divorced American cabaret singer named Aretha (Susan Sarandon). And
there are many others.

Hamlet has similarly lent itself to film adaptation. Edgar Ulmer's
Strange Illusion (1945) tells of a young man named Paul Cartwright
whose widowed mother marries a man who turns out to be the
murderer of Paul's father. Helmut Käutner's *Der Rest ist Schweigen*
(*The Rest is Silence*, 1959) is a tale of alienation set in modern times in
the Ruhrpott industrial belt of northwest Germany. In Akira Kurosa-
wa's *The Bad Sleep Well* (Japan, 1960) a thoughtful young businessman
named Koishi Nishi (Toshiro Mifune) suffers torments of conscience
as he ponders the heavy assignment of avenging the death of his father.
That death was a suicide, precipitated by the corrupt bribe-taking of
the villainous Iwabuchi (Takeshi Kato), now the powerful head of
Japan Land Corporation. Claude Chabrol's *Ophélia* (1962–3) is about a
young man, Yvan Lesurf, who, when his widowed mother quickly
remarries, becomes obsessively but wrongly convinced that he is
reliving Hamlet's story; he has been watching Olivier's *Hamlet*. In
Krsto Papic's *Acting Hamlet in the Village of Mrdusa Donja* (1974), a
Croatian village performance of *Hamlet* leads to the exposure of the
crimes of the local commissar. The Finnish film called *Hamlet Goes
Business* (1987), directed by Aki Kaurismäki, tells of an industrial
magnate in modern-day Helsinki who kills his brother to gain control

of a firm called Swedish Rubber Ducks, only to be foiled by his sex-starved, blithering nephew and a chauffeur (the Horatio equivalent) who is a trade union spy. In Dave Thomas and Rick Moranis's *Strange Brew*, 1983, Hamlet must do battle with the corrupt Elsinore Brewery. Spaghetti Western adaptations of *Hamlet* include Leopoldo Savona's *Apocalypse Joe* (1971, about a travelling actor and gunman who inherits a gold mine from his uncle), Richard Balducci's *Lust in the Sun* (also 1971, with a mute Hamlet), and Enzo G. Castellari's *Johnny Hamlet* (1972, fairly close in plot to Shakespeare's *Hamlet* for much of the story while exchanging Denmark for the Wild West). Walt Disney's award-winning animated feature *The Lion King* (1994), directed by Roger Allers and Rob Minkoff and subsequently making its debut as a stage musical in Minneapolis (1997) and then on Broadway, tells the story of a young African lion prince named Simba who, when his villainous uncle Scar has conspired with hyenas to kill Simba's father, King Mufasa, is deceived into believing that he, Simba, is responsible for that death. The American television series called "Sons of Anarchy," shown on cable network FX in 2008–9, makes use of Shakespeare's play in its saga of a close-knit outlaw motorcycle club in northern California.

Hamlet 2, directed in 2008 by Andrew Fleming, written by him and Pam Brady, is an irreverent Hollywood comedy film about a failed actor and recovering alcoholic, Dana Marschz (zanily played by British comedian Steve Coogan), who attempts to direct a musical sequel to *Hamlet,* written by himself, at the West Mesa High School in Tucson, Arizona, where he teaches drama. His apathetic, snarky students, who are in his class only because all other electives are closed, have their minds on higher things, such as cell-phone conversations and teen pregnancy. Nonetheless they rally at last to help Dana create his masterpiece, into which the author has introduced Jesus, Einstein, and Hillary Clinton along with Hamlet. The Tucson Gay Men's Chorus and a musical rendition of "Rock Me, Sexy Jesus" are so offensive to the school principal, the school board, and the community that the show is about to be quashed, but a lawyer from the American Civil Liberty Union (Amy Poehler) comes to the rescue, and the show finally achieves its triumphant realization in an abandoned railroad shed.

Tom Stoppard's *Rosencrantz and Guildenstern are Dead*, with its inside-out version of *Hamlet* giving the major parts to the Prince's

Tweedledum-and-Tweedledee friends, is a particularly fine example of shifting dramatic perspective. First produced at the Edinburgh Festival Fringe in August, 1966, this show was made into a film in 1990 with a film script by Stoppard. Gary Oldman and Tim Roth assume the title roles in the film. The stage version fits better with Shakespeare's original *Hamlet*. At Stratford, Canada, in 1986, a single acting company did both plays in rotating repertory, sometimes playing both on the same day, thereby demonstrating how practical it is to have large roles in *Rosencrantz and Guildenstern are Dead* for some of Shakespeare's minor characters, and conversely small parts in Stoppard's play for roles such as Hamlet, Claudius, Gertrude, and Polonius that impose heavy demands on the actors in the original *Hamlet*. This fine double production, with its intensely metatheatrical awareness of its taking place in the theatre, also showed how much better Stoppard's play is than the film adaptation, where "realistic" shots of journeying through a forest or traversing the seas on board ship interfere seriously with *Rosencrantz and Guildenstern*'s wittily profound metaphor of life and death as stage entrances and exits: "Now you see it, now you don't."[7]

A special favorite of British male academics is the obscene modernized short parody called *Skinhead Hamlet*, by Richard Curtis. The flavor and breakneck speed of this adaptation can perhaps be sampled from this quotation of act 2 in its entirety:

POLONIUS: Oi! You!
HAMLET: Fuck off, Grandad!
(*Exit Polonius. Enter Rosencrantz and Guildenstern.*)
ROSENCRANTZ AND GUILDENSTERN: Oi! Oi! Mucca!
HAMLET: Fuck off, the pair of you!
(*Exit Rosencrantz and Guildenstern.*)
HAMLET: (*Alone*) To fuck or be fucked.
(*Enter Ophelia.*)
OPHELIA: My Lord!
HAMLET: Fuck off to a nunnery! (*They exit in different directions.*)

A headnote assures us that the author's intention was "to achieve something like the effect of the *New English Bible*."

Although *Hamlet* has not enjoyed success as a musical equal to the successes of *Kiss Me Kate, West Side Story,* and *The Boys from Syracuse,*[8] a few attempts at rock opera have been made. Cliff Jones produced his *Rockaby Hamlet* in 1974. *Halliday Hamlet,* by Gilles Thibault (writer) and Pierre Groscolas (composer), 1976, starred the French rock star Johnny Halliday or Hallyday. In Eastern Europe, *Musikal Hamlet* (2000), composed and written by the Czech pop star Janek Ledecky, with himself in the lead role, has enjoyed some popularity. Rap versions of *Hamlet*, including *Hamlet Rap* (1994) by Moe Moskowitz and the Punsters, and *The Trage-D of Hammy-T* (1999) by Robert Krakovski, have opted for comic sendup. Orpheus's 1977 musicalized version of *Hamlet*, starring Richard E. Grant as Hamlet, is a campy, postmodern amalgam of Shakespeare and modern musical culture in a deliberately provocative style.

Hamlet has served as the model for classical musical interpretations in the years since 1900, as it had done in the two previous centuries (see chapters 4 and 5). Notable instances are Frank Bridge's *Hamlet*-based "Lament for Strings" in 1915 and "There Is a Willow Grows Aslant a Brook" in 1928.

The good-natured spoofing of Shakespeare that was so prominent a feature of eighteenth- and nineteenth-century enjoyment of his works (see chapter 5) continues to flourish after 1900. In George Bernard Shaw's "The Dark Lady of the Sonnets," written in 1910, Shakespeare, meeting with the Dark Lady and with Queen Elizabeth, jots down for his use in *Hamlet* some of the Dark Lady's well-phrased utterances, such as "Season your admiration for a while" and "I am of all ladies most deject and wretched." (Tom Stoppard and Mark Norman's *Shakespeare in Love* makes a similar joke when Shakespeare, abed with Viola de Lessups, hears from her mouth some especially good lines that will turn up in his *Romeo and Juliet*.)

More recently, a film spoof entitled *To Be Or Not To Be*, produced and directed by Ernst Lubitsch in 1942, features Jack Benny as a ham actor whose famous line "To be or not to be?" turns out to be a secret signal that, unbeknownst to Benny himself, informs a Polish flyer (Robert Stack), sitting midway in the second row of the audience, that Benny is now lengthily engaged in his stage performance and that the time has arrived for the flyer to hasten backstage and join Benny's wife (Carole Lombard) in her dressing room for an assignation. Benny collapses in a deep funk, not because of the threatened adultery of his wife (of which he has no inkling), but because during his "To be or not to be" soliloquy, of which he is particularly proud, a militarily dressed audience member keeps getting up to leave the auditorium, crossing over numerous pairs of knees as he proceeds toward the aisle. Benny is aghast: is he losing his touch as a great Shakespeare matinee idol? A color remake of this film in 1983 (not recommended) stars Mel Brooks in the Benny role. Lubitsch's original film contains a marvelous spoof of Adolf Hitler, who, in his chapter on "War Propaganda" in *Mein Kampf*, had made use of Shakespeare's famous phrase. "When the nations on this planet fight for existence," wrote Hitler, "when the question of destiny, 'To be or not to be', cries out for a solution, then all considerations of humanitarianism or aesthetics crumble into nothingness" (translated by Barry Gaines).

"To be or not to be" is once again the point of a joke in *Last Action Hero* (1993). At one point, Hamlet (Arnold Schwarzenegger) meditates on the hoary question only to conclude that it is "Not to be." As he speaks, Elsinore castle blows sky-high. Tom Stoppard has produced parodic stage versions of *Hamlet*, one running fifteen minutes, the other ninety seconds. In an episode of *Gilligan's Island,* "The Producer" (1966), some castaways on the island put on a short version of *Hamlet* set to famous operatic tunes. The Reduced Shakespeare Company's *The Compleat Works of Wllm Shkspr* (1994) devotes its second half to *Hamlet*. A skit called "Shamlet" by the Capitol Steps in 1988 has fun at the expense of a potential Democratic candidate for president who just can't make up his mind whether to run for office or not. An amateur film called *Green Eggs and Hamlet* (1995) recounts the story of Hamlet in Dr Seuss's signature doggerel style, notably in his *Green Eggs and Ham*. The first season of a Canadian television series called "Slings and Arrows" (2003), set at a fictional New Burbage Festival with obvious reference to Stratford, Ontario and featuring a number of actors from the Stratford Shakespeare Festival, tells of a former artistic Festival director named Oliver Gross (played by Stephen Ouimette) whose ghost comes back to haunt the new artistic director Geoffrey Tennant (Paul Gross) while that young man is doing is best to stage a star-crossed production of *Hamlet*.

Literary allusions to *Hamlet* in the last century attest to a never-ending fascination with this play as a central icon of culture in the English-speaking world, as in preceding centuries (see chapter 5). The speaker in T. S. Eliot's "The Lovesong of J. Alfred Prufrock" (1917) confesses self-abnegatingly that "I am not Prince Hamlet, nor was meant to be." Stephen Daedalus, in James Joyce's *Ulysses* (first American edition, New York: Modern Library, 1934), expounds his theories about *Hamlet*, among which are the ideas that the Son is "striving to be atoned with the Father" (in Haines's words) and that Gertrude committed adultery with Claudius before the murder. Buck Mulligan teases Stephen by parodying his Shakespearean obsessions: "He proves by algebra that Hamlet's grandson is Shakespeare's grandfather and that he himself is the ghost of his own father." Bloom poohpoohs the academic question as to whether Hamlet is Shakespeare or James I or Essex, and ponders the relationship of Shakespeare's son Hamnet to Hamlet. Joyce's text is plentifully enriched with quotations and paraphrases: "That beetles o'er his base into the sea," "nipping and eager air," "very like a whale," "a sable silvered," "tempting flood," "My cockle hat . . . my sandal shoon," "glimpses of the moon," "unweeded garden," "when churchyards yawn," "in the porches of mine ear," "the proud man's contumely," "method in his madness," and many more.

Iris Murdoch's *The Black Prince* (New York: Viking, 1973) is about an aging London novelist whose name, Bradley Pearson, bears the same initials as those of the Black Prince—that is, Hamlet, with whom Bradley strongly identifies to the extent of insisting that both Hamlet and Shakespeare are homosexual. Bradley discovers the compelling force of his own homosexuality when he is able to achieve sexual arousal with his mistress, Julian, only when she cross-dresses as Hamlet. Angela Carter's fascination with Shakespeare in her novel *Wise Children* (London: Chatto & Windus, 1991) culminates in a reworking of "To be or not to be" as a song and dance. In Alan Isler's *The Prince of West End Avenue* (Bridgehampton, NY: Bridge Works, 1994), some Jewish residents of New York stage *Hamlet* in their retirement home. In Margaret Atwood's "Gertrude Talks Back" (in *Good Bones*, Toronto: O. W. Toad, 1992), the title figure disabuses her unhappy son of the notion that Hamlet Senior was murdered by his brother: "It wasn't Claudius, darling, it was me!" John Updike's *Gertrude and Claudius* (New York: Knopf, 2000) is a prequel to Shakespeare's play, imagining what Gertrude's adolescence must have been like, her rejecting at first her father's choice of suitor, her ultimate acquiescence, her longing for freedom from a constraining marriage, and her affair with Claudius. Lisa Klein's *Ophelia* (London: Bloomsbury Children's Books, 2006) is a fictional account of a rowdy, motherless girl who becomes the Queen's most trusted lady-in-waiting; forced ultimately to choose between her love for Hamlet and her own safety, she feigns madness and survives by escaping Elsinore.[9]

Perhaps nothing can convey a sense of *Hamlet*'s astonishing universality today more readily than the extent to which its phrases have passed into the language. The word "ham" is derived from Hamlet's name and from the temptation that has afflicted too many actors to "ham up" the part. "Hamlet" can mean a daft person, one who is irresolute and can do nothing purposefully. "To be or not to be" is by now such a warhorse of an expression that actors are driven to desperate expedients in their search for a fresh approach (as in Robert Falls's modern-dress production of the play at Chicago's Wisdom Bridge Theatre in 1985, when Aidan Quinn as Hamlet spray-painted "To be or not to be" on a bulkhead, stood back to contemplate what he had done, and murmured admiringly, "Now *that* is the question!"). Other phrases have become no less proverbial. "More honored in the breach than the observance" (1.4.16) is a common way of characterizing a habit that one would better do without. "Neither a borrower nor a lender be" (1.3.75) sums up a bit of worldly advice offered to spendthrifts. Many such phrases in *Hamlet*, like this one, are quoted out of context as if they represent Shakespeare's thinking on the subject, when in fact we should remember that Polonius is speaking for himself and is not to be taken as a mouthpiece for the dramatist.[10]

This incredible knack of Shakespeare's for saying something appropriate to every imaginable situation has itself become proverbial. When, for example, a wealthy businessman named Tarlton in G. B. Shaw's *Misalliance* (1910) finds in his house a thief named Gunner who is the son of a woman whom Tarlton seduced and "ruined" some years ago, the thief shows Tarlton two photographs of the woman as she once was and as she is now, exclaiming as he does so, "Look here upon this picture, and on this!" The thief, intent on improving himself through self-education, has been reading *Hamlet*—in a public library built with Tarlton's money. Tarlton can only reply in ironic approval: "Good. Read Shakespear: he has a word for every occasion."

The phrase "Hamlet without the Prince" has entered the language as signifying a performance or an event lacking the principal actor or central figure. The origin of this phrase is an account in the London *Morning Post*, September 1775, telling of a touring company which suddenly discovered that its leading player had run off with the innkeeper's daughter. The company had to announce to the audience that "the part of Hamlet is to be left out, for that night."

In their various ways, then, literary criticism, teaching, stage productions, films, videos, translations, adaptations, and even spoofs all suggest how vital is the life of *Hamlet* today, more so perhaps than ever before. The play is central to our ever-changing cultural image of ourselves. It contributes to cultural evolution and is in turn transformed into many images by that ongoing change. *Hamlet* helps us to understand ourselves and who we are socially. Our conversation with the play shows no signs of slowing down. We continue to reinvent *Hamlet* to this day.

Notes

These notes are not citations of my sources, which are indicated in the text by parenthetical citation; the bibliography called "Further Reading" then provides further information on the publisher and place and date of publication for the items listed there. The notes here instead provide further material for a study of the history of *Hamlet*, especially on the Elizabethan playhouse and on productions not discussed in the main text of this book. I also include in these notes some instances of critical commentary on *Hamlet*, ones that supplement the illustrations of critical movements but that might seem a bit duplicatory in the main text of the book. To discuss more materials than I have done would risk the danger of losing the narrative and argument of the history. At the same time, the history of *Hamlet* does include a wealth of factual data worthy of brief notice. The information in these notes does not attempt to offer a complete history of productions on stage or in film and video; such a list would be too exhausting.

Citations throughout are to any edition of *The Complete Works of Shakespeare*, 6th ed., New York: Pearson/Longman, 2008.

CHAPTER I

1. Other early legends have contributed stories of a revenging figure or figures who disguise themselves by means of false names or an assumed madness. The anonymous Scandinavian *Saga of Hrolf Kraki* tells of two sons of the murdered King Halfdan named Hroar and Helgi who resort to disguise under false names. The *Ambales Saga* is not unlike that of Saxo Grammaticus. The legend of Brutus, deriving its name from the disguise motif of "dull, stupid," goes back to the early Roman history of the tyrannical L. Tarquinius the Proud, reportedly driven out of Rome by Lucius Junius Brutus, the heroic founder of republicanism and ancestor of the Marcus Brutus who figures prominently in Shakespeare's *Julius Caesar*. Sextus Tarquinius's rape of Collatinus's virtuous wife, Lucretia, a critical event leading to the expulsion of the Tarquins, is the subject of Shakespeare's *The Rape of Lucrece* (1594). See William F. Hansen, ed., *Saxo Grammaticus and the Life of Hamlet: A Translation, History, and Commentary* (Lincoln: University of Nebraska Press, 1983), pp. 1–37.

CHAPTER 4

1. See chapter 7 below, Zdenek Stribrny, *Shakespeare and Eastern Europe* (Oxford: Oxford University Press, 2000), and Anthony B. Dawson, "International Shakespeare," in *The Cambridge Companion to Shakespeare on Stage*, ed. Stanley Wells and Sarah Stanton (Cambridge: Cambridge University Press, 2002). George Frederick Cooke introduced a romantic style of acting Hamlet that was to become the hallmark of Edmund Kean in the early nineteenth century (see next chapter).

CHAPTER 5

1. The famed actress, Helen Modjeska played Ophelia in 1871 in her native Poland and subsequently in the United States to Edwin Booth's Hamlet in 1889–90. (She had begun her American acting career in 1877.) She and the American actor Joseph Hawarth were the toast of New York and on tour in the 1890s. A German touring company performed *Hamlet* in German at the St James Theatre in 1852, with Emil Devrient as the protagonist. The great Italian actor Tommaso Salvini also played Hamlet (in Italian), but not to the frenzy of enthusiasm that greeted his successful run with *Othello* in 1875. Salvini took this role to America in 1885–6. *Hamlet* inspired an opera by the French composer Charles-Louis-Ambroise Thomas in 1868, in which the emotional and musical highpoint was, for many audience members, the fourth act, devoted almost entirely to the madness and death aria of Ophélie. Thomas's librettists, Michel Carré and Jules Barbier, devised two endings, in one of which the avenging Ghost metes out just punishment to the offenders. The result is strikingly different from Shakespeare's text, and also from the earlier opera staged at the London's Haymarket theatre in 1712 (mentioned in chapter 4), based primarily on Saxo Grammaticus's *History of the Danes*.

2. Among other matters, Forrest and Macready quarreled over the interpretation of Hamlet's "I must be idle" as the play-within-the-play is about to begin (3.2.89). Macready danced about with a handkerchief, looking spooked and dotty, much to Forrest's disgust.
   Thomas W. Keene, having begun his theatrical career in stock theatre in San Francisco and then as a supporting actor with Edwin Booth, became well known on tour for a number of Shakespearean roles, including Hamlet, in the 1870s. A colorful poster, *c.* 1884, pictures him in favorite Shakespearean moments, including that of Hamlet leaning with his elbow against a mantelpiece, his hand held to his furrowed brow.
   E. H. Sothern had considerable success with *Hamlet*, beginning in New York in 1900, and then enjoying a twenty-year partnership (1904

and afterwards) with Julia Marlowe as his leading lady and his Ophelia. His elaborate stagings were in the Irving tradition.

CHAPTER 6

1. The Old Vic has gone on to house luminous performances of *Hamlet* by the likes of Robert Harris (1932, with Ralph Richardson as the First Gravedigger), Robert Helpmann (1934), Maurice Evans (1935), Laurence Olivier (1937–8), Alec Guinness (1938), Michael Redgrave (1950), Richard Burton (1953), John Neville (1957, with Judi Dench as Ophelia), Albert Finney (1975), Derek Jacobi (1977–9), and still more. Donald Wolfit played Hamlet at Stratford-upon Avon in 1936, directed by Ben Iden Payne, and at many times and in many places in later years.

2. Olivier's *Hamlet* was the first and only Shakespeare film to win an Academy Award for Best Picture, with Olivier as best actor, until the advent of *Shakespeare in Love* in 1998. (Max Reinhardt's 1935 color film of *A Midsummer Night's Dream* had won two Academy Awards for technical achievements.) From the start, the film had to win over those who were skeptical of the idea that anything so high-brow could sell tickets to mass audiences. Even the producer and financial backer to the tune of £600,000, J. Arthur Rank, was wary. The story goes that when one of Rank's executives was finally allowed by Olivier to see half an hour of the rushes, he reported back to his boss, in evident relief, "It's wonderful, Mr. Rank. You wouldn't know it was Shakespeare." To be sure, Olivier aimed at popular acceptance by shortening the script to a digestible film length, minus Fortinbras, Rosencrantz, and Guildenstern, thus following a stage tradition dating back to Thomas Betterton and David Garrick. Still, it was Shakespeare's *Hamlet*, and it sold (as had Olivier's *Henry V* in 1944).

3. The role of Hamlet is a defining supreme test of quality for any serious twentieth-century theatre artist. Besides the many performers already discussed, the years down to 1980 also include Alan Badel (Stratford-upon-Avon, 1956, directed by Michael Langham), Michael Redgrave (Stratford, 1958, directed by Glen Byam Shaw, with Dorothy Tutin as Ophelia), Martin Sheen (New York Public Theater, 1967–8, directed by Joseph Papp), Ian Richardson (Birmingham, 1959, directed by Bernard Hepton), Alan Howard (Stratford, 1970, directed by Trevor Nunn), Alan Bates (Cambridge Theatre, London, 1971, directed by Anthony Page), Stacy Keach (New York Public Theater, 1971–2, directed by Gerald Freedman, with Colleen Dewhurst as Gertrude, James Earl Jones as Claudius, Bernard Hughes as Polonius, Sam Waterston as Laertes, and Raul Julia as Osric), Ian McKellen (Cambridge Theatre, 1972, directed by Robert Chetwyn), Peter Eyre (Greenwich, 1974, directed by Jonathan Miller), Sam Waterston (New York Public Theater, 1975–6, directed by Michael Rudman), Jon Voight (California State University, North Ridge, Department of Theatre,

1976), Philip Bowen (Young Vic, 1977–8, directed by Michael Bogda-
nov), and Peter Siiteri (for the Riverside Shakespeare Company in New
York's upper west side, 1978, directed by W. Stuart McDowell, with
Kaeren Peregrin as Ophelia).

4. Much historical research has focused on the Elizabethan theatre and how
its conditions were necessarily an essential element in the writing and
staging of a play like *Hamlet*. Alfred Harbage insists, in *As They Liked It:
An Essay on Shakespeare and Morality* (New York: Macmillan, 1947) that
Shakespeare was a popular dramatist who wrote for an alert, enthusiastic,
socially diversified audience. Ann Jennalie Cook offers a significant quali-
fication, based on a study of demographics in the early modern period:
Shakespeare's London audience was, to be sure, composed of "groundlings" along with the more well-to-do who sat in the Globe seats, but those
standing spectators were hardly proletarian: they tended to be apprentices
or younger members of London's powerful trade guilds who could afford
to take off from work on occasion and pay the penny price of admission,
roughly equivalent to the hourly wage of a skilled workman. The audience
was thus more affluent and socially consequential, as is implied in Cook's
title: *The Privileged Playgoers of Shakespeare's London, 1576–1642* (Princeton:
Princeton University Press, 1981). More recently, Andrew Gurr
has learnedly surveyed the topic in his *Playgoing in Shakespeare's London*
(Cambridge: Cambridge University Press, 1987, 2nd ed. 1996).

   Studies of the Elizabethan playhouse have advanced our knowledge of
early London theatres in many ways. John Cranford Adams's influential
model of the Globe Playhouse, as featured in Irwin Smith's *Shakespeare
Globe Playhouse: A Modern Reconstruction* (New York: Scribner, 1956) and
still occasionally reproduced photographically in textbooks, represents a
tendency of scholarship in the mid-twentieth century to cling to a picturesque ye-olde-England image of the Globe, with wattle and daub construction and, in the acting area, an elaborate curtained "inner stage" backstage
and an "upper stage" above. A resemblance of this idea can be seen in
Laurence Olivier's 1944 film of *Henry V*, where, following the Prologue's
appearance on the main stage, the play's first brief scene involving the
Archbishop of Canterbury and the Bishop of Ely takes place in the "upper
stage" so that it can occupy a space separate from that used in the next long
scene on the main stage, Henry's response to the French Dauphin's challenge. More up-to-date studies opt for a less hampered and compartmenta-
lized stage, with action "above" only on occasion and the "inner stage"
reduced to a "discovery space." Influential works here include Bernard
Beckerman's *Shakespeare at the Globe* (New York: Macmillan, 1962, 1967),
several essays by Richard Hosley, T. J. King's *Shakespearean Staging,
1599–1642* (Cambridge, MA: Harvard University Press, 1971), and Andrew
Gurr's *The Shakespearean Stage, 1574–1642* (Cambridge: Cambridge University Press 1970, 3rd ed. 1992). These studies include information about the

acting companies, their styles of acting, their methods of doubling, and much more.

Questions about *Hamlet* have, of course, been raised by such research. Did Shakespeare have his leading actor, Richard Burbage, in mind, when he wrote of Hamlet that (in the Queen's words) he is "fat and scant of breath" (5.2.289)? Did Shakespeare play the Ghost in 1601, as theatre tradition maintains? He seems to have played old Adam in *As You Like It*, and is credited with having taken "Kingly parts"; was this his line of work as an actor? Does this have anything to do with the death of Shakespeare's own father in 1601? Did the Ghost in original performances emerge from a trap door in the stage? In any event, how did his company arrange for the Ghost to cry "Swear" from the "cellerage," presumably under the stage (1.5.158–60)? Could the audience hear the Ghost? (See chapter 2 on staging.)

Other valuable background information on theatres and acting companies has been assembled, thanks to the efforts of E. K. Chambers, *The Elizabethan Stage* (4 volumes, Oxford: Clarendon Press, 1923), G. E. Bentley, *The Jacobean and Caroline Stage* (Oxford: Clarendon Press, 1941–68), John H. Astington, *The Development of Shakespeare's Theater* (New York: AMS Press, 1962), G. E. Bentley, *The Profession of Dramatist in Shakespeare's Time, 1590–1642* (Princeton: Princeton University Press, 1971) and *The Profession of Player in Shakespeare's Time, 1590–1642* (Princeton: Princeton University Press 1984), Herbert Berry, *Shakespeare's Playhouses* (New York: AMS Press, 1987), and David Bradley, *From Text to Performance in the Elizabethan Theatre: Preparing the Play for the Stage* (Cambridge: Cambridge University Press, 1992), to name only some. Alan C. Dessen's *Recovering Shakespeare's Theatrical Vocabulary* (Cambridge: Cambridge University Press, 1995) provides insight as to how his stage directions are to be interpreted. R. A. Foakes and R. T. Rickert have edited *Henslowe's Diary* (Cambridge: Cambridge University Press, 1961), and Foakes has edited *The Henslowe Papers* (London: Scolar Press, 1977), both providing invaluable insights into the business practices of one of London's busiest theatre entrepreneurs. Marie Channing Linthicum has assembled a trove of materials on costuming in her *Costume in the Drama of Shakespeare and His Contemporaries* (Oxford: Clarendon Press, 1936). Roland Mushat Frye learnedly reconstructs what Elizabethan audiences would have known, and how such knowledge might have afforded them various means of interpreting the play (*The Renaissance "Hamlet,"* 1984). All of this scholarship has contributed extensively to the ways in which we are to imagine *Hamlet* in its own day.

The story of Shakespeare criticism during the early twentieth century from a philosophical perspective is well told in Morris Weitz's *Hamlet and the Philosophy of Literary Criticism* (1964).

5. Shakespeare editing in the twentieth century is a story of historical and scholarly advances that have subsequently been challenged in more recent days. The so-called New Bibliography, championed by Alfred W. Pollard (*Shakespeare Folios and Quartos*, London, Methuen, 1909, *Shakespeare's Fight with the Pirates*, 2nd ed., Cambridge: Cambridge University Press, 1920, R. B. McKerrow (*An Introduction to Bibliography for Literary Students*, Oxford: Clarendon Press, 1928, *Prolegomena for the Oxford Shakespeare*, Oxford: Clarendon Press, 1939), W. W. Greg, *The Editorial Problem in Shakespeare* (3rd ed., Oxford: Oxford University Press, 1954), Alice Walker, *Textual Problems of the First Folio* (Cambridge: Cambridge University Press, 1953), and Fredson Bowers, *Bibliography and Textual Criticism* (Oxford: Clarendon Press, 1964), among others, developed what they saw as a scientific and scholarly method for analyzing how Shakespeare's plays evolved from the author's working papers (called "foul papers" by these scholars) to fair copy in some cases, and sometimes to playhouse scripts. Various forms of these papers might be sold to publishers, especially the author's manuscripts, which the acting company would generally regard as less valuable than "prompt" copies marked up for stage production and licensed for performance. The two members of Shakespeare's acting company who undertook to edit the Folio collection of 1623, John Heminges and Henry Condell, thus had various materials at their disposal from which to choose. A modern textual scholar needs to determine as accurately as possible what sort of copy lies behind a given printed text. Inconsistencies might point to a partly unfinished authorial manuscript behind the printed text; plentiful stage directions and a consistent handling of speech prefixes and the like might point to a playhouse document, on the assumption that the acting company would require a more complete preparation of the script. Since no manuscripts of the plays assigned to Shakespeare have survived other than an insertion he may have written for a play called *The Book of Sir Thomas More* (*c.* 1595), the published texts have been looked at closely for inferences of this sort. In the case of *Hamlet* the quartos of 1603 and 1604 and the Folio of 1623 vary substantially in their readings; see chapter 3. The job of the textual editor preparing a scholarly "critical" edition is to sort out the evidence as dispassionately as possible and thereby produce an edition that represents, as nearly as can be determined, what the author would have wished the text to say.

This New Bibliographical method, once the prevailing ideology of textual scholars, has been the subject of intense criticism since 1980 or so (see chapter 7). The method presupposes that the editor can come up with a "definitive" edition of a play like *Hamlet*, whereas the historical record suggests that the play existed at various times in different forms. Should we try to produce a single text of *Hamlet*, as did Harold Jenkins in his monumental edition for Arden 2 in 1982, still very much in the New Bibliographical mode despite its late date, or should we represent all three

early printed texts in their own right, as Ann Thompson and Neil Taylor
have done in their splendid edition of *Hamlet* for Arden 3 in 2006? The
point can, of course, be debated; especially for student editions intended for
classroom use, the advantages of having a single *Hamlet* are substantial.

6. See also Murray M. Schwartz and Coppélia Kahn, eds. *Representing Shakespeare: New Psychoanalytic Essays* (Baltimore: Johns Hopkins University
Press, 1980), William Beatty Warner, *Chance and the Text of Experience:
Freud, Nietzsche, and Shakespeare's "Hamlet"* (Ithaca, NY: Cornell University Press, 1986), and Peter Gay, *Reading Freud: Explorations and Entertain-
ments* (New Haven: Yale University Press, 1990).

CHAPTER 7

1. Among the critics and scholars who have been most incisive in pointing
out the reasons for reassessing the claims of the New Bibliography are Paul
Werstine, William B. Long, Stanley Wells, Gary Taylor, Michael Warren,
Peter Blayney, and Steven Urkowitz. Newer methods of critical editing
have emerged in, among others, the *Oxford Shakespeare*, edited by Wells
and Taylor (Oxford: Clarendon Press, 1985), separate play editions also
published by the Oxford University Press, the new Cambridge Shakespeares, the New Folger Library Shakespeares, and the Arden 3 Shakespeares; all of these series are still in the process of being updated and
re-edited. A team of editors headed up by Bernice Kliman and Eric
Rasmussen is assembling a Variorum *Hamlet*, with internet capability, to
replace the "New Variorum" *Hamlet* (Philadelphia: Lippincott, 1877,
1905, 1918) of H. H. Furness. Working files are online at www.hamlet-
works.org. Paul Bertram and Bernice Kliman have published a handy
facsimile edition of Q1, Q2, and the 1623 Folio (*The Three-Text "Hamlet,"*
New York: AMS Press, 1991) laid out side by side. The Arden 3 *Hamlet*
(London: Thomson Learning, 2006) also provides fully edited texts of all
three early versions. Comparative study is now more easy than it was.

2. New Historicists often pay particular attention to the ways in which a
culture expresses and defines itself through rituals, ceremonies, dance,
song, and drama. Influenced in part by Mikhail Bakhtin's *Rabelais and
His World* (translated 1984, Bloomington: Indiana University Press), these
modern critics erase distinctions between "high" and "low" culture, and
are intent on dethroning canonical texts, emphasizing instead the cultural
function of art as deeply imbedded in the social practices of its time.
Michael D. Bristol, for example, declares his critical purpose in the title
of his *Carnival and Theater: Plebeian Culture and the Structure of Authority in
Renaissance England* (New York: Methuen, 1985). In some writers, the
Marxist point of view is central, as for example in Robert Weimann's
Shakespeare and the Popular Tradition in the Theater; Studies in the Social

Dimension of Dramatic Form and Function (translated from the German, Baltimore: Johns Hopkins University Press, 1978).

3. For other perspectives on gender conflict in *Hamlet*, see Carolyn G. Heilbrun, "The Character of Hamlet's Mother," *Shakespeare Quarterly* 8 (1957), 201–6; Elaine Showalter, "Representing Ophelia: Women, Madness, and the Responsibilities of Feminist Criticism," in *Shakespeare and the Question of Theory*, ed. Patricia Parker and Geoffrey Hartman (New York and London: Methuen, 1985), 77–94; Dympna C. Callaghan, *Shakespeare Without Women: Representing Gender and Race on the Renaissance Stage* (London: Routledge, 2000); Dympna C. Callaghan, Lorraine Helms, and Jyotsna Singh, *The Weyward Sisters: Shakespeare and Feminist Politics* (Oxford: B. Blackwell, 1994); Peter Erickson, *Patriarchal Structures in Shakespeare's Drama* (Berkeley: University of California Press, 1985); Ania Loomba, *Gender, Race, Renaissance Drama* (Manchester: Manchester University Press, 1989); and Valerie Wayne, ed. *The Matter of Difference: Materialist Feminist Criticism of Shakespeare* (Ithaca, NY: Cornell University Press, 1991). Queer theory, a no less insistent topic under the rubric of gender studies, is the focus of Bruce R. Smith's *Homosexual Desire in Shakespeare's England* (Chicago: University of Chicago Press, 1991) and *Shakespeare and Masculinity* (Oxford: Oxford University Press, 2000), and of Valerie Traub's *Desire and Anxiety: Circulations of Sexuality in Shakespearean Drama* (London: Routledge, 1992). On related questions of race and colonialism, see Catherine M. S. Alexander and Stanley Wells, eds., *Shakespeare and Race* (Cambridge: Cambridge University Press, 2000); Thomas Cartelli, *Repositioning Shakespeare: National Formations, Postcolonial Appropriations* (London: Routledge, 1999); Jean E. Howard and Scott Cutler Sershow, eds., *Marxist Shakespeares* (London: Routledge, 2001); and Ania Loomba and Martin Orkin, eds., *Postcolonial Shakespeares* (London: Routledge, 1998).

4. For well-informed accounts of structuralist debates in recent years, see David Scott Kastan, *Shakespeare After Theory* (New York: Routledge, 1999), and Arthur F. Kinney, ed., *Hamlet: New Critical Essays* (New York: Routledge, 2002). Some recent readings of *Hamlet*, to be sure, show a heightened interest in the protean flexibility of Shakespeare's language without endorsing a strenuous poststructuralist position. Indeed, a softening of stances that were fiercely maintained in the early days of the postmodern revolution (in the 1980s particularly) has lent itself to a critical movement toward synthesis. The distinctions between New Criticism and deconstruction begin to dissipate, reminding us of ways in which the New Criticism did after all herald the advent of deconstruction. Stephen Booth provides an early instance. His careful reading of the beginning of *Hamlet* aims at demonstrating how the protagonist's uncertain quest for meaning becomes the audience's problem as well. "*Hamlet*," Booth concludes, "is a tragedy of an audience that cannot make up its mind" ("On the Value of *Hamlet*," *Reinterpretations of Elizabethan Drama*, ed. Norman Rabkin, New

York: Columbia University Press, 1969). Robin Headlam Wells argues against the more intemperate claims of deconstruction and New Historicism by insisting that Shakespeare, like his fellow Elizabethans, did indeed have a well-developed sense of humanism and objective moral standards (*Shakespeare's Humanism*, Cambridge: Cambridge University Press, 2005).

   Similarly, the critical phenomenon of "metadramatic criticism" in the 1980s has offered a measured way of looking at indeterminacy in Shakespeare. James L. Calderwood's *To Be and Not to Be: Negotiation and Metadrama in "Hamlet"* (New York: Columbia University Press, 1983) focuses on a set of oppositions in the play, such as illusion versus reality and negation versus assertion, in ways that accentuate ambiguity and yet lead ultimately to a synthesis of these opposites. Michael Goldman, in his "'To Be or Not to Be' and the Spectrum of Action" (*Acting and Action in Shakespearean Tragedy*, Princeton: Princeton University Press, 1985), proposes that Hamlet and spectators alike must attempt to unravel what appear to be contradictory pieces of evidence in order to arrive at a coherence of meaning or meanings that is all the more persuasive and wonderful for having been arrived at through a complex uncertainty. Mark Rose's "Hamlet and the Shape of Revenge" (*ELR*, 1, 1971, 132–43) argues metatheatrically that the play is in a sense about itself, that is, about acting. Hamlet must find a way of fulfilling his father's dread command that is consistent with his own sense of what constitutes the proper style of the avenger. Hamlet's concept of "style" in this sense thus rules out killing a defenseless man kneeling at prayer, validating instead an ending in which Hamlet does what he must do but without killing in cold blood.

5. Other stage Hamlets of the 1980s and 1990s include Christopher Walken (for the American Shakespeare Festival, 1982); Roger Rees (Stratford-upon-Avon, 1984, directed by Ron Daniels), Richard Thomas (the Hartford Stage, 1987, directed by Mark Lamos), Mark Rylance (Stratford-upon-Avon, 1989, directed by Ron Daniels), Ian Charleson (shortly before he died of AIDS, replacing Daniel Day-Lewis, in Richard Eyre's production at the Olivier Theatre, London, 1989), Jeremy Northam (as an understudy in that same production who got his big chance when Day-Lewis suffered a nervous breakdown), Stephen Lang (for the Roundabout Theatre Company, 1992, with Lang as Hamlet and director), Ralph Fiennes (directed by Jonathan Kent in New York, 1995, for which Fiennes won the Tony Award for Best Actor that year), Alex Jennings (Stratford-upon-Avon, 1997, Brooklyn Academy of Music, 1998, directed by Matthew Warchus), and Liev Schreiber (New York Public Theater, 1999–2000, directed by Andrei Serban).

   Ingmar Bergman directed *Hamlet* for the Royal Dramatic Theatre of Stockholm in 1984, transferred to the Lyttleton Theatre of London's National Theatre in 1987 and to the Brooklyn Academy of Music in New York. Entirely in Swedish with no subtitles, this production featured a Hamlet (Peter Stormare) who sulked in sunglasses and a black leather coat and who dragged out the body of Polonius from behind the arras to stab it repeatedly in full view of the audience; an Ophelia who observed many scenes in which she was not a participant and through whose eyes the audience was invited to interpret the play; and a fascistic Fortinbras who had Horatio killed offstage and then unceremoniously disposed of Hamlet and the other dead figures on stage.

Stage Hamlets of the years 2000–2010 include Wallace Acton (Shakespeare Theatre Company, Washington DC, 2001, directed by Gale Edwards), Tobias Menzies (Royal Theatre, Northampton, 2005, directed by Rupert Goold), Santino Fontana (the Guthrie Theater, Minneapolis, 2006, directed by Joe Dowling), Ben Carlson (Chicago Shakespeare Theater, 2006, directed by Terry Hands), Richard Stacey (on tour, Actors from the London Stage, 2006), and William Hurt (at the Circle Repertory Theatre, New York, in 2009).

A production at Princeton's McCarter Theatre in 2005 distributed the play's roles among eight actors in a resolutely modern setting. The cast sat at the start around two tables as though for a first read-through; a little later, Hamlet faced his father's ghost as they were seated in two chairs for a tête-à-tête about death. Rob Campbell as Hamlet, looking like a Princeton undergraduate, was humorous, young, impulsive, self-critical, and informally dressed. The Ghost (Michael Emerson) materialized to the strains of Duke Ellington's "Don't Get Around Much Anymore," played on an LP turntable. Osric (Emerson again) turned out to be a fop in Jacobean attire, with a sonorous mannerism of speech reminiscent of John Gielgud.

Janet Suzman directed the play at the Baxter Theatre Centre, Cape Town, South Africa, in 2006, with Vaneshran Arumugam as Hamlet and John Kani as Claudius. A *Hamlet* at the San Diego Summer Shakespeare Festival in 2007, directed by Darko Tresnjak, was more traditionally Elizabethan in decor, with a handsome and vulnerable Hamlet (Lucas Hall) and a fiery, hot-blooded Gertrude (Celesta Ciulla). The acting company called Creation staged *Hamlet* in Oxford in that same summer, on a long outdoor platform and with crackling loudspeakers and spooky musical effects for the Ghost. Ophelia, spaced out on drugs and outfitted in mod attire, considered her father Polonius a cretin. Laertes, of a similar opinion, mockingly recited Polonius's "Neither a borrower nor a lender be" in chorus with the old man; Laertes had heard all this before. No doubt because it is such a familiar play, *Hamlet* has become a virtually inexhaustible resource for innovative touches like these.

6. Two rather traditional productions for television deserve brief notice here. In a Hallmark Hall of Fame condensed production directed by Peter Wood for NBC television in 1970, Richard Chamberlain's Hamlet is a thoughtful young idealist who is deeply distressed by his mother's sexual relationship with Hamlet's uncle and her seemingly having forgotten her first husband.

(Chamberlain had played Hamlet in 1969 in Peter Dews's production at the Birmingham Repertory Theatre.) The cast features many seasoned and distinguished Shakespearean actors from both sides of the Atlantic, especially from Great Britain: Michael Redgrave as Polonius, Margaret Leighton as Gertrude, Richard Johnson as Claudius, Ciaran Madden as Ophelia, and John Gielgud as the Ghost, replaying the role he took in the Electronovision version he had directed with Richard Burton as Hamlet in 1964. Regrettably, Gielgud, though often seen on stage as Hamlet since his first appearance in the role in 1930, never acted Hamlet on film. The 1970 Hallmark Hall of Fame version, though substantially cut in an adaptation by John Barton to meet the procrustean and remorseless scheduling requirements of television, stands as a very worthy attempt, too often forgotten today. This production illustrates how a familiar approach to interpretation, costuming, set design, and the rest need not result in a tired and uninspiring performance. The play itself is so remarkable that it can breathe life into an astonishing range of staging choices from traditional to innovative and back again.

The 1980 BBC *Hamlet* for Time-Life Television, produced by Cedric Messina and directed by Rodney Bennett, makes a choice similar to that of the Hallmark Hall of Fame production, and with equally satisfactory, if unsurprising, results. That is to say, it is a straightforward reading of the play, aiming at a high degree of expertise and clarity in the performance rather than at novelty. The text is nearly intact. The camera work unadventurously gives us a lot of talking heads, as in other productions of the series. A relatively uncluttered set keeps the focus on the well-chosen cast. Derek Jacobi as Hamlet explores a wide range of emotions: he is at various times hysterical, troubled, impetuous, sometimes introspective, always thoughtful. Claire Bloom is an intelligent and sympathetic Gertrude, Patrick Stewart is a politically capable Claudius, and Eric Porter is a warm and sensitive Polonius. This is one of the best of the BBC Plays of Shakespeare—a bland series overall. Jacobi had played Hamlet on stage under the direction of Toby Robertson at the Old Vic in 1979 and then on tour. Later, in 1988, he directed *Hamlet* for the Renaissance Theatre Company, and in 1996 played Claudius in Kenneth Branagh's four-hour film (described in chapter 7).

7. Other film adaptations of *Hamlet* from a novel perspective include Ragnar Lyth's Swedish film-for-television, 1984, not commercially available, featuring an Ophelia conceived of in the context of the feminist movement; Ken Gass's *Claudius* (1993); Stacy Title's *Let the Devil Wear Black* (2000, exploring intergenerational conflict from a rebelliously youthful point of view); and Janusz Glowacki's *Fortinbras Gets Drunk* (1990), a macabre retelling of *Hamlet* from a Norwegian perspective. Feminist dramatizations based on the sad tale of Ophelia include Jean Betts's *Ophelia Thinks Harder*

(1993), Byrony Lavery's *Ophelia* (1997), Jurgen Vsych's *Ophelia Learns to Swim* (2000), and Stephen Berkoff's *The Secret Love Life of Ophelia* (2001).

8. The musical is, in its origins at least, a distinctively American genre, and nowhere has the musical succeeded more brilliantly than when its energies have been harnessed to a first-rate Shakespearean text. *The Boys from Syracuse*, a popular musical adaptation derived from *The Comedy of Errors* in 1938 by George Abbott and with music by Richard Rodgers and Lorenz Hart, was made into a rollicking and campy film in 1940. *Kiss Me Kate*, produced on stage in 1948 as a musical version of *The Taming of the Shrew*, was freely refashioned into an enduringly popular film in 1953. With its show-stopping numbers like "I Hate Men" and "Brush up your Shakespeare," this musical has done much to bring Shakespeare alive in the popular imagination, and with an ineffably American flavour, suggesting that Shakespeare really swings. The hugely successful *West Side Story* (1957), with book by Arthur Laurents, lyrics by Stephen Sondheim, music by Leonard Bernstein, and direction by Robert Wise and Jerome Robbins, translated *Romeo and Juliet* into a drama of ethnic conflict in New York City between the white American Jets and the Puerto Rican Sharks, with obvious relevance to the contemporary scene. It was made into an excellent film in 1961.

9. *Hamlet* has also been adapted to the purposes of fiction in such novels and short stories as *Lillie Buffum Chace Wyman's Gertrude of Denmark: An Interpretive Romance* (Boston: Marshall Jones Co., 1924), John Turing's *My Nephew Hamlet* (a journal of events at Elsinore, London: Dent, 1967), Alethea Hayter's *Horatio's Vision* (London: Faber, 1972), Margaret Atwood's "Gertrude Talks Back" in her *Good Bones* (Toronto: O. W. Toad, 1992), and Salman Rushdie's "Yorick" in his *East, West: Stories* (New York: Pantheon, 1994). These are only a few instances of a rich literary tradition reaching back to *Hamlet*.

Sometimes *Hamlet* has been incorporated into a modern play or film not as an adaptation of the whole work but as an element of the plot. In Eldar Ryazonov's *Beregis Automobilya* (Russia, 1974), an insurance agent's pursuit of a car thief takes on the dimensions of Laertes's pursuit of Hamlet. Terrence Ortwein's *Flights of Angels* (1991) picks up where Hamlet's last words to his best friend leave off: Horatio is to tell Hamlet's story, assisted by a group of actors. Lee Blessing's zany comedy *Fortinbras* (1991) similarly imagines what might take place in the aftermath of *Hamlet*. In Penny Marshall's *Renaissance Man* (1994, available on video with Danny DeVito and Ed Begley), a down-on-his-luck former executive named Bill Rago tries to teach *Hamlet* to a bunch of army recruits. Paul Rudnick's droll comedy, *I Hate Hamlet* (Broadway, 1994), tells of a discontented sitcom actor named Andrew Rally who needs the assistance of John Barrymore's ghost to attempt the role of Hamlet. Kenneth Branagh's film *In the Bleak Midwinter* (1995) is about an unemployed, thirty-ish actor named Joe

Harper (Michael Maloney), who, at the cost of losing a lucrative contract in a Hollywood sci-fi film, plays Hamlet in a hilariously amateurish local production at Christmastime in order to assist his sister Molly (Hetta Charnley) in saving her church from demolition. The use of *Hamlet* to resist dictatorial authority is a motif in Don Chaffey's slapstick comedy *Breakout*, set in an Italian prisoner-of-war camp during World War II (1958), and David L. Cunningham's *To End All Wars*, similarly set in a Japanese prisoner-of-war camp (2001).

10. Some other memorable and by-now-proverbial phrases include "they are actions that a man might play" (1.2.84), "frailty, thy name is woman" (1.2.146), "the apparel oft proclaims the man" (1.3.72), "There needs no ghost... come from the grave / To tell us this" (1.45.131–2), "'tis true 'tis pity, / And pity 'tis 'tis true" (2.2.97–8), "Words, words, words" (2.2.193), "what is this quintessence of dust?" (2.2.309), "'twas caviar to the general" (2.2.436–7), "The play's the thing" (2.2.605), "Ay, there's the rub" (3.1.66), "conscience does make cowards of us all" (3.1.84), "Get thee to a nunnery" (3.1.122), "The lady doth protest too much" (3.2.228), "'tis the sport to have the enginer / Hoist with his own petard" (3.4.213–14), "Rightly to be great / Is not to stir without great argument" (4.4.54–5), "Alas, poor Yorick!" (5.1.183–4), "There's a divinity that shapes our ends, / Rough-hew them how we will" (5.2.10–11), "The readiness is all" (5.2.220), and "purposes mistook / Fall'n on the inventors' heads" (5.2.387–8). There are many more.

A postscript: Jonathan Miller's 2011 production of *Hamlet* at the Tobacco Factory in Bristol billed itself as an attack on London's obsession with the celebrity casting of David Tennant, Jude Law, and the like; Miller chose instead to work with regional and lesser-known actors, including a mercurial and idiosyncratic Jamie Ballard in the title role. Jay Villiers played Claudius as a man much in love with the wife for whom he has committed a terrible murder, who is forced at last to confront his own guilt. With a nearly uncut text, the Elizabethan-dress production relied on a minimum of props, other than three church pews. Reviewers found the production memorable and well paced. Miller's previous stagings of *Hamlet* include productions at the Cambridge Arts Theatre, Cambridge, in 1970, the Greenwich Theatre Company, 1974, and the Warehouse Theatre, 1982, noted in chapter 7 above.

Further Reading

The following list offers reading suggestions for anyone who would like to follow up on questions that have been raised by this book. It also acknowledges at least some of my indebtedness, which is very great.

Throughout this book, act-scene-and-line references to the plays of Shakespeare are to my edition of *The Complete Works of Shakespeare*, 6th ed., New York: Pearson/Longman, 2008. The line numberings may differ from those of other editions, owing chiefly to different column widths in the printing of prose and to differing editorial views as to where line breaks occur in verse, but generally the user of any reputable edition of Shakespeare ought to be able to find a particular passage close to where it is cited in this book.

BOOKS OF GENERAL INTEREST IN THE TOPIC

Bate, Jonathan. *The Genius of Shakespeare.* Oxford: Oxford University Press, 1997.
———. *Soul of the Age: A Biography of the Mind of William Shakespeare.* New York: Random House, 2009.
Buell, William Ackerman. *The Hamlets of the Theatre.* New York: Astor-Honor, 1968.
Dawson, Anthony B. *Hamlet: Shakespeare in Performance.* Manchester: Manchester University Press, 1995.
Duncan-Jones, Katherine. *Ungentle Shakespeare: Scenes from this Life.* London: The Arden Shakespeare (Thomson Learning), 2001.
Erne, Lukas. *Shakespeare's Modern Collaborators.* London: Continuum, 2008.
Furness, Horace Howard, ed. *Hamlet.* A New Variorum Edition of Shakespeare. 2 vols. Philadelphia: J. B. Lippincott, 1877, 1905, 1918.
Odell, George C. D. *Shakespeare from Betterton to Irving.* 2 vols. New York: C. Scribner's, 1920. New ed. New York: Dover, 1966.
Taylor, Gary. *Reinventing Shakespeare: A Cultural History, from the Restoration to the Present.* New York: Weidenfeld & Nicolson, 1989.
Trewin, J. C. *Five and Eighty Hamlets.* London: Hutchinson, 1987.
Warner, William Beatty. *Chance and the Text of Experience: Freud, Nietzsche, and Shakespeare's "Hamlet."* Ithaca: Cornell University Press, 1986.
Weitz, Morris. *Hamlet and the Philosophy of Literary Criticism.* Chicago: University of Chicago Press, 1964.

———. and Sarah Stanton, eds. *The Cambridge Companion to Shakespeare on Stage.* Cambridge: Cambridge University Press, 2002.

Wells, Stanley, *Shakespeare For All Time.* Oxford: Oxford University Press, 2003.

Williamson, C. H., compiler. *Readings on The Character of Hamlet, 1661–1947.* London: George Allen and Unwin, 1950.

For working files of the new *Variorum Hamlet* project, visit www.hamlet works.org

CHAPTER I PROLOGUE TO SOME GREAT AMISS:
THE PREHISTORY OF *HAMLET*

Bullough, Geoffrey, ed. *Narrative and Dramatic Sources of Shakespeare.* 8 vols. London: Routledge and Kegan Paul; New York: Columbia University Press, 1957–1975.

Hansen, William F. *Saxo Grammaticus and the Life of Hamlet.* With translation. Lincoln: University of Nebraska Press, 1983.

CHAPTER 2 ACTIONS THAT A MAN MIGHT PLAY:
HAMLET ON STAGE IN 1599–1601

Beckerman, Bernard. *Shakespeare at the Globe, 1599–1609.* New York: Macmillan, 1962.

Bevington, David. *Action Is Eloquence: Shakespeare's Language of Gesture.* Cambridge, MA: Harvard University Press, 1984.

Fergusson, Francis. *The Idea of a Theater.* Princeton: Princeton University Press, 1949; Garden City, NY: Doubleday, 1953.

Gurr, Andrew. *Playgoing in Shakespeare's London.* 2nd ed. Cambridge: Cambridge University Press, 1996.

———. *The Shakespearian Playing Companies.* Oxford: Oxford University Press, 1996.

———. *The Shakespearean Stage, 1574–1642.* 2nd ed. Cambridge: Cambridge University Press, 1980.

———, and Mariko Ichikawa. *Staging in Shakespeare's Theatres.* Oxford: Oxford University Press, 2000.

Pollard, Tanya. *Shakespeare's Theater: A Sourcebook.* Oxford: Blackwell, 2004.

Wilson, John Dover. *What Happens in "Hamlet."* New York: Macmillan; Cambridge: Cambridge University Press, 1935.

CHAPTER 3 THE PLAY'S THE THING: PHILOSOPHICAL
AND RELIGIOUS CONTEXTS OF *HAMLET* IN 1599–1601

Bowers, Fredson T. "Hamlet as Minister and Scourge," *PMLA* 1970 (1955), 740–9.

Bradley, A. C. *Shakespearean Tragedy.* London: Macmillan, 1904.

Erickson, Peter. *Patriarchal Structures in Shakespeare's Drama.* Berkeley: University of California Press, 1985.

Frye, Roland Mushat. *The Renaissance "Hamlet": Issues and Responses in 1600*. Princeton: Princeton University Press, 1984.

Greenblatt, Stephen. *Hamlet in Purgatory*. Princeton: Princeton University Press, 2001.

Jenkins, Harold, ed. *Hamlet*. The Arden Shakespeare, 2nd series. London: Methuen, 1982.

Kliman, Bernice W., ed. *The Enfolded Hamlets: Parallel Texts of F1 and Q2, Each with Unique Elements Bracketed*. New York: AMS, 2004.

——, and Paul Bertram, eds. *The Three-Text Hamlet: Parallel Texts of the First and Second Quartos and First Folio*. New York: AMS, 1991.

Levin, Harry. *The Question of Hamlet*. London, New York: Oxford University Press, 1959, 1970.

Mack, Maynard. "The World of *Hamlet*," *Yale Review* 41 (1952), 502–23.

Mullaney, Steven. "Mourning and Misogyny: *Hamlet, The Revenger's Tragedy*, and the Final Progress of Elizabeth I, 1600–1607," in *Centuries' Ends, Narrative Means*, ed. Robert D. Newman. Stanford, CA: Stanford University Press, 1996, 238–60.

Rose, Mark. "*Hamlet* and the Shape of Revenge," *English Literary Renaissance* 1 (1971), 132–43.

Shapiro, James. *1599: A Year in the Life of William Shakespeare*. New York: HarperCollins, 2005.

Thompson, Ann, and Neil Taylor, eds. *Hamlet*. The Arden Shakespeare, 3rd series. 2 vols: Q2 in vol. 1, Q1 and the 1623 Folio in vol. 2. London: Thomson Learning, 2006.

CHAPTER 4 THE MIRROR UP TO NATURE: *HAMLET* IN THE SEVENTEENTH AND EIGHTEENTH CENTURIES

Benedetti, Jean. *David Garrick and the Birth of Modern Theatre*. London: Methuen, 2001.

Brewer, John. *The Pleasures of the Imagination: English Culture in the Eighteenth Century*. New York: Farrar, Straus, and Giroux; Chicago: University of Chicago Press, 1997.

Hogan, Charles B. *Shakespeare in the Theatre, 1701–1800*. 2 vols. Oxford: Clarendon Press, 1952–7.

Spencer, Hazelton. *Shakespeare Improved: The Restoration Versions in Quarto and on the Stage*. Cambridge, MA: Harvard University Press, 1927.

CHAPTER 5 THE VERY TORRENT, TEMPEST, AND WHIRLWIND OF YOUR PASSION: *HAMLET* IN THE NINETEENTH CENTURY

Coleridge, Samuel Taylor. *Coleridge on Shakespeare: The Text of the Lectures of 1811–12*, ed. R. A. Foakes. Charlottesville: University Press of Virginia, 1971.

Dowden, Edward. *Shakspere: A Critical Study of His Mind and Art.* London: K. Paul, Trench, Trübner, & Co., 1875.

Downer, Alan S. *The Eminent Tragedian, William Charles Macready.* Cambridge, MA: Harvard University Press, 1966.

Hazlitt, William. *Characters of Shakespear's Plays.* London: C. H. Reynell for R. Hunter, 1817.

Hughes, Alan. *Henry Irving, Shakespearean.* Cambridge: Cambridge University Press, 1981.

Schlegel, August Wilhelm von. *Lectures on Dramatic Art and Literature,* 1846, rev. A. J. W. Morrison. London: G. Bell, 1889.

Schoch, Richard W. *Not Shakespeare: Bardolatry and Burlesque in the Nineteenth Century.* Cambridge: Cambridge University Press, 2002.

Wells, Stanley. *Nineteenth-Century Shakespeare Burlesques.* London: Diploma Press, 1977–8.

CHAPTER 6 REFORM IT ALTOGETHER: *HAMLET,*
1900–1980

Bevington, David, ed. *Twentieth Century Interpretations of "Hamlet": A Collection of Critical Essays.* Englewood Cliffs, NJ: Prentice-Hall, 1968.

Bowers, Fredson T. "Hamlet as Minister and Scourge," *PMLA* 1970 (1955), 740–9.

Bradley, A. C. *Shakespearean Tragedy.* London: Macmillan, 1904.

Calderwood, James L. *To Be and Not To Be: Negation and Metadrama in "Hamlet."* New York: Columbia University Press, 1983.

Charney, Maurice. *Style in "Hamlet."* Princeton: Princeton University Press, 1969.

Crosse, Gordon. *Shakespearean Playgoing, 1890–1952.* London: Mowbray, 1953.

Eissler, K. R. *Discourse on Hamlet and "Hamlet": A Psychoanalytic Inquiry.* New York: International Universities Press, 1971.

Eliot, T. S. "Hamlet and His Problems," *Selected Essays, 1917–1932.* London: Faber & Faber, 1932.

Erlich, Avi. *Hamlet's Absent Father.* Princeton: Princeton University Press, 1977.

Granville-Barker, Harley. *Hamlet.* In his series of *Prefaces to Shakespeare.* Originally 1936, reprinted, Portsmouth, NH: Heineman, 1995.

Jones, Ernest. *Hamlet and Oedipus: A Classic Study in the Psychoanalysis of Literature.* Rev. ed., New York: W. W. Norton, 1949; Garden City, NY: Doubleday, 1954.

Kennedy, Dennis. *Looking at Shakespeare: A Visual History of Twentieth-Century Performance.* Cambridge: Cambridge University Press, 1993.

Lidz, Theodore. *Hamlet's Enemy: Madness and Myth in "Hamlet."* New York: Basic Books, 1975.

Mack, Maynard. "The World of *Hamlet,*" *Yale Review* 41 (1952), 502–23.

Mazer, Cary. *Shakespeare Refashioned: Elizabethan Plays on Edwardian Stages.* Ann Arbor, MI: UMI Research Press, 1981.

Russell, John. *Hamlet and Narcissus.* Newark: University of Delaware Press; London and Toronto: Associated University Presses, 1995.

Shattuck, Charles H. *Shakespeare on the American Stage.* 2 vols. Washington: Folger Books, 1976 and 1987.

Trewin, J. C. *Shakespeare on the English Stage, 1900–1964.* London: Barrie and Rockliff, 1964.

Wells, Robin Headlam. *Shakespeare's Humanism.* Cambridge: Cambridge University Press, 2005.

Wilson, John Dover. *What Happens in "Hamlet."* New York: Macmillan; Cambridge: Cambridge University Press, 1935.

Winter, William. *Shakespeare on the Stage.* 3 vols. New York: Moffat, Yard & Co., 1915.

Woodfield, James. *English Theatre in Transition, 1881–1914.* London: Croom Helm; Totowa, NJ: Barnes & Noble, 1984.

CHAPTER 7 THERE IS NOTHING EITHER GOOD OR BAD BUT THINKING MAKES IT SO: POSTMODERN *HAMLET*

Adelman, Janet. "Man and Wife Is One Flesh: *Hamlet* and the Confrontation with the Maternal Body," *Suffocating Mothers; Fantasies of Maternal Origin in Shakespeare's Plays, "Hamlet" to "The Tempest."* New York and London: Routledge, 1992.

Artaud, Antonin. *The Theatre and Its Double.* Translated by Victor Corti. London: Calder & Boyars, 1970.

Bulman, J. C. and Herbert Coursen, eds. *Shakespeare on Television.* Hanover, NH: University Press of New England, 1988.

Cavell, Stanley. *Disowning Knowledge in Six Plays of Shakespeare.* Cambridge: Cambridge University Press, 1987. A second edition, 2003, *in Seven Plays*, adds a study of *Macbeth*.

de Grazia, Margreta. *"Hamlet" without Hamlet.* Cambridge: Cambridge University Press, 2007.

Dollimore, Jonathan. *Radical Tragedy: Religion, Ideology and Power in the Drama of Shakespeare and His Contemporaries.* Chicago: Chicago University Press, 1984; 2nd ed., 1989.

—— and Alan Sinfield. *Political Shakespeare: New Essays in Cultural Materialism.* Manchester: Manchester University Press, 1985.

Drakakis, John, ed. *Alternative Shakespeares.* London, New York: Methuen, 1985; Routledge, 1988; 2nd ed., 2002.

Dusinberre, Juliet. *Shakespeare and the Nature of Women.* London: Macmillan, 1975. 2nd ed., New York: St Martin's, 1996.

Eagleton, Terry. *Shakespeare and Society: Critical Studies in Shakespearean Drama.* London: Chatto & Windus, 1967.

———. *William Shakespeare*. Oxford: Oxford University Press, 1986.

Felperin, Howard. *The Uses of the Canon: Elizabethan Literature and Contemporary Theory*. Oxford: Clarendon Press, 1990.

Garber, Marjorie. *Coming of Age in Shakespeare*. London and New York: Methuen, 1981.

Geertz, Clifford. *Negara: The Theatre State in Nineteenth-Century Bali*. Princeton: Princeton University Press, 1980.

Greenblatt, Stephen. *Renaissance Self-Fashioning*. Chicago: University of Chicago Press, 1980.

———. *Hamlet in Purgatory*. Princeton: Princeton University Press, 2001.

———. *Will in the World: How Shakespeare Became Shakespeare*. New York: Norton, 2004.

Grotowski, Jerzy. *Towards a Poor Theatre*. New York: Simon and Schuster, 1968.

Jardine, Lisa. *Still Harping on Daughters: Women and Drama in the Age of Shakespeare*. Sussex: Harvester; Totowa, NJ: Barnes & Noble, 1983; 2nd ed., New York: Columbia University Press, 1989.

Kahn, Coppélia. *Man's Estate: Masculine Identity in Shakespeare*. Berkeley: University of California Press, 1981.

Kastan, David Scott. *Shakespeare After Theory*. New York: Routledge, 1999.

Kinney, Arthur F., ed. *Hamlet: New Critical Essays*. New York and London: Routledge, 2002.

Kliman, Bernice W. *"Hamlet": Film, Television, and Audio Performance*. Rutherford, NJ: Fairleigh Dickinson University Press; London, Cranbury NJ: Associated University Presses, 1988.

Kott, Jan. *Shakespeare Our Contemporary*. Translated from the Polish by Boroslaw Taborski. Garden City NY: Doubleday, 1964.

Landau, Aaron. " 'Let Me Not Burst in Ignorance': Skepticism and Anxiety in *Hamlet*," *English Studies* 82, 2001, 218–29.

Lanier, Douglas. *Shakespeare and Modern Popular Culture*. Oxford and New York: Oxford University Press, 2002.

Lenz, Carolyn Ruth Swift, Gayle Greene, and Carol Thomas Neely, eds. *The Woman's Part: Feminist Criticism of Shakespeare*. Urbana: University of Illinois Press, 1980.

Lévi-Strauss, Claude. *The Elementary Structures of Kinship*. Paris: Presses universitaires de France, 1949 (*Les structures élémentaires de la parenté*); translated into English, Boston: Beacon Press, 1969.

Litvin, Margaret. *Hamlet's Arab Journey: Shakespeare's Prince and Nasser's Ghost*. Princeton: Princeton University Press, 2011.

Marcus, Leah. *Puzzling Shakespeare: Local Reading and Its Discontents*. Berkeley: University of California Press, 1988.

Neely, Carol Thomas. *Broken Nuptials in Shakespeare*. New Haven: Yale University Press, 1985.

Novy, Marianne. *Love's Argument: Gender Relations in Shakespeare*. Chapel Hill: University of North Carolina Press, 1984.

Parker, Patricia, and Geoffrey Hartman, eds. *Shakespeare and the Question of Theory*. New York, London: Methuen, 1985.

Patterson, Annabel. *Shakespeare and the Popular Voice*. Oxford: Blackwell, 1989.

Rothwell, Kenneth S. *A History of Shakespeare on Screen: A Century of Film and Television*. Cambridge: Cambridge University Press, 1999.

—— and Annabella Henkin Melzer. *Shakespeare on Screen: An International Filmography and Videography*. New York: Neal-Schuman, 1990.

Russell, John. *Hamlet and Narcissus*. Newark: University of Delaware Press; London, Cranbury NJ: Associated University Presses, 1995.

Stone, Lawrence. *The Crisis of the Aristocracy, 1558–1641*. Oxford: Clarendon Press, 1965.

——. *The Family, Sex, and Marriage in England, 1500–1800*. London: Weidenfeld & Nicolson, 1977.

Taylor, Gary and Warren, Michael, eds. *The Division of the Kingdoms*. Oxford: Clarendon Press, 1983.

Turner, Victor. *The Ritual Process: Structure and Anti-Structure*. Ithaca: Cornell University Press, 1969, 1977.

van Gennep, Arnold. *The Rites of Passage (Rites de Passage)*. Translated into English. Chicago: University of Chicago Press, 1960.

Index